Second Language Acquisition in Action

Also available from Bloomsbury

The Bloomsbury Companion to Second Language Acquisition, edited by Ernesto Macaro

Key Terms in Second Language Acquisition, by Bill VanPatten and Alessandro G. Benati

The Interactional Feedback Dimension in Instructed Second Language Learning: Linking Theory, Research, and Practice, by Hossein Nassaji

Language Learner Strategies: Contexts, Issues and Applications in Second Language Learning and Teaching, by Michael James Grenfell and Vee Harris

Online resources to accompany this book are available at: www.bloomsbury.com/second-language-acquisition-in-action-9781474274869. Please type the URL into your web browser and follow the instructions to access the Companion Website. If you experience any problems, please contact Bloomsbury at: companionwebsites@bloomsbury.com

Second Language Acquisition in Action

Principles from Practice

Andrea Nava and Luciana Pedrazzini

BLOOMSBURY ACADEMIC
LONDON • NEW YORK • OXFORD • NEW DELHI • SYDNEY

BLOOMSBURY ACADEMIC
Bloomsbury Publishing Plc
50 Bedford Square, London, WC1B 3DP, UK

BLOOMSBURY, BLOOMSBURY ACADEMIC and the Diana logo are trademarks of
Bloomsbury Publishing Plc

First published in Great Britain 2018

Cover design by Olivia D'Cruz
Cover images © Getty Images/Andrew Baker

A catalogue record for this book is available from the British Library.

Library of Congress Cataloging-in-Publication Data
Names: Nava, Andrea. | Pedrazzini, Luciana author.
Title: Second language acquisition in action : principles from practice /
Andrea Nava and Luciana Pedrazzini.
Description: London ; New York : Bloomsbury Academic, 2018. |
Includes bibliographical references and index.
Identifiers: LCCN 2017042655 (print) | LCCN 2017046591 (ebook) |
ISBN 9781474274883 (ePub) | ISBN 9781474274890 (ePDF) | ISBN 9781474274869
(pbk. : alk. paper) | ISBN 9781474274876 (hardback : alk. paper)
Subjects: LCSH: Second language acquisition.
Classification: LCC P118.2 (ebook) | LCC P118.2 .N385 2018 (print) |
DDC 401/.93–dc23
LC record available at https://lccn.loc.gov/2017042655

ISBN: HB: 978-1-4742-7487-6
         PB: 978-1-4742-7486-9
         ePub: 978-1-4742-7488-3
         ePDF: 978-1-4742-7489-0

Typeset by Integra Software Services Pvt. Ltd.
Printed and bound in Great Britain

To find out more about our authors and books visit www.bloomsbury.com
and sign up for our newsletters.

Contents

List of Figures

List of Tables

Acknowledgements

This book is the result of a research project which in its initial stages was supported by a generous scholarship provided to us by the University of Michigan. We are thus highly indebted to Diane Larsen-Freeman for being an inspiring mentor and helping us identify the 'principles' which are shown 'in action' in the book and the staff of the English Language Teaching Institute for providing us with a stimulating environment during our stay as Morley scholars. We are also very grateful to Maria Cecilia Rizzardi, one of the leading Italian experts in TESOL and our supervisor, for sparking our interest in language teaching research; Luciano Mariani, a teacher, teacher trainer and textbook author, for sharing his expertise in teacher education and material development; and Alessandro Benati, for giving us an opportunity to present and discuss our work during our stay at the University of Greenwich.

We wish to thank the director of the Multimedia Centre of the University of Milan (CTU) and the producers of the videorecorded lessons included in the book – Daniela Scaccia, Marco Carraro and Davide Biscuola.

Special thanks are due to the teachers (Alessandro Mencarelli, Stefania Madella, Tim Quinn, Ilaria Orsini and Elena Vergani) and students who took part in the videorecorded lessons. Teresa Grassi, Elisa Vannucci, Laura Doria and Sara Villa provided invaluable help in transcribing the lesson extracts.

Thanks also to all at Bloomsbury, particularly Gurdeep Mattu and Helen Saunders for their advice and help in the production of this book.

Last but not least, a big thank you to our families.

Introduction

The purpose of this book is to raise second language teachers' awareness of key findings of Second Language Acquisition (SLA) research. What does SLA research have to offer teachers? How can teachers become aware of the possible relevance of SLA findings for their teaching? How can they be challenged to think differently and experiment new options in their teaching? The idea for the book has originated from our attempt to answer these questions.

SLA research and L2 pedagogy

SLA is a broad and constantly expanding field of research. It aims to study and explain how learners acquire a second or additional language (L2). The term 'additional' barely accounts for the diversity of issues SLA research aims to address, as Long (2007: 4) points out:

> the simultaneous and sequential learning and the loss of second (third, fourth, etc.) languages (L2) and dialects, by children and adults, with different motivations, abilities, and purposes, as individuals or whole communities, with varying access to the L2, in formal, informal, mixed, foreign, second, and lingua franca settings.

SLA research is characterized by a variety of theories, hypotheses, models and theoretical frameworks, which make this field particularly challenging for non-specialists. For this reason, it may still be unchartered territory for many second language teachers.

Although 'SLA theories and SLA theorists are not primarily interested in language teaching' (Long 2007: 19), the relationship between SLA research and language pedagogy has been debated extensively among SLA researchers and teacher educators alike. Two main issues concerning this controversial 'relationship' have seemed to emerge from the debate:

a. the differences in approaches and perspectives which are mainly due to the inherent gap between these two fields: with SLA research relying on technical and theoretical knowledge and language teaching drawing mainly on practical experience and what seems to work in a particular situation (Ellis 1997, 2010; Bartels 2003; Ellis and Shintani 2014);

b. the disputable applicability of SLA research findings to language classroom practice (Kramsch 2000; Lightbown 2000; Freeman 2007; Erlam 2008; Larsen-Freeman 2015) also on account of the risk of possible 'misapplications' (Spada 2015).

The debate on these issues has led teachers and researchers to take different positions. For example, findings from studies aimed at exploring what teachers actually think about this relationship suggest that, although their views on SLA research are on the whole positive, they remain sceptical about its applicability and straightforward relevance to teaching (Tavakoli and Howard 2012) and tend to believe that the knowledge they gain from teaching experience has more of an impact on their teaching practices than the knowledge they gain from research (Nassaji 2012). These views seem to be supported by researchers and practitioners in language teacher education, who have started to question the role of 'technical' knowledge from applied linguistics in the process of 'learning to teach' (Burns and Richards 2009; Wright 2010), arguing that much of teachers' knowledge originates from their previous experience of learning and teaching and is added to through reflection on actual teaching practice.

In the SLA research field, researchers have called for a fruitful and reciprocal relationship between SLA research and L2 pedagogy and put forward suggestions about ways in which relevance of SLA findings can be 'appraised' by teachers (Pica 1997; Ellis 1997, 2009, 2010, 2012; Long 2007, 2009; Larsen-Freeman 2009, 2015; Borg 2010; Ortega 2012). According to Long (2007: 19), 'the theories themselves might not say anything to teachers about how to teach, but perhaps something about who and what it is they are trying to teach'; for example, 'about whether depending on L1–L2 relationships, drawing students' attention to some contrasts is essential, facilitative, or not needed at all'. In particular, SLA theories 'may provide insight into putatively methodological principles for language teaching', that is, general 'desirable instructional design features motivated by theory and research findings in SLA [...], which show them either to be necessary for SLA or facilitative of it' (Long 2009: 376). Providing negative feedback, for example, 'may or may not turn out to be necessary for language development, but numerous studies have shown it to be facilitative'. The theoretical and empirical evidence underpinning these principles makes them suitable 'candidates for any approach to language teaching'.

In an attempt to define a framework for examining the so-called 'SLA-Language Pedagogy nexus', Ellis (2010: 194) highlights the crucial roles of classroom researchers and teacher educators 'who function as mediators between SLA researchers and teachers'. He also argues that 'the topics [...]

teacher educators choose to include in their courses need to be filtered through teachers' own ideas about what is important for learning' but 'these ideas need to be fine-tuned by a better understanding of SLA'. The guiding principles he proposes for the design of programmes in SLA are first concerned with 'what SLA topics are of relevance to teachers and how technical knowledge drawn from SLA can interface with the practical knowledge that informs actual teaching' (Ellis 2010: 195).

Suggestions for possible syllabuses and methodological principles of teacher-oriented SLA courses have also been advanced in a number of studies, many of which have provided empirical evidence that teachers' knowledge of SLA theories and findings acquired during a course may help them develop their own ideas of language learning and have some bearing on their teaching (e.g. Kerekes 2001; Angelova 2005; Lo 2005; Erlam et al. 2006; Busch 2010). Taking stock of these principles and proposals, the authors of this book undertook a research project aimed at devising an approach to English Language Teaching training which would activate a dynamic interplay between teachers' beliefs and their experiential knowledge about teaching and insights from SLA research (Nava and Pedrazzini 2011; Nava, 2012; Pedrazzini 2012). The idea for this book originated from the experimentation of this approach with MA students and teachers during the project.

Second language acquisition 'in action'

Students and teachers in SLA courses in teacher education and language teaching degrees often report struggling to bridge the gap between SLA theories and their applications in the classroom. Indeed, most introductory SLA textbooks and courses tend to prioritize a thorough review of SLA theories and research studies, leaving students and teachers with the challenging task of 'making practical use' of their knowledge about these theories in their teaching. In order to overcome this 'transfer' problem, this book aims to involve readers in an 'experiential' approach which enables them to approach a number of SLA principles 'in action' – not only through the words of the actual proposers of the principles but also through the experience of teachers who have been involved in awareness-raising activities (including planning and delivering actual lessons) aimed at exploring the implications of the principles for their teaching.

In keeping with what have been defined as the main observable phenomena that SLA research needs to explain (Long 1990; VanPatten and Williams 2015), the authors have identified eight SLA principles for readers to explore throughout the book. Each principle or tenet is expressed through a concise statement, for example: 'The form, meaning and use components of lexicogrammar are learnt through different psycholinguistic processes' (Chapter 1), 'Comprehensible input is the essential ingredient for second language acquisition' (Chapter 2). The principles have been selected on account of their possible relevance to issues teachers may find problematic (Ellis 2010). Readers are involved in an awareness-raising process of the relevance of each SLA principle to teaching practice through three stages: a stage of reflection, a stage of conceptualization and a final stage of restructuring and planning. Each stage is briefly illustrated below.

During the first stage, through a number of 'reflection' tasks readers are asked to tap their previous knowledge, beliefs and attitudes about language and language learning and teaching. This is in keeping with findings from teacher cognition research that point to the fact that teacher training programmes which do not take into account trainees' beliefs may turn out to be less effective at developing their knowledge and changing their practices (Borg 2005). As a 'bridge' from the first to the second stage, a review of the key theoretical positions surrounding each of the eight principles and their main learning and teaching implications is provided.

The tasks for the second stage are aimed at favouring the 'conceptualization' of the principles. Readers are first presented with a video extract of a lesson in which a principle is operationalized in the teaching of a specific language skill or lexicogrammatical area. The video extract is aimed at providing tangible experience of the teaching implications the tenet lends itself to, highlighting the constraints and affordances inherent in the view of language learning and teaching encapsulated in the tenet as well as the practical constraints of actual classroom teaching. Being exposed to an actual 'teacher case study' is also thought to foster the development of 'situated' knowledge, which has been shown to be more amenable to transfer (Bartels 2005). Through discussion questions and tasks, readers are then lent the opportunity to analyse extracts of the lesson transcripts illustrating specific process features related to the operationalization of the principle. Data-based tasks are indeed deemed 'more effective in helping teachers making the link between technical and practical knowledge than more traditional, transmission modes of teacher education' (Ellis 2010: 196). Selected data from the authors' qualitative research with EFL teachers provide additional material for reflection and analysis.

The aims of the final stage – 'restructuring and planning' – are twofold: to stimulate critical thinking as regards the principles and to engage readers in tasks aimed at having them reflect on the application of the principles vis-à-vis their specific teaching context with a view to developing possible plans for action. By devising 'plans for action' teachers are given an opportunity to 'own' the newly acquired knowledge: the complex technical knowledge encapsulated in the tenet and its teaching implications are matched with the familiarity of both the context of application and the activity of planning teaching tasks and evaluating and designing teaching materials, thereby favouring the restructuring process.

The structure of the book

The book features six chapters. The structure of each chapter was devised according to the methodological approach illustrated above. Each chapter, which targets one or two SLA tenets, includes the sections described below.

1. Key questions

After a short introduction to the chapter, a number of key questions draw the readers' attention to the main issues related to the SLA principle that will be further explored.

2. Experience

This section involves readers in 'reflection' tasks aimed at tapping their previous knowledge, beliefs and attitudes about specific issues of language learning and teaching related to the SLA principle. Extracts from teacher and learner narratives, learner language data, transcriptions of classroom interactions and other types of materials are used in the tasks.

3. The principle

The SLA principle targeted in the chapter is introduced and explored through different types of resources (short quotations, diagrams and tables) aimed at analysing the main theoretical constructs and concepts underpinning the tenet. A following section weighs in on the learning and teaching implications the tenet lends itself to and illustrates key methodological principles and procedural options together with examples of learning and teaching activities.

4. The principle in the classroom

In this section the SLA principle is further explored through the lens of practice. Readers are led to analyse a lesson aimed at the operationalization of key methodological principles and procedural options stemming from the SLA tenet. The lessons selected for this section showcase a number of EFL teachers – native and non-native – teaching at different levels of schooling. The lesson activities are first introduced through a short video extract and further analysed through transcripts supported by examples of teaching materials. All the video extracts are provided on a website that accompanies the book.

5. Restructuring and planning

The section engages readers in tasks aimed at having them reflect on the application of the methodological principles and procedural options issuing from the SLA tenet vis-à-vis their specific teaching context. Readers are provided with opportunities to try their hands in different areas of a language teacher's professional expertise: task planning, materials evaluation and design.

6. Further reading

Following the body of the chapter are selected references related to the SLA principle introduced.

Starting from 'practice', from the issues that teachers often struggle with, and trying to find possible answers in SLA 'principles', this book is a modest proposal for building a bridge between SLA research and teaching practice. We would like to end this introduction with a quotation from a recent article by Larsen-Freeman (2015: 274) who provides a much-needed cautionary note to applied linguists:

> Seeing research findings as 'applicable' to pedagogy might not be a helpful way to think of them. In my opinion, perhaps the most important contribution of research to practice is to challenge teachers to think differently, to experiment with new practices, and to help them make the tacit explicit by cultivating new ways of talking about their practice.

We hope that viewing SLA 'in action', as we have attempted to do in this book, will help second language teachers to think and talk about themselves, their students and their work 'differently'.

Note

The book was planned jointly by the two authors. Andrea Nava wrote the Introduction, Chapters 1, 4 and 6. Luciana Pedrazzini wrote the Introduction, Chapters 2, 3, 5 and 6.

Chapter 1
Form, meaning and use

1.1 Key questions

In the centuries-long tradition of teaching second languages on the basis of one or another method (Howatt 2004; Howatt and Smith 2014), the acquisition of a second language has often been thought to be triggered by a single learning process underpinning a given method. For example, in audiolingual teaching, language acquisition was held to result from the process of repetition of language patterns. On the other hand, according to the grammar translation method, it is the conscious understanding of grammatical rules and the comparison of the grammar of the L1 and the L2 that were thought to lead to acquisition. The object of learning – the (second) language – has also traditionally been viewed as a monodimensional construct (Larsen-Freeman 2003) – e.g. a series of form-based structural patterns (Audiolingualism) or morphosyntactic rules with their exceptions (Grammar Translation). In recent decades, however, researchers have pointed to the 'complexity' of language and its dynamic nature (Larsen-Freeman 1997; Ellis and Larsen-Freeman 2009). Such complexity is mirrored in the fact that no single process is now thought to account for language acquisition. This chapter will introduce a framework for viewing the core of a second language (its 'lexicogrammar') from a more complex and dynamic perspective than has traditionally been the case. According to this framework, any linguistic element is multidimensional. Each 'dimension' is learnt and needs to be taught differently. The following key questions will be addressed in the chapter:

- Is lexicogrammar only about form?
- Can lexicogrammar be learnt through a single learning process?
- Should lexicogrammar be taught through written and/or spoken (

1.2 Experience

(a) Grammar is an aspect of language learning which as learners and teachers we often feel very strongly about. Read these statements about second language learning and teaching and say if you (1) strongly agree, (2) agree, (3) neither agree nor disagree, (4) disagree or (5) strongly disagree (Table 1.1).

Table 1.1 Language learning beliefs.

Beliefs	Strongly agree	Agree	Neither agree nor disagree	Disagree	Strongly disagree
Learning a second language is mostly a matter of learning a lot of grammatical rules.					
Presenting language in a meaningful context can help students learn grammar.					
Written drills are essential for learning grammar.					
Role plays can be an effective way to learn grammar.					

(b) The passive voice is a topic of English grammar that very often features in coursebooks and grammar books for EFL students. Below you will find an exercise targeting the passive voice. Read the exercise and consider the following questions.

- What aspect of the passive voice is the exercise supposed to teach? What aspect(s) of the passive voice is/are *not* targeted by the exercise?
- What is a student supposed to do to carry out the exercise according to the instructions?

- What do you expect a student will learn about the passive voice in English when carrying out the exercise? What will they *not* learn?
- What possible problems might a student encounter when carrying out the exercise?

Complete the following sentences by placing the verbs in brackets in the correct form of the passive voice.

1. Unfortunately, my washing machine _____.
   (not repair) (present perfect)
2. 'Alice in Wonderland' _____
   by Lewis Carrol. (write) (past simple)
3. As you can see, the message _____
   to Mr Jones. (fax) (present progressive)
4. Most of the tea we drink _____
   from China. (import) (present simple)

(c) Miss Wong is a secondary school teacher who often uses exercises like the one above in her classes. Read this extract from an interview with Miss Wong and consider the following questions.

- What does Miss Wong's frustration stem from?
- What aspects of the passive voice in English do you think Miss Wong is less familiar with?
- How does Miss Wong teach the passive?
- What do Miss Wong's students learn when carrying out her activities on the passive?

It's easy if you ask them to rewrite the sentences, because they find it easy to follow. However … they just don't know when we are supposed to use passive voice and when we are supposed to use active voice. And one of the students even asked me 'Miss Wong, why do we have to use passive voice in our daily life?' And I find this question difficult to answer, ha, and I said 'Oh, I'll tell you next time' … and then I asked my colleagues 'Why do we use and teach passive voice?' and no one can give me the correct answer. And then I go home and think about it. But even now I really don't know how to handle that student's questions. I finish the worksheets with them and they know how to rewrite the sentences. But I don't know how to explain to them.

(Andrews 1999: 169)

1.3 The principle

The complex and dynamic nature of lexicogrammar and its acquisition will be explored through an SLA principle which originates from Diane Larsen-Freeman's research:

> **The form, meaning and use components of lexicogrammar are learnt through different psycholinguistic processes**.
> (Larsen-Freeman 2003)

The word 'lexicogrammar' refers to the fact that viewing vocabulary (or lexis) and grammar as two completely separate areas of language no longer reflects what we know about language. Lexis and grammar are not discrete language domains but are intertwined not only in the way we use a language but also in the way we learn it (Celce-Murcia and Larsen-Freeman 2015). The term 'lexicogrammar' is meant to account for this changed perspective on language use and language learning.

In an attempt to account for what recent research has shown about the complex, multifaceted nature of language and the main linguistic approaches to its analysis, Diane Larsen-Freeman, an American linguist and teacher educator, has put forward a principle whereby any lexicogrammatical feature (e.g. the passive voice) can be viewed from three different perspectives: the perspective of 'form', 'meaning' and 'use'. Different areas of linguistics provide us with the tools for analysing language from each of these perspectives. For example, we may draw on phonology, orthography, morphology and syntax to describe form, semantics to describe meaning and pragmatics to describe use. Each of these 'dimensions' interacts with the others in the actual use of the language and in its dynamic development over time so much so that when one dimension changes, the others are affected too. The isolation of one or another dimension is thus only warranted for research or pedagogical purposes.

The multidimensionality of lexicogrammar is mirrored in the diversity of psycholinguistic processes that learners engage in when learning lexicogrammar. To learn the form of a lexicogrammatical item, it is assumed that several repeated encounters are usually needed while learning meaning may only require one or a limited number of instances of associative learning. Learning use involves developing context-related appropriateness and this is believed to come about through experiencing the real conditions of language use in different contexts (Johnson 1996).

1.3.1 The form, meaning and use dimensions of lexicogrammar

If we flip through the pages of a grammar practice book, we will very likely be struck by the fact that most of the exercises aiming to teach specific lexicogrammatical topics target formal features. For example, transformation exercises are often used to teach that the passive voice in English requires a verb made up of an auxiliary (*be* or *get*) and a past participle (e.g. *checked*) and that the 'doer' is not in its usual initial position in the sentence but is placed after the verb (if it is mentioned at all), as in the sentence *Each room is checked by one of the hotel's supervisors every evening.* In other words, lexicogrammar is viewed as mainly a matter of form (prefixes and suffixes added to words, changes in word order, etc.). However, this view of lexicogrammar does not pay justice to the complexity and the resources afforded by language to language users. Lexicogrammatical items '[…] not only have a morphosyntactic form, they are also used to express meaning (semantics) in context-appropriate use (pragmatics). We refer to these as the dimensions of form, meaning and use' (Celce-Murcia and Larsen-Freeman 1999: 4).

When we refer to an item of lexicogrammar, we thus need to think beyond its form. Form itself is not only a matter of morphosyntax – whether words change their shape (e.g. add prefixes or suffixes, modify their internal vowels) and in what order they are used (e.g. auxiliary before past participle, *does* before or after the subject). Lexicogrammatical form also entails spelling and pronunciation (the domains of orthography and phonetics/phonology). Consider, for example, in how many different ways we can pronounce the *-ed* morpheme that shows up in the past participle form of many English verbs (*changed* vs *helped* vs *started*) and the changes to the orthography of a verb it may bring about (*preferred* vs *offered*).

The fact that lexicogrammar conveys meaning (the domain of semantics) is perhaps self-evident if we consider what are traditionally viewed as vocabulary items (e.g. the phrasal verb *bump into*). However, all the grammatical areas that appear in second language teaching syllabuses also express meanings of their own. A common grammatical meaning has to do with time. Although not all linguists would agree, the core meaning conveyed by verb tenses in English can be thought of as temporal (the present, past and present perfect, e.g., locate situations in the present, past or pre-present time spheres, respectively) (cf. e.g. Declerck 2006; Depraetere and Langford 2012). Other lexicogrammatical items may express more abstract meanings. The English passive voice, for instance, is often said to convey a focus meaning: it de-focuses (de-emphasizes) the 'doer', which does not appear at the start of the sentence but shows up after the verb.

The last aspect that we need to take into account to understand the nature of lexicogrammar is how lexicogrammatical features are used in context (the domain of pragmatics). When speakers or writers use lexicogrammar for a communicative purpose in a specific context (e.g. in making a formal vs informal request, in writing an academic essay vs delivering an oral presentation), they consciously or unconsciously make a choice among alternative lexicogrammatical items based on the features of the context. Any lexicogrammatical item, then, is associated with specific use features that make it more likely to be chosen in a given context. The historically past forms of English central modal auxiliary verbs (*could, might, would, should*) are often used in place of their present forms (*can, may, will, shall*) when the context calls for tentativeness in making a request, an offer or a suggestion. As the act of requesting/offering/suggesting is metaphorically located in the past, the request/offer/suggestion takes on a less forceful and direct undertone. The passive voice is preferred to the active voice in lab reports as it enables writers to foreground procedures and results and to omit mentioning the actual 'doers' that have carried out the procedures. To understand how the use of an item of lexicogrammar works, it is thus necessary to view it not on its own, in isolation, but vis-à-vis other lexicogrammatical items that express a similar meaning. To investigate the use dimension, Larsen-Freeman (2014: 258) suggests considering the following questions:

1. When or why does a speaker/writer choose a particular grammar construction over another that could express the same meaning or accomplish the same purpose? For example, what factors in the social context might explain a paradigmatic choice such as a speaker choosing a *yes/no* question rather than an imperative to serve as a request for information (e.g. *Do you have the time?* vs *Please tell me the time*)?

2. When or why does a speaker/writer vary the form of a particular linguistic construction? For instance, what linguistic discourse factors will result in a syntagmatic or word sequence choice such as the indirect object being placed before the direct object (e.g. *Jenny gave Hank a brand-new comb* vs *Jenny gave a brand-new comb to Hank*)?

Although each of the three aspects of form, meaning and use of any lexicogrammatical feature can be singled out and described, they are deployed in actual language use at the same time. Each aspect – or, to borrow Larsen-Freeman's term, 'dimension' – interacts with the others and this accounts for the complex nature of language. To help teachers view lexicogrammar from a perspective that is more in keeping with the nature of language and language use, Larsen-Freeman has developed a tool – the three-dimensional pie chart – which she has used in the creation of pedagogical grammars (Celce-Murcia

Figure 1.1 The 'form, meaning and use' pie chart.

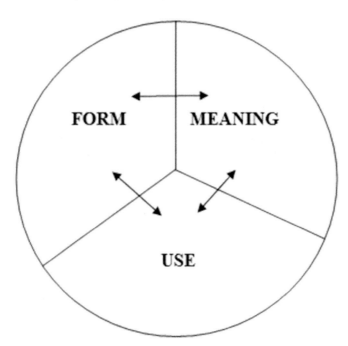

and Larsen-Freeman 1999, 2015; Larsen-Freeman 2007) as well as in several teacher education materials (Larsen-Freeman 2001, 2003, 2014). As shown in Figure 1.1, each wedge of the three-dimensional pie chart represents a different dimension – form, meaning or use. The arrows connecting the wedges show that the dimensions are interrelated.

The three-dimensional pie chart in Figure 1.2 illustrates the main formal, semantic and pragmatic features of the English genitive (Larsen-Freeman 2014) – in its prenominal (*Jennifer's* book, *a women's* magazine) and postnominal (the end *of the book*) alternatives.

The 'form' wedge of the pie presents the information that the prenominal genitive is created by adding the morpheme *'s* to the end of a noun. Plural nouns ending in -*s* only add an apostrophe. Proper names add *'s* or, if they end in -*s*, writers usually have the option of adding *'s* or only an apostrophe (*James's* or *James'*). An important feature of the form of the genitive is the fact that the *'s* morpheme has three different allomorphs (/s/, /z/, /iz/ or /əz/), which are phonologically conditioned in that /s/ is used after a voiceless consonant, /z/ after a voiced consonant or a vowel and /iz/ or /əz/ after a sibilant. In the 'meaning' wedge, some of the main meanings realized by

Figure 1.2 The multidimensional pie chart for the English genitive.

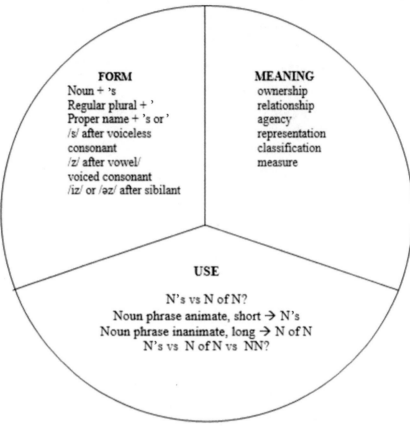

FORM
Noun + 's
Regular plural + '
Proper name + 's or '
/s/ after voiceless
consonant
/z/ after vowel/
voiced consonant
/iz/ or /əz/ after sibilant

MEANING
ownership
relationship
agency
representation
classification
measure

USE

N's vs N of N?
Noun phrase animate, short → N's
Noun phrase inanimate, long → N of N
N's vs N of N vs NN?

the so-called determinative genitive are identified: *Paul's car* (ownership), *Paul's brother* (relationship), *Shakespeare's poem* (agency), *Shakespeare's picture* (representation). The classifying genitive (*a man's sweater*), on the other hand, identifies a category or class, rather than determining a noun. Finally, a genitive can convey a meaning of measure (*six months' leave*). The 'use' wedge identifies the choices that a speaker/writer has to make when trying to express one of the meanings conveyed by the genitive. The most basic one entails choosing between the prenominal version (N's) and the postnominal version (N of N). This choice may be determined by the degree of animacy of the head noun and its relative length. Another possible alternative is the N N construction (*London's art scene/the art scene of London/the London art scene*). A pedagogical grammar book for English language teachers (Cowan 2008: 202) explains the fact that native speakers may choose to use the postnominal vis-à-vis the prenominal genitive in a specific context with reference to the principle of *end-weight*, which is a general principle that reflects how speakers and writers tend to structure information in a message:

> [T]here appears to be a tendency for relatively short noun phrases to have the inflected noun form, as in (57a) and relatively long noun phrases to have the *of*-phrase form, as in (57b). The latter choice seems to reflect the information-structuring principle referred to as *end-weight,* which states that long phrases should be put at the end of a phrase, clause, or sentence (in this case after a head noun). Apparently, native speakers feel that longer, more complex modifiers should appear after the head noun rather than before it.
>
> (57) a. [The designer's creations] were on display.
>
>   b. [The creations of a relatively young designer from Italy] were on display. *preferred*
>
>   c. [A relatively young designer from Italy's creations] were on display. *not preferred*

1.3.2 Form, meaning and use: learning and teaching implications

To counter the monodimensional view of language underpinning language teaching methods, Larsen-Freeman has posited that lexicogrammar – both vocabulary items and grammatical structures – should be considered from the perspectives of form, meaning and use. This section will explore the implications that a multidimensional view of lexicogrammar has for learning and teaching second languages.

Contrary to what has often been assumed, a single psycholinguistic process – e.g. habit formation or rule development – is unlikely to account for the acquisition of lexicogrammar as a multidimensional phenomenon. Learning form is thus held to come about through a different process from learning meaning or use.

To learn the form of a lexicogrammatical feature, repeated instances of exposure to the feature are usually needed. Multiple encounters with a feature of lexicogrammar may trigger the process of 'pattern detection' (Celce-Murcia and Larsen-Freeman 2015: 5), which is believed to underpin the acquisition of formal features of a language:

> Through encountering repeated instances of patterns, learners, with their capacious memories, adaptively imitate them, an innovative and recursive process that involves perceiving and transforming a pattern in

accordance with co-textual and contextual constraints to meet the user's goals. (Larsen-Freeman 2015: 229)

On the other hand, learning meaning sometimes only requires a single exposure to an item of lexicogrammar, which is enough to engage 'associative memory' (Celce-Murcia and Larsen-Freeman 2015: 5):

> Countless cases in the research literature attest to the existence of instantaneous learning, where very few instances of a particular phenomenon are needed for it to be learned. I think this is often the case with semantics. A few instances of associating a lexical item or a grammatical structure with its meaning is sometimes all it takes. A colleague once told me that he learned the Japanese word for *pear blossom* from one exposure to it. Now, I would think that *pear blossom* is probably not very frequent in the input, nor especially communicatively useful. However, sometimes we can make such strong semantic bonds that they stick. (Larsen-Freeman 2003: 42)

Finally, in order to learn use, learners need to 'develop a sensitivity to context' (Larsen-Freeman 2003: 43) – to the fact that the way we express a message is dependent not only on what has just been said in a communicative exchange, but also on the characteristics of the situation in which the exchange takes places and the people involved in the exchange. Learning how to make language choices appropriate to the context involves experiencing the actual conditions, or as close an approximation as possible, in which language use in context takes place ('real operating conditions', Johnson 1996) (cf. Chapter 6).

For any lexicogrammatical feature, one of the three dimensions usually proves to be the most challenging to learn. This represents the long-term 'learning challenge' for that specific aspect of lexicogrammar, which a teacher needs to be able to pinpoint and address:

> [F]or a given group of students, the immediate challenge may differ from the overall long-term challenge, depending on the characteristics of the students, such as their native language and their level of target language proficiency. However, it is possible to anticipate which dimension is likely to afford the greatest long-term challenge for all students, and it is important to do so, for being clear about the overall challenge will give you a starting point and suggest an approach that is consistent with the long-term challenge. (Larsen-Freeman 2003: 45)

The 'form, meaning, use' principle also prompts teachers to view the classroom teaching of lexicogrammar from a different perspective. While language teaching methodology traditionally opposes the teaching of lexis and grammar to the teaching of the four skills (listening, speaking, reading, writing), Larsen-Freeman argues that lexicogrammar should be viewed as a fifth skill. This shifts the emphasis from 'knowing' grammar to 'using' or 'doing' grammar – which Larsen-Freeman (2003: 13) captures with the term 'grammaring':

> I think that it is more helpful to think about grammar as a skill rather than an area of knowledge; this underscores the importance of students developing an ability to do something, not simply storing knowledge about the language or its use. I have coined the term *grammaring* (Larsen-Freeman 1992) to highlight the skill dimension of grammar. I also find this term helpful in reminding us that grammar is not so fixed and rigid as the term *grammar* implies.

Grammaring thus refers to 'the ability to use grammar structures accurately, meaningfully, and appropriately' (Larsen-Freeman 2003: 143). As with teaching any other skill, such as playing the piano and driving, teaching grammaring entails providing students with opportunities to 'practise' the form, meaning and use of lexicogrammar. Traditionally, language practice has been associated with mechanical written or spoken drills. These require learners to produce correct instances of a lexicogrammatical item by modifying the form of cues provided by the teacher or a textbook, as in the examples shown below.

Write the verb in the past.
1. John _____ Mary. (meet)
2. I _____ my sister some money. (give)

Write what Betty and Sam said using reported speech.
1. Betty: 'I'm living in London.' Betty said …
2. Sam: 'I have never seen it.' Sam said …

Write full answers in the present perfect, using the words given.
1. I can't find my bag. (someone/steal/it) _____
2. Jessie isn't here. (she/not/arrive yet) _____

(Ur 2016: 109)

As any teacher or learner who has experienced traditional mechanical drills is well aware, this type of language practice has several shortcomings. First, it tends to focus predominantly on the formal dimension of lexicogrammar, neglecting the meaning and use aspects. It usually requires minimal engagement on the part of the learner (and teacher!) – in order to carry out an exercise correctly, it is often not even needed to understand the meaning of the cues provided. The major drawback of traditional practice, however, which explains why it has been heavily criticized by SLA researchers (DeKeyser 2007) is that it does not seem to have much of an impact on spontaneous language use. In other words, what has been practised intensively through mechanical drills often does not seem to transfer to free written or spoken language production or, if transfer does take place, this does not have a long-lasting effect (Larsen-Freeman 2013).

Grammaring practice departs from traditional mechanical practice in four respects, as will be discussed below.

a. Broader remit. Grammaring practice may target any of the three dimensions of lexicogrammar, not just the formal aspect. It may engage both spoken and written modalities and involve students in comprehension, production and/or interaction (Ortega 2007).

b. Meaningfulness. Grammaring practice is meaningful. As happens in authentic language use, students are required to use the language for 'some meaningful purpose' (Larsen-Freeman 2013: 117) other than practising a given lexicogrammatical item. Meaningful practice also enhances students' level of engagement, both cognitive and affective, as Larsen-Freeman (2003: 117) explains:

> Meaningful practice activities also serve to engage learners. [...] If they are not engaged, then they are probably not attending, and their attention is important. Thus, any practice activities have to be independently motivating, seen by learners as worth doing.

c. Transfer-appropriate processing. In order to overcome the problem of lack of transfer of what is practised in the classroom to spontaneous language use, grammaring practice engages 'transfer-appropriate processing'. Larsen-Freeman (2003: 111) explains that the concept of transfer-appropriate processing is based on the idea that 'we can better remember what we have learned if the cognitive processes that are active during learning are similar to those that are active during retrieval'. In other words, the conditions in which practice is carried out should match as much as possible the actual conditions in which spontaneous language use takes place (Larsen-Freeman 2013). This means, for example, that practice should not be based exclusively on decontextualized written exercises if it is meant to prepare learners for spoken production in authentic contexts of language use (cf. Chapter 6).

d. Focus on a specific dimension. Grammaring practice is designed in such a way that it not only focuses on a lexicogrammatical area but also targets a specific dimension (form, meaning or use). Hence, once a teacher has identified the dimension that needs practising, they should plan activities that trigger the psycholinguistic process that is believed to foster the learning of the targeted dimension.

If a teacher wishes to target form, they should plan activities that allow 'purposeful iteration' (rather than 'rote repetition') of a given lexicogrammatical feature (Celce-Murcia and Larsen-Freeman 2015: 7). An example of a meaningful and naturally iterative activity targeting form is the game 'Twenty questions'. The teacher or a student thinks of a famous person, an animal or an object, and the class has to guess what person, animal or object it is by asking twenty yes/no questions (Larsen-Freeman 2003: 118). Unlike mechanical drills, this activity has a meaningful purpose other than practising a grammatical structure. The targeted lexicogrammatical feature is not simply repeated parrot-fashion by the students, but it is 'iterated' in slightly different contexts (each new question has to take account of the information about the mystery person/animal/object provided by the 'knower'). Larsen-Freeman (2012: 204) highlights the advantages of 'iteration' over straight 'repetition' (i.e. 'identical performance'):

> [G]iving learners an opportunity to do something a little bit different each time they engage in a (repeated) particular activity is good training not only for creating and perceiving alterity, but also for being able to make the adaptations learners need when faced with a different context or task.

If the target is meaning, the ideal teaching activity should foster the association between the form of an item and its essential semantic features. For example, Larsen-Freeman (2014: 264) suggests using 'miming' exercises. To learn the meaning of phrasal verbs, the students can be asked to practise carrying out a sequence of actions (such as making a telephone call – using e.g. *look up, call up, pick up, hang up*), naming each action as they mime it. If the learning challenge is use, the teacher's choice should be an activity which leaves learners free to select the most appropriate among several, equally meaningful lexicogrammatical options within a given communicative context. An ideal activity for this purpose is the role play. Students could practise asking for and giving advice in different communication contexts (patient asking advice from their doctor; husband asking advice from his wife, etc.).

1.4 The principle in the classroom

1.4.1 Stefania teaching the form, meaning and use of 'can'

Video Extract 1

This section aims to provide examples of the way a multidimensional view of lexicogrammar and of its learning and teaching can be implemented in actual teaching practice. The examples refer to an EFL teacher who has carried out a series of grammaring activities targeting the form, meaning and use of *can* with her elementary level students.

(a) The multidimensional pie chart is a useful tool for analysing the form, meaning and use dimensions of any lexicogrammatical feature. It can be used by teachers as a 'self-evaluation' instrument – to find out how much they actually know about the three dimensions of a lexicogrammatical item. Before watching Stefania's lesson, try and find out how much you know about the form, meaning and use of *can*. How would you describe the main features of the modal auxiliary *can* according to the three dimensions of form, meaning and use? In Figure 1.3

Figure 1.3 The multidimensional pie chart for the English modal auxiliary *can*.

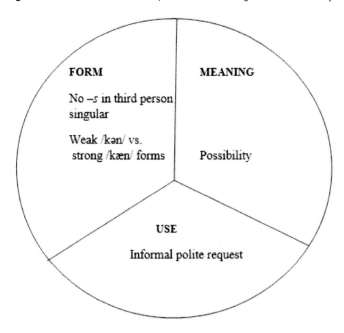

you will find a three-dimensional pie chart for *can* completed by a teacher. What other features of *can* would you add to the chart?

(b) Stefania's lesson develops through four main stages:

1. Sketch
2. Game
3. Drama
4. Role play

Watch the extracts of her lesson. Which dimension of *can* does she address at each stage?

1.4.2 Learning form, meaning and use

According to Larsen-Freeman's principle, given that lexicogrammar is a complex multidimensional phenomenon, a single psycholinguistic process is unlikely to account for the acquisition of the different dimensions of lexicogrammatical items. It is thus hypothesized that each dimension (form, meaning and use) is learnt through a specific psycholinguistic process. Such specific psycholinguistic processes should thus be activated in the classroom in order for the acquisition of lexicogrammar to take place (cf. Subsection 1.3.2).

(a) Analyse an extract from stage 1 of Stefania's lesson. How does she help her students learn the meaning of *can* at this stage? What makes the activity she uses suitable for this purpose? How else might Stefania have implemented this activity? For example, by asking for another object? By engaging two students in a similar interaction?

> T: *ok. so ehm I have to write something on the board but can you lend me a pen? yes? can you lend me your pen, please? thank you (writes on the board). can you lend ok? can you understand this? can you lend me?*

(In the transcripts in the Section *The Principle in the classroom*, T identifies the teacher; S identifies the student; Ss identifies two or more students.)

(b) How does Stefania help her students learn the form of *can* at Stage 2 of her lesson? What makes the activity she uses suitable for this purpose? Would you have introduced the game in the same way? What other games with a similar iterative design might have been used?

> T: *[...] alright so I have to go to buy something, where can I go to buy something? where can I go? if I need to buy something, where can I go? to? to a shop, for example? a big shop [...]. a shopping centre. do you understand shopping centre? yes? [...]*
>
> Ss: *yes*
>
> T: *ah, yes. ok, so you go to shopping centres and so, can you buy, can you buy something for me, right? [...] what? you buy something with a letter... so I'll tell you a letter of the alphabet [...] so Fabio. you go to the shopping centre, please. can you buy me something that begins with letter c? something that begins with letter c? what is it? [...]*
>
> S: *a cherry*
>
> T: *a cherry? oh, yes, ok, good. what is the question that I've asked? [...] can you buy me something that begins with letter c? ok? and I say alright, sure! I'll buy a calculator mm? sure, I'll buy a calculator right? so let's repeat together. can you buy me something that begins with letter c?*
>
> Ss: *sure, I'll buy a calculator*

(c) At stage 3 of her lesson, Stefania introduces two short dialogues in which *can* and *could* are used to make informal and formal requests. At stage 4, she engages the students in a role-play activity. She first introduces the situations for each role play. After going over the differences between the two situations, she asks a number of students to act out the interaction required in each role play. What makes this activity suitable for teaching the use of *can* and *could*? How would you have introduced the role-play situations? How else might the role-play interactions have been implemented?

> T: *ok boys and girls. so let's go on. let's revise a little while the two dialogues. do you remember the two dialogues we did before?*
>
> Ss: *yes*
>
> *[...]*
>
> T: *now, as you can see on the board there are two role play cards. role play number one. [...] so in the first role play, role play number one, there are two people. so who are the people?*
>
> S: *you and your teacher*
>
> T: *[...] and you have to do what? read the task over there. 'ask for...'*
>
> S: *ask for a phone number*
>
> T: *ask for a phone number. for your teacher's phone number. [...] so tell me. which of the two dialogues would you use, Lucrezia?*

> do you remember, dialogue one or dialogue two? in this situation
> here. you are you and your teacher. you have to ask. Sorry?
> S: dialogue two
> T: [...] so what would you say?
>   [...]
> S: ah, could you your phone number?
> T: could you?
> S: could you tell me your phone number?
> T: exactly! repeat
> S: could you tell your phone number?
> T: oh yes, sure. there it is. 334960...
> S: thank you
> T: ok. you're welcome. very well. who wants to be the teacher and
>   the student? to try this dialogue? [...]

(d) Although all three dimensions of lexicogrammar may be challenging to learn especially for low-level students, for a given lexicogrammatical item, one of the three dimensions of lexicogrammar is usually more difficult to learn irrespective of the student's L1 or their L2 proficiency. Which of the three dimensions of the modal auxiliary *can* represents a long-term learning challenge for EFL students? Why?

1.4.3 Practising form, meaning and use

The main teaching implication of the 'form, meaning and use' principle is that teaching lexicogrammar should involve providing 'grammaring' practice. A key requirement of grammaring practice activities is that they be focused and engage dimension-specific learning processes. Different types of activities trigger different psycholinguistic processes and hence lend themselves to practising different dimensions of lexicogrammar (cf. Subsection 1.3.2).

(a) Complete the chart with the most suitable activities for each 'dimension' choosing among those listed below.

Guessing game/Total Physical Response/Find someone who.../Letter writing/ Listen and draw/Find the differences/Label objects in pictures

Lexicogrammatical dimension	Psycholinguistic process	Activities
Form	Iteration	
Meaning	Association	
Use	Choice in context	

(b) Look at these pairs of activities. Which dimension does each pair target? Which psycholinguistic process is fostered in each activity to learn a specific dimension?

1a ... ...   1b......................................

A hobby is an activity we do in our free time. Look at the pictures. Match each person to a hobby and write a statement about the person's hobby. (Picture of a woman holding a camera) Helen *Helen's hobby is photography* *Gardening playing the guitar dancing surfing the Internet travelling* 1. (Picture of a man with a guitar) Mark 2. (Picture of children dancing) the children (Adapted from Badalamenti and Henner-Stanchina 2007: 85–87)	Work in a group of four to six people. Find out who in your group can do the following things. Take turns asking questions. *Who/play a musical instrument?* S1: Who can cook? S2: I can cook. S1: What can you cook? S2: I can cook spaghetti.

2a ... ...   2b ....

Look at the pictures and answer the questions. 1. (Picture of a horse; arrow pointing at the tail) What's this? 2. (Picture of a house; arrow pointing at the roof) What's this? (Adapted from Cowan 2008: 209)	Congratulations! You have just won a certificate for Easy-Does-it-Housecleaning Services. You will get three hours of housecleaning service for your room. First make a list of what you want the housecleaner to do in your room (clean the windows, mop the floor, etc.). Then write these requests in a polite note to your housecleaner. (Adapted from Wisniewska et al. 2007: 259)

3a ....   3b ....

Look at the pictures and write statements about Tom Dylan and Sara Jones. (picture of a CD) Tom Dylan *This is Mark Dylan's CD.* 1. (picture of a guitar) Tom Dylan 2. (picture of a secretary at work) Sara Jones 3. (picture of a woman) Sara Jones	Look at the situations below and complete the sentences to show how certain the speaker is about each one. She always wears a purple hat. (50% certain)→ She *may* like purple. She always wears a purple hat and a purple coat. (80% certain)→ She .... like purple. She always wears purple clothes, she drives in a purple car and lives in a purple house. (100% certain)→ She .... purple. (Adapted from Wisniewska et al. 2007: 73)

(c) Whether aiming at form, meaning or use, grammaring practice needs to be meaningful (have a purpose other than practising an item of lexicogrammar) and engage transfer-appropriate processing (reproduce as much as possible the real operating conditions of spontaneous language use). Analyse the following two activities targeting the form of *can*. Which is more meaningful and is more likely to engage transfer-appropriate processing (prepare students to use the lexicogrammatical item in spontaneous conversation)?

Activity 1
Work with a partner.
Ask each other questions like this:
Can Mike ride a bike? ᵛ *Yes, he can.*
Can Susan play the piano? X No, she can't.

Mike/ride a bike ᵛ
Susan/play the piano X
the children/swim X
Tom's sister/speak French X
John's grandparents/use a computer X

Activity 2
One student goes out of the classroom. The teacher chooses the name of an animal or a person and tells the class what it is. The student who has gone out of the classroom comes in and has to guess, with the help of hints suggested by the others, based on what the subject *can* or *can't* do. For example, if the subject is 'koala bear' students might say
It can climb trees.
It can carry its babies.
The guesser may also ask *can/can't* questions.
                                                                    (Ur 1988: 172)

1.5 Restructuring and planning

In this section, you will be involved in the evaluation of two examples of materials for teaching lexicogrammar according to the implications of the 'form, meaning and use' principle (cf. Subsection 1.3.2 and Section 1.4). The lexicogrammatical area you will be asked to consider is the passive voice in English.

(a) Which of the three dimensions of the passive voice might represent the long-term learning challenge for EFL students?

(b) The activity below is aimed at teaching the use of the English passive. Which of the following specific uses of the passive are targeted by the activity?

1. Use the passive when you don't know who performed the action.
2. Use the passive when the person who performed the action is obvious.
3. Use the passive when you don't want to say who performed the action.
4. The passive is more formal than the active. It is more common in writing, especially in scientific and technical reports, and in newspaper articles. It is less common in conversation.

The police are currently investigating a robbery that took place in a hotel room a few nights ago. Look at the pictures of the room before the robbery (A) and after the robbery (B). Seven different things were done to the room. Find what these seven things were and complete the report below.
(A) Picture of a room before a robbery
(B) Picture of a room after a robbery

ROBBERY AT HOTEL PARAISO
Last night the police were called to investigate a robbery that took place at the Hotel Paraiso. The identity of the thief is still unknown. The police took note of seven unusual occurrences. For example,

_____

_____

_____

_____

The public has been asked to contact the police with any information about the identity of the thief. Any information leading to an arrest will be rewarded.

(Adapted from Wisniewska et al. 2007: 317)

(c) Go over the activity again. Which learning process does it foster? If you were to use this activity with a group of intermediate level students, what type of extra support would you provide to enhance the learning of the use of the passive?

(d) Review activity (b) targeting the passive voice in the 'Experience' section (cf. Section 1.2). Evaluate the effectiveness of the activity according to the 'form, meaning and use' principle for your teaching context/a teaching context you are familiar with. How is the form of the passive taught? Are students provided with enough opportunities for iteration of the form? Are they asked to use the language in a meaningful and engaging way? Is transfer-appropriate processing of the language engaged? Is the metalanguage provided a help or a possible obstacle? How would you adapt the activity to make it more effective at teaching the form of the passive?

1.6 Conclusions

In this chapter, we have explored how lexicogrammar may be viewed as a more complex phenomenon than the language teaching tradition has often assumed. Using lexicogrammar as a communicative tool means being able to express messages that are accurate, meaningful and appropriate to the communicative context. If lexicogrammar is a multidimensional phenomenon, no single process is likely to account for its learning, and teaching activities should also be differentiated in accordance to whether the targeted dimension is form, meaning or use.

Throughout the chapter we have been using the term 'lexicogrammar' to refer to the fact that lexis and grammar are intertwined in actual language use. A logical consequence of this changed perspective is that words and grammar 'rules' are no longer viewed as completely distinct linguistic categories. Indeed, linguists have identified 'constructions' as the core of lexicogrammar (Celce-Murcia and Larsen-Freeman 2015). In a construction, morphosyntactic rules or rather 'patterns' and lexis work together to convey specific meanings. An example of a construction is the ditransitive one (Goldberg 2006), as instantiated in the examples *He gave me his phone number* or *Can you buy me something that starts with the letter C?*. The underlying meaning of the construction is one of 'transfer'. Any construction is subject to specific constraints: for example, the verb *donate*, while conveying the meaning of transfer, cannot be used in the ditransitive construction **He donated a charity part of his inheritance*. Through playing the 'buying' game, Stefania's learners not only practised the 'rule' for asking questions with the modal auxiliary *can* but also became familiar with the ditransitive construction (*Can you buy me...?*). It goes without saying that any construction can be analysed, and may pose learning challenges, from the perspectives of form, meaning and use.

As well as complex and multidimensional, language is also dynamic, changing not only over time but as it is being used by its speakers (Larsen-Freeman 1997). It is thus sometimes difficult to describe, and keep apart, the meaning and use dimensions of lexicogrammatical features, which are the aspects that are more prone to language change. A useful resource for keeping abreast of how a language may be described for teaching purposes are pedagogical grammars for language teachers. In addition to teacher-oriented descriptions of the core topics of lexicogrammar for a specific language, a pedagogical grammar for language teachers usually features information on learning challenges and suggestions of teaching activities for each topic presented (Nava 2008, 2017). For teachers of English, recently published pedagogical grammars are Cowan (2008), Parrott (2010) and Celce-Murcia and Larsen-Freeman (2015).

1.7 Further reading

Celce-Murcia, M. and D. Larsen-Freeman (2015), *The Grammar Book: An ESL/EFL Teacher's Course*, 3rd edn, Boston: Thomson Heinle.

Cowan, R. (2008), *The Teacher's Grammar of English*, Cambridge: Cambridge University Press.

Larsen-Freeman, D. (2003), *Teaching Language. From Grammar to Grammaring*, Boston: Heinle.

Larsen-Freeman, D., ed. (2007), *Grammar Dimensions*, 4th edn, Boston: Heinle.

Larsen-Freeman, D. (2009), 'Teaching and testing grammar', in M. Long and C. Doughty (eds), *The Handbook of Language Teaching*, 518–542, Oxford: Wiley-Blackwell.

Larsen-Freeman, D. (2014), 'Teaching grammar', in M. Celce Murcia, D. Brinton and M. A. Snow (eds), *Teaching English as a Second or Foreign Language*, 4th edn, 256–270, Boston: Heinle.

Nava, A. (2012), 'SLA in action: raising teachers' awareness of English lexicogrammar and its acquisition', in L. Pedrazzini and A. Nava (eds), *Learning and Teaching English. Insights from Research*, 91–115, Monza: Polimetrica.

Parrott, M. (2010), *Grammar for English Language Teachers*, 2nd edn, Cambridge: Cambridge University Press.

Ur, P. (2009), *Grammar Practice Activities*, 2nd edn, Cambridge: Cambridge University Press.

Chapter 2
Comprehensible input

2.1 Key questions

What is input to language learners? Input is the language available to them and to which they are exposed. It can come in written or spoken form, or from visual mode, such as sign language. Input needs to have some kind of communicative intent: this means that there is a message that the learner is supposed to understand and respond to (VanPatten 2003: 25). Input can be non-interactive in the form of texts that learners listen to or read or it can arise out of interaction, as when learners take part in conversations. Input can also provide opportunities to speak or write and to receive feedback (Ellis 2008: 205) (cf. Chapter 5). Input is also needed for the 'maintenance' and development of what has been previously been learned (Verspoor et al. 2009: 71).

One of the 'accepted findings' in SLA research is that exposure to input is necessary for SLA. This chapter aims to analyse the role of input in SLA by exploring a principle derived from Krashen's Input Hypothesis (1985). The hypothesis posits that comprehensible input serves as the basis for SLA. The following main questions will be addressed in the chapter:

- What kind of input are language learners exposed to?
- Why do learners need access to input that is comprehensible?
- How can input be made comprehensible?
- How does comprehensible input support second language learning?

2.2 Experience

Before exploring the SLA principle that will be targeted in this chapter, we will consider which role input may have in teaching practice.

(a) Language input can be derived from a wide range of sources in both spoken and written form. Refer to your experience as a learner and/or a teacher. Which materials among those listed below are used as a source of language input in the L2 classroom? What other types of sources are used or can be used?

Listening/viewing materials
TV commercials, quiz shows, cartoons, news clips, comedy shows, movies, soap operas, audio-taped short stories, radio ads, songs, documentaries, etc.

Printed/written materials
Newspaper articles, movie advertisements, astrology columns, sports reports, lyrics to songs, restaurant menus, street signs, tourist information brochures, maps, TV guides, comic strips books, etc.

(b) Materials written specifically for language teaching do not always prepare learners for coping with the language used in the 'real world'. Which materials, in particular, do not seem to provide 'natural' or 'authentic' input for language learning? Which texts or materials instead are more likely to provide input that will engage learners in interesting and real-life activities?

(c) Stefania, a lower secondary school teacher, was asked how she deals with input in her teaching.[1] Read through Extracts 1-3 from her interview and consider the following questions:

- What are her main problems in providing 'authentic' and interesting input in her lessons?
- How does she cope with these problems?

---

(1) *Coursebooks on the market are pretty disappointing and boring [...] They lack listening materials and those ones afforded are not suitable. They are either too difficult or too easy [...] sometimes I prepare extra materials with a song or something related to it to get the students involved.*

(2) *Listening from an audio-recorded source is certainly the most difficult thing because you can't adapt the speed of speech and there is no interaction.*

(3) *My students start with a limited knowledge of English [...] So in my first and second year classes I speak Italian most of the time. I start using more English in the third year class when they understand a bit more.*

2.3 The principle

The principle targeted in this chapter originates from Krashen's Input Hypothesis (1985: 4). The hypothesis is aimed at highlighting the role of 'comprehensible' input in the acquisition process:

> **Comprehensible input is the essential ingredient for second language acquisition.**

The Input Hypothesis, later referred to as the Comprehension Hypothesis (1994), is considered the central part of one of the early theories in SLA, the Monitor Theory, which was developed by Stephen Krashen in the 1970s and 1980s (Krashen 1981, 1982, 1985). On account of the considerable influence that the Monitor Theory has had in language pedagogy, we will illustrate the more general framework in which the Input Hypothesis is embedded through a brief presentation of the other hypotheses comprising the theory.

- The Acquisition-Learning Hypothesis: learners have two distinct and independent ways of developing competence in a second language: through 'acquisition' – a subconscious process similar to the way children acquire their first language and through 'learning' – a conscious process which implies 'knowing about' language, namely knowing its grammar and being able to talk about it. These two processes lead to two types of knowledge that can be seen as separate: the 'acquired' knowledge is used to produce language while the 'learned' knowledge is used to check the correctness of the learner's utterances.

- The Natural Order Hypothesis: learners acquire the rules of a language in a predictable order. Some forms tend to be acquired earlier than others; for example the progressive marker -*ing* and the plural marker -*s* are among the first morphemes to be acquired, while the third person singular marker -*s* and the possessive *'s* are typically acquired later. Similarly, learners tend to pass through predictable stages in the acquisition of grammatical structures such as negation and questions. The order of acquisition does not appear to be determined by the complexity of the structures to be acquired or the order in which lexicogrammar is taught.

- The Monitor Hypothesis: learners' ability to produce utterances comes from their 'acquired' knowledge. Conscious knowledge plays only a limited role in second language performance and functions as an editor or 'monitor', but only under certain conditions: learners need to have sufficient time, be consciously focused on form, or concerned about correctness.

- The Affective Filter Hypothesis: for acquisition to take place, learners need to be 'open' to the input. The 'affective filter' is a mental block that prevents them from fully using input for acquisition. This happens when learners are unmotivated, lacking in self-confidence or anxious.

The Input Hypothesis, which completes the framework of the Monitor Theory, will be analysed in greater depth in the following sections (cf. Subsections 2.3.1 and 2.3.2).

2.3.1 The Input Hypothesis

The basic claim of the Input Hypothesis is that 'humans acquire language in only one way – by understanding messages, or by receiving "comprehensible input"' (Krashen 1985: 2). What does this imply for SLA? Learners are supposed to make progress by understanding input that contains structures at a stage a bit beyond their current level of competence. This is how Krashen (1985: 2) illustrates the process:

> We progress along the natural order [...] by understanding input that contains structures at our next 'stage' – structures that are a bit beyond our current level of competence. (We move from i, our current level, to $i+1$, the next level along the natural order, by understanding input containing $i+1$.)

What kind of explanation does Krashen (1985: 2) provide in support of his hypothesis?

> We are able to understand language containing unacquired grammar with the help of context, which includes extra-linguistic information, our knowledge of the world, and previously acquired linguistic competence. The caretaker provides extra-linguistic context by limiting speech to the child to the 'here' and 'now'. The beginning-language teacher provides context via visual aids (pictures and objects) and discussion of familiar topics.

Krashen and Terrell (1983: 33) compare this process to a 'net' which is cast around the learners' current level (their i) when the teacher talks to them in a language they have not yet acquired completely and wants to help them understand what is said: this net includes many instances of $i+1$ (cf. Subsection 2.3.2).

The Input Hypothesis also has a number of 'corollaries', as Krashen (1982: 2) points out:

(a)   'Speaking is a result of acquisition and not its cause'; it cannot be taught directly but 'emerges on its own as a result of building competence via comprehensible input'.

(b)   If input becomes 'comprehensible', namely it is understood by learners and is available in sufficient amount, then 'the necessary grammar is automatically provided'; this implies that learners will not need to be deliberately taught the specific structures they are due to acquire.

Although comprehensible input is the 'essential' ingredient for language acquisition, it is not considered sufficient by itself. According to Krashen, two additional factors need to be taken into account. First, learners do not simply acquire what they hear – the contribution of an 'internal language processor' (Chomsky's Language Acquisition Device, or LAD), that is an innate mental structure that handles the process of acquisition is also assumed. Second, learners need to be 'open' to the input for acquisition to take place. They, therefore, need to lower their 'affective filter', which may prevent them from fully utilizing the input they receive for language acquisition.

In support of his Input Hypothesis, Krashen (1985, 1994) reports evidence from method comparison research showing that students at beginning stages in Total Physical Response (TPR) classes and Natural Approach classes (cf. Subsection 2.3.2) outperform students in traditional classes on communicative tests, and do at least as well, or better, on grammar tests. These methods have one major characteristic in common: they provide a great deal of comprehensible input and aim for a low-anxiety environment. Likewise, research on extensive reading programmes, in which texts are at an appropriate level of complexity and interesting in content, has shown that those who read more do better on a variety of tests. Recent studies reviewed by Verspoor et al. (2009: 75) have confirmed that 'an input-only approach may be equally effective for teaching general language knowledge, although 'in the long run interaction, feedback and output may be needed for accuracy in the output' (cf. Chapters 5 and 6).

The following section illustrates a pedagogical approach that directly draws on Krashen's views about SLA. The analysis of the approach will focus on the implications of the Input Hypothesis for teaching.

2.3.2 Comprehensible input: Learning and teaching implications

Both in the illustration of his hypothesis (Krashen 1985, 1994) and in earlier publications, Krashen discusses the main implications of his Monitor Theory for classroom practice. As said, the central claim of the theory, which also informed the Input Hypothesis, is that language acquisition occurs only in one way, that is, by understanding messages or by getting comprehensible input (cf. Subsection 2.3.1). Krashen and Terrell's (1983) Natural Approach is based on this theory of SLA and was designed to address the needs of elementary students and help them achieve an intermediate level. The aim of this approach is then to supply learners with comprehensible input that will allow them to learn the language implicitly.

The Natural Approach assumes four principles (Krashen and Terrell 1983: 20–21):

- Comprehension precedes production: this follows from the hypotheses presented above that 'acquisition is the basis for production ability' and that in order for acquisition to take place, the learner must understand messages. Some of the implications of these principles are that teachers always use the target language, will focus on a topic of interest for the student and will help students understand.

- Production will emerge in stages and 'students are not forced to speak before they are ready'; these stages typically consist of nonverbal responses, responses with a single word, combinations of two or three words, sentences and more complex discourse. Errors that do not interfere with communication are not corrected.

- The teaching syllabus consists of communication goals: the focus of each classroom activity is organized by topic, not by a specific grammatical structure. 'Grammar will be effectively acquired if goals are communicative.'

- The classroom activities aimed at acquisition 'must foster a lowering of the affective filter': they will focus on topics which are interesting and relevant to the students and encourage them to express their ideas, opinions, desires, emotions and feelings.

The requirement that input be comprehensible has several relevant implications for classroom practice, as Krashen and Terrell (1983: 55) underline:

First, it implies that whatever helps comprehension is important. This is why visual aids are so useful. Pictures and other visuals [...] supply the extra-linguistic context that helps the acquirer to understand and thereby to acquire. Second, it implies that vocabulary is important [...] with more vocabulary there will be more comprehension and with more comprehension, there will be more acquisition. [...] A third implication is that in giving input, in talking to students, the teacher needs to be concerned primarily with whether students understand the message.

Moreover, Krashen and Terrell (1983: 155) maintain that 'comprehensibility is dependent directly on the ability to recognize the meaning of key elements in the utterance. Thus, acquisition will not take place without comprehension of vocabulary'. Since the early stages, teachers should give complete attention to vocabulary recognition so that learners develop listening strategies based mainly on the ability to recognize key lexical items. Classroom activities should aim at continual comprehension of lexical items in which language is used for meaningful and communicative purposes.

Given that speaking is not essential for language acquisition, Krashen and Terrell (1983: 56) think that 'the best way to teach speaking is to focus on listening (and reading) and spoken fluency will emerge on its own'. In situations where there is some need for early communication, the teacher can encourage some limited early production through routines and patterns in dialogues. Finally, the study of grammar has a limited role: only certain rules need to be taught for most learners and will be used as a 'supplement' to acquisition.[2] Learners are not expected to be concerned with points of grammar while they are speaking in free conversation; the time to use grammar is in writing and in prepared speech, when monitoring is a relatively simple task. Grammar is, therefore, acknowledged a role as a subject of study in programmes at an advanced level addressed to future linguists and language teachers.

Krashen and Terrell (1983: 73) suggest three stages for the planning of a syllabus aimed at the learners' development of basic oral and written communication skills. The stages involve personalization and the use of familiar topics. At the first stage ('personal identification'), students learn how to talk about themselves, their family and their friends; this stage is aimed primarily at getting students to know each other better thus lowering the affective filter. At the second stage, students will get comprehensible input about experiences and have opportunities to engage in conversations about their own experiences (holidays, common situations, etc.). The third stage consists of input and discussion concerning opinions about family, friends, relationships, society, media and so forth.

Since the priority of the Natural Approach is to afford comprehensible input, Krashen and Terrell (1983: 76–77) also suggest a number of techniques that are considered particularly effective for the purpose: (1) giving commands to students and having them act out what is said; (2) using physical characteristics and clothing of the students; (3) using visuals, for example pictures, charts and advertisements and (4) using repetition and paraphrase. Each technique will be briefly explained below.

(1) The technique of giving commands to students and asking them to act out what is said forms the basis of the TPR, a language teaching method developed by James Asher in the 1960s.[3] The method attempts to teach language through physical activity and emphasizes the development of comprehension skills. At first, the commands are quite simple (*Stand up, turn around*); then parts of the body and body actions can be taught, together with a number of vocabulary items (*Put your hands on your shoulders, pick up the pencil and put it on the table*). Commands can also be combined with statements (*If Tom walks to the door, then stand up*).

(2) The use of contextual information related to the physical characteristics and clothing of the students themselves provides additional opportunities to make input comprehensible (*Barbara is wearing glasses. Who else is wearing glasses? Who is wearing a yellow shirt today?*).

(3) The use of visuals of different types can also serve the same purpose; for example, the teacher uses a picture or a visual focusing on specific features or information and introducing new words or expressions. Students can then be involved through questions. The use of visuals can be used with commands (*Find the picture of the pop star and show it to the class*).

(4) Teachers can also aid comprehension by making some 'adjustments' in the language used in the classroom. These modifications may include slowing down, repeating, restating, changing *wh*-questions to *yes/no* questions. It was observed that teacher talk shows indeed similar features to other types of simplified speech such as caretaker speech (used by mothers, fathers and others with children) and foreigner talk used by native speakers when talking to non-native speakers. Input is therefore 'roughly tuned' to facilitate the understanding of what is said. Several features of simplified or modified second language input have been investigated (cf. Chaudron 1988 for a comprehensive review). Table 2.1 describes the features of simplified input employed in second language situations according to five categories: rate of speech, vocabulary, syntax, discourse and speech setting.

Table 2.1 Characteristics of simplified second language input (adapted from Hatch 1983).

Rate of speech	Longer and more frequent pauses; fewer reduced vowels and contractions; extra stress on nouns
Vocabulary	More basic and high-frequency vocabulary; fewer idioms; fewer pronoun forms; extra lexical information related to morphology (*miracle, anything that's miraculous*), or semantic features (*a cathedral usually means a church that has very high ceilings*); marked definitions (*This is a …/It's a kind of a …*)
Syntax	Short sentences; lower degree of subordination; repetition and restatement; more declaratives and statements; expansion of learner's utterance
Discourse	Choice of responses is provided (*Where did you go? Did you go to the beach or to the mountains? What did he want? A book?*); correction (*You mean he left?*)
Speech setting	Repetition of scenarios

Lee and VanPatten (2003: 30) also underline that simplified input provides learners with language that is not only more comprehensible, but also easier to process: 'the forms and structure of the language are more easily perceived, and the learner has a greater chance to hear and process the form-meaning connections that are contained in the input' (cf. Chapter 3).

The deployment of the techniques illustrated above seems to suggest that it is relatively simple to enhance comprehension without requiring more than minimal production. The transition to a stage of early production can be facilitated through gradual techniques within the normal comprehension activities, such as asking simple questions which require '*yes-no*' replies, using '*either-or*' questions or asking for the identification of items that have already been introduced (Krashen and Terrell 1983: 79). Production can be further extended by feeding prefabricated patterns, for example, open-ended sentences with a slot or open dialogues that students complete, or through association, that is, by relating the meaning of a new lexical item not only with its target language form but also with the experiences or opinions of a particular student (Krashen and Terrell 1983: 84–85).

Krashen and Terrell (1983: 97) also identify specific types of acquisition activities that constitute the core of the Natural Approach classroom. We will first consider what the term 'activity' implies:

By activity we mean a broad range of events which have a purpose other than conscious grammar practice. Thus, we refer to activities as opposed to audiolingual drills or cognitive learning exercises. For acquisition to take place, the topics used in each activity must be intrinsically interesting or meaningful so that the students' attention is focused on the content of the utterances instead of the form.

While in the early stages the most important function of activities is to provide comprehensible input and mainly develop listening skills, at a later stage oral production takes a more important role. Each activity focuses on a particular topic and/or situation and students will normally be made aware of the content of the activity. As regards the format, Krashen and Terrell point out that an activity may also often have a specific form or structure that can be used repeatedly. This will provide learners with a familiar cognitive 'frame' to rely on. However, it is important to remember that the purpose of activities is to supply comprehensible input, not to teach a specific structure, 'since conscious concentration on structure and form may prevent focusing on the message and may thus impede acquisition' (Krashen and Terrell 1983: 98). Moreover, the effectiveness of any activity can be measured by the interest it evokes: 'discussing topics that are of interest to the students is not just a frill: it is essential if language acquisition is to take place'.

The activities that best qualify for the Natural Approach fall into the following four types, although many of them contain elements of more than one type (see Table 2.2).

Table 2.2 Types of acquisition activities according to the Natural Approach (adapted from Krashen and Terrell 1983).

Affective-humanistic activities	Dialogues, interviews, preference ranking, personal charts and tables, activities using the imagination
Problem-solving activities	Carrying out a practical task, making a story using pictures, sorting out a problem using charts, graphs, ads, maps
Games	'Illogical combination' games, guessing games, action games, contests, problem-solving games, etc.
Content activities	Presentations, reports, 'show and tell' activities, films, music and drama activities, subject-based activities, etc.

These activities are designed to further the acquisition process by making input comprehensible in two ways: 'through student interlanguage', that is the language used by the students themselves, and 'from the teacher talk included in the activity as well as in the follow-up to the activity' (Krashen and Terrell 1983: 99). We will briefly illustrate each type of activity.

Affective-humanistic activities involve students' feelings, opinions, desires, ideas and experiences. Within this group, open dialogues and role plays provide repeated opportunities to focus on particular conversational situations. As for interviews, the most successful ones are those which focus on interesting events in the students' lives or on their wants, needs, feelings or opinions. They can also be constructed around a particular grammatical structure: 'if the conversational exchange is interesting enough, the grammatical focus will probably not interfere with the interaction and the activity' (Krashen and Terrell 1983: 102). Preference ranking consists of a simple lead-in statement (*My favourite summer activity is ...*) followed by three or four possible responses that students rank from 1 to 4 according to their own preference. It should be noted, though, that the point of this activity is not the initial ranking itself, but the follow-up conversation between the teacher and the students (*Who ranked swimming as number one? Where do you swim? When did you first learn to swim?*). The construction of tables and charts with information about the students can serve as the basis for class discussions. In the last type of activities in this group, students are asked to imagine some situation or some person and describe what they 'saw' and 'said'. As Krashen and Terrell (1983: 107) state, visualizations can provide comprehensible input in two ways: the teacher may guide visualizations explicitly (*Think of ... It may be outdoors or indoors. Look around. What can you see?*) or imagine some hypothetical situation and ask the students to report what happened.

Problem-solving activities aim to focus the learners' attention on finding a correct answer to a question, a problem or a situation. Comprehensible input is supplied in a variety of ways: by explaining the problem to be solved, discussing the problem and comparing the solutions to the problem. Learners can be involved in different types of activities in which, in pairs or small groups, they are asked to carry out a specific task (e.g. washing a car, painting a room), build up a story using pictures or sort out a problem using charts, graphs, ads, maps (find a place, the time of an event, the price of something, etc.).

According to Krashen and Terrell (1983: 121), games are not simply a way of enhancing students' interests but 'can serve very well as the basis for an acquisition activity and are therefore not a reward nor a "frill", but an important experience in the acquisition process'. They can be used to provide comprehensible input in various ways either through teacher talk or student interlanguage, or both. For example, in games that focus on particular words, learners have to answer the teacher's questions and find out what is wrong about illogical combinations or expressions (*What is strange about a bird swimming? What kind of birds swim?*); in guessing games they have to guess what another student is thinking or miming, or the activity he/she normally does (*Do you do this activity in evening? Do you do this activity with your friends?*), or what particular famous person he/she is thinking about

(*Is he an actor? Is he married?*); in action games they have to find a person with specific characteristics (*Find someone who is going to visit Spain this summer/ has never been abroad/ likes to watch thrillers*); in contests, which may replicate television formats, students can be involved in 'question and answer sessions'.

In content activities the purpose is to learn something new other than language, for example through reports, presentations, 'show and tell' activities, films, discussions and so forth: the important characteristic of these types of activities is maintaining students' interest and ensuring comprehensible input (Krashen and Terrell 1983: 123).

Finally, although reading does not play a major role in the Natural Approach, it can serve at any rate as an 'additional' source of comprehensible input. The texts for the reading activities need to meet two main criteria: they must be at an appropriate level of complexity and be interesting. Learners will be trained to develop and use 'meaning-getting' strategies both within the text (looking ahead and back, illustrations, headings) and outside the text (real-world information and knowledge of the language).

2.4 The principle in the classroom

This section aims to provide examples of the way a number of techniques and activities illustrated above with reference to Krashen's Input Hypothesis can be implemented in actual teaching practice. The examples refer to a teacher who attempts to make input comprehensible in a speaking task and a listening task. Both tasks involve a group of students at an elementary level.

2.4.1 Stefania trying to make input comprehensible in a speaking task and a listening task

Video Extract 2

(a) Before watching the tasks from Stefania's lesson, think of what you do or you would do to make oral input 'comprehensible' for your students.

(b) Look at the techniques listed below. Which ones do you or would you consider particularly effective in facilitating comprehension?

1. reference to real-world information/personal experience
2. use of visuals, objects etc.
3. miming and use of gestures
4. repetitions
5. paraphrase
6. simplification
7. use of questions
8. metalinguistic information
9. intonation emphasis
10. use of the L1

(c) Watch the tasks in Stefania's lesson:

- In the first task, 'Matchmaker', the students are involved in a problem-solving activity and they have to find the perfect partners for some people shown by the teacher.
- In the second task, 'New Year's resolutions', the students have to watch a group of people celebrating New Year's Eve and find out what their resolutions are.

What type of input is provided in each task? What materials are used as a source of input?

2.4.2 Personalization

One of the main assumptions of Krashen's Input Hypothesis is that dealing with topics that are familiar or of interest to the students together with the use of specific techniques that facilitate comprehension will ensure optimal input language acquisition to take place. This will also contribute to the lowering of the students' affective filter as students will be concerned with the message, not with the form, and will be encouraged to express their ideas, opinions, desires, emotions and feelings (cf. Subsection 2.3.1). The choice of familiar or interesting topics is thus linked to the selection of tasks that would involve 'personalization' so that students can engage in conversations about familiar situations, personal experiences and opinions (cf. Subsection 2.3.2).

(a) Focus on the transcriptions of two extracts of Stefania's lesson. Which is the topic in each task? How does Stefania involve her students in a process of personalization in each task?

   (1) 'Matchmaker': Stefania is showing the picture of a woman who is looking for a partner.

> T: *[...] so I will <u>pretend</u>. do you understand ↑<u>pretend</u>? pretend means that what I I am a teacher but from now on I am not a teacher any more so I will be someone else mm ok? [...] I want to find a partner do you understand <u>partner</u>? (gestures) [...] who is a partner? for example is a ↑friend. [...] a very close friend I want to go out with. or a girlfriend or a boyfriend so I'm looking for my ↑<u>ideal</u> partner ehm? the <u>best</u> partner I can choose*

(2)   'New Year's resolutions': after showing a video, Stefania is talking about New Year's resolutions.

> T: *this is the <u>last</u> day of December the <u>last</u> night of December [...] it's the last <u>day</u> of the year. and what do you usually <u>do:</u> on the thirty first? you usually? ↑celebrate! ok? you go to <u>parties</u>, or you stay at home. but you <u>celebrate</u>. [...] with your family. or?*
> S: *friends.*
> T: *[...] do you understand flatmate? Ok? you probably don't have a flatmate because you live with your ↑<u>family</u>. [...] they are not a family. they are just friends. they <u>share</u> the <u>same</u> flat. they <u>share</u>. they live together. ok? do you understand?*

(In the transcripts, an upward arrow and a downward arrow denote marked rising and falling shift in intonation respectively. Underlined words indicate louder volume. One or more colons indicate lengthening of the preceding sound.)

2.4.3 Communication and meaning-getting techniques

Within the Natural Approach, input can be made comprehensible through a number of communication and meaning-getting techniques, such as having students act out what the teacher says, using physical characteristics and clothing of the students, using different types of visuals, repetition and paraphrase (cf. Subsection 2.3.2). Krashen and Terrell (1983: 75) also point out that learners can be facilitated in their job of understanding if they are led to pay attention to the context and the keywords in the sentences: 'this contextual inferencing is the secret to learning to understand a second language and to the eventual success of the student in the acquisition process'.

(a) Analyse the following three short extracts from Stefania's lesson. Identify the techniques she uses at different stages to facilitate her students' comprehension. Which particular technique(s) does she seem to rely on?

---

(1) ↑*first of all I am this young lady here (she shows the picture). m?
how can I describe ↓this young lady? m? what do you think? I am
quite* <u>*tall*</u> *(gesture) m? and and* <u>*slim*</u> *(gesture) yes fortunately I'm
slim.*

(2) *[...] what is this? (she shows a calendar) [...] this is a (she shakes
the calendar) calendar. And this month is* <u>*December*</u>*. this is
the* <u>*last*</u> *day of December the* <u>*last*</u> *night of december it is very
important. [...]*

(3) *so I'm quite sporty. a sporty person. m? do you understand*
<u>*sporty*</u>*? what is a sport? a sport is an* <u>*activity*</u> *that you can do in a
game you play something ok. so I'm sporty.*

(b) Go through the above extracts again. By referring to Table 2.1, determine
what types of adjustments Stefania makes to 'simplify' her speech and aid
students' comprehension.

(c) Vocabulary plays a key role in the process of enhancing comprehension.
Look at the two extracts below from another stage of Stefania's lesson and
analyse how she focuses on the comprehension of vocabulary. What types of
vocabulary does she target (single word, derived word, compound, phrasal
verb, collocation)? Which technique does she use to draw the students'
attention on a specific word and make input comprehensible?

---

(1) T: *our new year's* <u>*resolutions*</u> <u>*resolutions*</u> *what should*
<u>*resolutions*</u> *(she writes it on the flip chart) do you understand
this word? what is a resolution? what I want to do ↑*<u>*next*</u>*.
what I want to do ↑*<u>*different*</u>*. in ↑this case this is the end
of the year so for the next year I want to do something
↑different. this is* <u>*my*</u> *resolution. do you understand this?
can you translate into Italian? [...] how can you translate a
resolution?*

S: *soluzione* [solution]

T: *not exactly no*

(2) T: *he wants to* <u>*give up*</u> *fast food. do you understand? of course*
<u>*fast food*</u> *you understand* <u>*fast food*</u>*. but ↑*<u>*give up*</u> *↓fast food?
(she writes it on the flip chart) [...] give up. and what did he
say? and become more healthy. something like that. m so to
give up something. what is? I want to* <u>*give up*</u> *eating fast food.
does it mean that he wants to ↑*<u>*go on*</u> *eating fast food or ↑*<u>*to
stop*</u> *eating fast food? what do you think? [...]*

(d) As mentioned earlier in the chapter (cf. Subsection 2.3.2), according to the Natural Approach speaking is not considered a priority. Early production can be enhanced within the normal comprehension activities through simple questions which require 'yes-no' replies, using 'either-or' questions or asking for the identification of items that have already been introduced. Look at the extract below. Which techniques does Stefania use to enhance students' response to the topic she introduced?

T: *love. a new partner. love. and but she used an adjective.*
     gorgeous. gorgeous. do you think it's positive or negative?
     someone gorgeous.
Ss: *positive.*
T: *positive. gorgeous. (she writes it on the flip chart) so she wants*
     to find someone gorgeous. someone that she likes very much.
     ok? and [...]
S: *but ↑gorgeous is one word or two?*
T: *it is one word sorry. one word. gorgeous. ↑you're gorgeous!*
     when you are wearing something very smart. very elegant
     you're gorgeous.
S: *yes.*

2.5 Restructuring and planning

In this section you will be involved in the evaluation of three examples of listening and speaking tasks and asked to implement them according to the implications derived from Krashen's Input Hypothesis and the guidelines provided by the Natural Approach (cf. Subsection 2.3.2 and Section 2.4).

(a) Look at an example of a listening task addressed to an elementary level class. Go through the spoken description of the room provided during the listening task.

This is a nice comfortable room, with a sofa, chairs, television, rug. What a lovely little dog under the table. And there are plates and glasses on the table… and spoons, forks and knives…and a jug of water. Behind the table on the wall there's a picture of a horse, and if you look out of the window you can see the full moon shining on the sea…

How would you implement the description in order to aid students' comprehension during the task? For example: *Look at the room in the picture. It is a nice room. It is also comfortable. It has....*

Look at the room in the picture. Listen to the description of the room. Circle the objects that do not match with the description.

(Adapted from Ur 1984: 82)

(b) Adapt the previous task. Use the same picture and ask the students to colour some objects in the room. Prepare a spoken description with the necessary instructions:

You have a black and white picture of a room. I'm going to tell you how to colour some objects in the room. Are you ready? ...

Include all the suitable modifications to make the description comprehensible for students at an elementary level.

(c) Look at the following listening task from a coursebook for an intermediate level class.

- Go through the transcription of the conversation and identify the keywords or expressions that are essential for the comprehension of what is said. Which of them may be unfamiliar to intermediate level students?

- Which techniques would be necessary to support learners' comprehension before and during the listening task?

Poor Carl has had an accident. He is speaking to his friend, Andy, on the phone. Listen to their conversation and answer these questions.

    a. What type of accident did he have? Has he recovered yet?

    b. Where did the accident happen?

    c. How did it happen?

A = Andy   C = Carl

A Hi! Carl? It's Andy.

C Andy!

A Yeah. How are you? Feeling better?

C No! Not a lot. I have to sit down most of the time. It's too tiring - walking with a crutch.

A Really? Still using a crutch, eh? So you're not back at work yet?

C No. And I'm bored to death. I don't go back to the hospital for two more weeks.

A Two more weeks! That's when the plaster comes off, is it?

C Well, I hope so. I can't wait to have two legs again! Anyway. How are you? Still missing all that snow and sun?

A No, I'm fine. The suntan's fading though. Josie's is too. She sends love, by the way.

C Love to her, too. I miss you all. By the way, have you got any holiday photos back yet?

A Yes, yes, I have. I got them back today. They're good. I didn't realize we'd taken so many.

C What about that one you took of that amazing sunset behind the hotel?

A Yes, the sunset. It's a good one. All of us together on Bob and Marcia's balcony, with the mountains and the snow in the background. It's beautiful. Brings back memories, doesn't it?

C Yeah. The memory of me skiing into a tree!

A Yes, I know. I'm sorry. At least it was towards the end; it could have been the first day. You only came home two days early.

(Adapted from Soars, L. and J. Soars 1996: 88–89)

(d) Exploit the topic of the conversation in the listening task above for a follow-up speaking task:

Tell the class about an accident which happened to you or someone in your family when you were on holiday.

How would you prepare the students for the speaking task? What kind of questions would you ask? Would you use any visuals? Would you provide a list of words related to the topic?

2.6 Conclusions

This chapter has aimed to explore the role of input in SLA according to one of the early hypotheses – Krashen's Input Hypothesis (1985). The principle originating from this hypothesis is that 'comprehensible input is the essential ingredient for SLA'. The main learning and teaching implications of the hypothesis were also highlighted through the guidelines provided by Krashen and Terrell in their Natural Approach (1983), a teaching method which translates Krashen's theory of SLA into practice. Additional examples of actual classroom activities based on Krashen's hypothesis were also provided.

However, since its onset, Krashen's Input Hypothesis has left a number of questions unanswered and soon became the object of debate and considerable criticism among SLA researchers. White (1987: 108) argued that the hypothesis shows a number of flaws. Where 'comprehensible input' is interpreted as 'simplified' input, 'one is in danger of providing less than adequate input to the acquirer'. Moreover, the emphasis on the role of meaning and of extra-linguistic factors in making input comprehensible underestimates the role of psycholinguistic factors. Finally, the hypothesis 'fails to consider cases where the input does not help at all, and underestimates the problem of the acquisition of form'. In conclusion, White's critique calls for 'a far more precise characterization of the possible interactions between learner and input'. On the other hand, VanPatten and Williams (2015: 31), among others, underline the difficulty of testing the specific constructs of Krashen's Monitor Theory. In the specific case of the Input Hypothesis, they argue that 'if we wanted to do research, for example, to see if the provision of $i+1$ in the input really does facilitate acquisition, how should we define i, and how do we subsequently operationalize $i+1$?' In a similar vein, Gass and Selinker (2008: 310) observe that 'the hypothesis is not specific as to how to define levels of knowledge' so it is not clear how it will be possible to gear the input provided one degree beyond the actual learner's level of competence. Issues of 'quantity' and 'quality' of the input, therefore, raise the crucial question of determining what is to be considered 'sufficient' and what is not. According to Ellis (2008: 251) 'perhaps the major problem is that Krashen paid little attention to what comprehension entails', that is, 'what processes are needed for acquisition to take place'. Given that learners need access to input that is comprehensible, it may be argued that 'simplifying input does not guarantee that it is comprehended' and that 'acquisition will automatically take place if learners comprehend input' (Ellis and Shintani 2014: 177).

Notwithstanding a number of flaws, Krashen's Hypothesis succeeded in raising a lot of interest among second and foreign language teachers by drawing their attention to the role of 'input' for both comprehension and acquisition. It can't be argued that the teaching approach underlying the hypothesis has supplied practitioners with examples of 'good' sources of input, engaging activities as well as specific techniques for enhancing comprehension. Although it is a given fact that learners do need input to learn and some level of comprehension of the input is required for acquisition to take place, SLA researchers have questioned the fact that comprehensible input is a 'sufficient' condition to trigger language acquisition. In the wake of Krashen's hypothesis, they further investigated the complex interplay between input and other cognitive, interactional and sociocultural factors, as will be discussed in the following chapters.

2.7 Notes

1   The interview data are from Pedrazzini (2012).
2   Krashen and Terrell (1983: 31–32) refer here to those rules defined as 'simple', which 'do not require elaborate or complex movements of permutation', but only the attachment of a morpheme. The third-person singular is an example of 'simple rule': 'it is relatively easy to describe and learn, and it is late acquired'.
3   Asher's TPR is sometimes linked to a movement in foreign language teaching referred to as the Comprehension Approach (Winitz 1981). Comprehension-based teaching is built on similar principles: comprehension abilities precede productive skills; speaking should be delayed until learners are ready to speak; skills acquired to listening transfer to other skills; teaching should emphasize meaning rather than form and teaching should minimize learner stress.

2.8 Further reading

Krashen, S. (1981), *Second Language Acquisition and Second Language Learning*, Oxford: Pergamon.
Krashen, S. (1982), *Principles and Practice in Second Language Acquisition*, Oxford: Pergamon.

Krashen, S. (1985), *The Input Hypothesis: Issues and Implications*, London: Longman.

Krashen, S. (1994), 'The input hypothesis and its rivals', in N. Ellis (ed.), *Implicit and Explicit Learning of Languages*, 45–77, London: Academic Press.

Krashen, S. and T. D. Terrell (1983), *The Natural Approach*, New York: Pergamon.

Pedrazzini, L. (2012), 'SLA principles from practice: the Input Hypothesis', in L. Pedrazzini and A. Nava (eds), *Learning and Teaching English. Insights from Research*, 117–144, Monza: Polimetrica.

White, L. (1987), 'Against comprehensible input: the Input Hypothesis and the development of second-language competence', *Applied Linguistics*, 8 (2): 95–110.

Chapter 3
Input processing

In the previous chapter (see Chapter 2) we explored one of the main givens in SLA research; that is, comprehensible input is a necessary ingredient for SLA. As VanPatten (2015: 113) highlights, 'acquisition is, to a certain degree, a by-product of comprehension' and 'although comprehension cannot guarantee acquisition, acquisition cannot happen if comprehension does not occur'. However, making input comprehensible was soon deemed insufficient to fully account for acquisition to take place. As a matter of fact, a good deal of acquisition is also dependent upon learners using appropriate strategies to interpret what is heard or read. This involves making appropriate form-meaning connections during comprehension.

In this chapter we will describe how learners make sense of the language they hear or read and how they connect (or do not connect) particular forms of a language (e.g. the inflectional suffix -*ed*) with corresponding meanings (e.g. past time reference); that is how they 'process' data in the input. The principles that will be presented are grounded in Input Processing (IP), a theory or model that explains what happens during comprehension that may interact with other processes and affect acquisition (VanPatten 1996, 2004, 2015). Underlying the model is the assumption that 'connecting formal features to their meanings and functions is part of acquisition' (VanPatten 2012: 269). The teaching implications for this model will be examined in relation to Processing Instruction (PI), a pedagogical approach whose purpose is to optimize the ways in which learners attend to input and help them use appropriate processing strategies.

The following main questions will be addressed in the chapter:

- What aspects of the language do learners spontaneously focus on when they try to understand a message? What language features do they not attend to?
- What strategies and mechanisms do learners use in processing new data in the input?
- How can teachers help learners optimize their processing strategies and make appropriate form-meaning connections?

3.2 Experience

(a) Understanding something in a language that we do not know is indeed a challenging experience. Try this quick experiment. Below are five sentences in five different languages. Cover the sentence(s) in the language(s) you know. Try to understand the sentence(s) in the language(s) you do not know. Then answer the questions provided.

1. German: *Sylvia ist nicht nur intelligent, sondern auch fleissig.*
2. French: *Sylvia n'est pas seulement intelligente mais aussi travailleure.*
3. Italian: *Sylvia non è solo intelligente ma anche diligente.*
4. Polish: *Sylwia nie jest tylko mądrą, ale także sumienną.*
5. Swedish: *Sylvia är inte bara intelligent men också flitig.*

What were you able to understand in the language(s) you do not know? Did you recognize any words that are similar in your language? Which words were easier to understand? Are they mainly content words (nouns, verbs, adjectives, adverbs) or grammatical words (articles, prepositions, pronouns, auxiliaries, etc.)? Was sentence structure a clue you used? Without looking back, what do you remember about verb forms used, word order or how negation is formed?

(Adapted from VanPatten 2003: 29–30)

(b) Look at this listening task addressed to a pre-intermediate level class. What is the lexicogrammatical focus of the task? Does the task help students focus on the lexicogrammatical feature?

Listen to the following story that a student told about his first day in London. Tick the places the student visited.

Buckingham Palace   Hyde Park   Tower Bridge Madame Tussaud's
Trafalgar Square   Covent Garden   The National Gallery

(Transcription)

I really wanted to see Madame Tussaud's so early in the morning I took a quick shower and travelled by train to Baker Street station. I had my picture taken with David Beckham, well the wax model that is. I also visited Trafalgar Square and saw Nelson's Column. There were so many pigeons there! In the afternoon I waited for a train to take me to Covent Garden. I really hated London trains; they are awful. Covent Garden was fantastic, I watched the different street performers, and I really enjoyed listening to the music. I finished my exploration and sunbathed for a bit in Hyde Park – London's most famous and largest open space. I arrived home quite late and called my parents back in China and talked about my day. All in all, I had a wonderful time!

(Adapted from Benati 2015)

3.3 The principles

What happens when learners hear (or read) something in an L2 that they need to understand? As VanPatten (2009: 48) points out, two things must simultaneously happen:

(1) They must attempt to understand what the other person is saying and (2) their internal processors must map what said (meaning) onto how it was said (form, i.e. the formal properties of language). This is a tremendous challenge.

In the 1970s and 1980s, SLA researchers came to agree that exposure to 'meaning-bearing' input is essential to SLA. This implies that learners must be exposed to samples of language (and possibly in great amounts) that has some communicative intent. It was also suggested that the input must be comprehensible (cf. Chapter 2) or modified through interaction (cf. Chapter 5). However, VanPatten (2012: 269) argues that researchers 'were looking at the role of input globally […] and not psycholinguistically in terms of processing'. IP (VanPatten 1996, 2004, 2015) thus emerged as a theory or model aiming to explain how the learner's mind interacts with input, that is, which psycholinguistic strategies and mechanisms are used to derive linguistic data in the input. VanPatten (1996: 7) motivates his theory of IP as follows:

From a purely psycholinguistic perspective, we note that what language learners hear and see may not be what gets processed. […] What is clear is that learners filter input; they possess internal processors that act on the input and only part of it makes its way into the developing system at any given time. […] What learners do to input during comprehension – that is how intake is derived – is called input processing.

'Intake', a term first coined by Corder (1967), thus constitutes the part of 'comprehended' input that learners process and will be incorporated into the learner's developing system or interlanguage through further processing. To put it simply, it is the part of input that can be used for learning. However, as VanPatten (2004: 7) explains, 'intake is not just "filtered" data but it may include data processed incorrectly (i.e. the wrong form-meaning connection may be made)'. IP thus involves making appropriate form-meaning/function connections during real-time comprehension (VanPatten 2004: 7). That is to say, a learner notices a form (e.g. the inflectional suffix -*s* in the word *boys*) and at the same time determines its meaning (plurality of a noun). The strategies that learners use to map forms to meanings are 'largely unconscious' and psycholinguistic; these types of strategies are not synonymous with 'learning strategies', a term used to define tools, techniques and behaviours learners rely on to control and enhance their learning (VanPatten 1996: 10).

It should also be noted that in the IP model, 'processing' is not equivalent to phenomena such as attention or noticing, which have been posited to play a role in L2 development (cf. Chapters 4 and 5). As VanPatten (2004: 6) explains, 'processing is not the same as perception of a form or noticing'. A learner may perceive and notice a form but not connect it to any function or meaning. But what does noticing involve? The concept, which is strictly related to that of attention, was defined by Schmidt (e.g. Schmidt 1990, 2001) in his Noticing Hypothesis. Schmidt (1990: 142) argues 'you can't learn a foreign language [...] through subliminal perception'. Attention to input is required and noticing – the registration of formal features in the input – is an essential process in L2 acquisition. Attention is therefore responsible for the subjective experience of noticing. This means that to learn any linguistic feature of the L2, learners need to notice this feature; that is, they have to pay 'focal attention' to it; this entails that learners are aware of aspects of the linguistic feature although they may not be able to assign any meaning or function to it. As Schmidt (2001: 5) posits:

> the objects of attention and noticing are elements of the surface structure
> of utterances in the input – instances of language, rather than any
> abstract rules or principles of which such instances may be exemplars.

Noticing is therefore 'the first step in language building, not the end of the process' (Schmidt 2001: 31). According to VanPatten (2004: 7) 'processing implies that perception and noticing have occurred'. Thus, the main issue from an IP perspective is how learners allocate attentional resources during online processing and in particular 'what causes certain (linguistic) stimuli in the input to be detected and not others?' (VanPatten 1996: 17).

IP aims to address three core questions (VanPatten 2015: 114):

1. Under what conditions do learners make initial form-meaning connections?
2. Why, at a given moment in time, do they make some and not other form-meaning connections?

3. What internal strategies do learners use in comprehending sentences and how might this affect acquisition?

Underlying these issues is the idea that an integral part of language acquisition is making form-meaning connections during comprehension. The following example will help contextualize the questions above:

> In English as an L2, learners must, at some point, map the meaning of PASTNESS onto the verb inflection /t/ (or -ed in written form). How does this happen and why don't learners do this from the first time they encounter this form in a context in which the speaker is clearly making reference to the past?

IP makes a number of claims to explain what guides learners' processing of linguistic data in the input as they try to understand a message. These claims are summarized below (VanPatten 2015: 115):

(1) Learners are driven to get meaning while comprehending.
(2) Comprehension for learners is initially quite effortful in terms of cognitive processing and working memory and [...] may tax the computational resources as learners engage in the millisecond-by-millisecond analysis of a sentence.
(3) At the same time, learners are limited capacity processors and cannot process and store the same amount of information as native speakers can.
(4) Learners make use of certain universals of IP but may also make use of the L1 input processor (or parser).

The above claims have led VanPatten (1996) to codify two major IP principles, with a set of subprinciples for each. The principles aim to explain how learners – left on their own – use their attentional resources when they process input data during comprehension:

- The Primacy of Meaning Principle (P1) (see Subsection 3.3.1)
- The First Noun Principle (P2) (see Subsection 3.3.2).

These principles, which have been slightly revised over time (VanPatten 2004, 2007, 2015), are not thought to act in isolation: sometimes they may act together or one may take precedence over the other. As VanPatten (2004: 19) argues,

> one must look at a variety of factors that influence processing rather than at one single principle or problem to determine why a form may be difficult to process in the input.

The principles also provide the theoretical basis for a pedagogical approach known as PI aimed at helping learners optimize their default processing strategies during comprehension (cf. Subsection 3.3.3).

3.3.1 The Primacy of Meaning Principle

According to 'the Primacy of Meaning Principle' (P1), learners process input for meaning before they process it for form. As explained above, the term 'process' refers to making connections between meaning and form. What the principle posits is that during the act of comprehension, learners will look for whatever meaning they can from the input: 'this "push to get meaning", combined with limited resources for processing input, means that certain elements of form will not get processed for acquisitional purposes' (VanPatten 2004: 7). The fact that learners are driven to get meaning from input has a number of consequences in terms of IP that will be illustrated in the following four subprinciples (VanPatten 2004).

Let us consider the first subprinciple:

> P1 (a) The Primacy of Content Words Principle: learners process content words in the input before anything else.

For example, if learners hear the sentence 'The cat is sleeping', which is said in a context in which a cat is actually sleeping, they will try to isolate the lexical forms that encode the meanings of *cat* and *sleep* (VanPatten 2015: 115). The fact that learners will first isolate lexical items and process them for meaning is aided by prosodic factors: in most natural languages content words tend to receive stronger stress than non-content words or inflections. According to VanPatten (2012: 270), 'in the early stages, processing lexical items is "good enough" and gets the learners through most of the tasks they need to perform in and out of classrooms'.

The second subprinciple is a consequence of the 'The Primacy of Content Words Principle':

> P1 (b) The Lexical Preference Principle: learners will tend to rely on lexical items as opposed to grammatical forms to get meaning when both encode the same semantic information.

Meanings are often encoded more than once in a sentence or in discourse. For example, in the sentence *I called my mother yesterday* the meaning of pastness is both encoded in the inflectional suffix *-ed* of the verb and the adverb of time *yesterday*. If learners rely on lexical items first to get meaning, grammatical forms such as inflections (if they are redundant) will not get processed. To interpret the subprinciple correctly, VanPatten (2004: 9) points out that 'the learner may very well perceive the form and notice it, but because no connection to meaning or function is made, the form is dropped from further processing'. Thus, in the previous example learners will not process the past inflectional suffix *-ed* but derive the meaning of pastness from their processing of the adverb of time. According to VanPatten (2015: 116) a possible consequence of this principle is that 'learners will begin to process redundant grammatical forms only when they have processed and incorporated corresponding lexical forms into their developing linguistic system'. This also explains why redundant grammatical items take the longest for learners to acquire.

Principle 1(c) posits that when meaning is not redundant and is not encoded in a lexical item, learners will turn to grammatical forms to see if a semantic notion is expressed there:

P1 (c) The Preference for Nonredundancy Principle: learners are more likely to process non-redundant meaningful grammatical forms before they process redundant meaningful forms.

For example, -*ing* is the sole marker of the semantic notion of an event in process, as in *What are you doing? I'm baking a cake. Why are you asking?* As such, this marker conveys high semantic information because there are no lexical items that carry the same information (VanPatten 2004: 10).[1] For example, as VanPatten (2015: 117) suggests, if we compare the sentences *The cat is sleeping* and *The cat sleeps ten hours every day*, in the first sentence there is no lexical indication of the meaning of 'in progress' conveyed by the grammatical marker -*ing*; in the second sentence, instead, the meaning of -*s* of *sleeps* is encoded lexically in *the cat* (third personal, singular) and *every day* (iterative or habitual). For this reason, as VanPatten concludes,

[I]f learners are confronted with something like -*ing* on verb forms, they will be forced to make this form-meaning connection sooner than say third person -*s* because the latter is redundant and the former is not.

However, there are some grammatical forms that do not carry meaning. In the sentence *John thinks that Mary is smart*, we cannot define what semantic information *that* encodes. It has a grammatical function, which is to link two sentences, but it does not encode any semantic information. This leads to the following subprinciple:

P1 (d) The Meaning-Before-Nonmeaning Principle: learners are more likely to process meaningful grammatical forms before nonmeaningful forms irrespective of redundancy.

The model of IP posits that such grammatical features 'will be processed in the input later than those for which true form-meaning connections can be made' (VanPatten 2015: 118).

3.3.2 The First Noun Principle

Besides explaining how learners make form-meaning connections, IP aims to account for how learners determine the basic meanings of sentences during comprehension:

> When a person hears a sentence, whether in the L1 or the L2, that person also does a micro-second-by-micro-second computation of the syntactic structure of that sentence. This is called parsing. (VanPatten 2015: 118)

This means that learners must assign the roles such as agent and patient or subject and object to the nouns they process. For example, when a person hears *The cat...*, the parsing mechanism or 'parser' will assign it the role of subject. If a verb follows (*The cat chased....*), the parser may continue in this path: *the cat* = NP = subject, *chased* = verb. If the phrase *the mouse* follows, the parser may continue: *the cat* = NP = subject, *chased* = verb, *the mouse* = NP =object. This is an example of a sentence computed and understood. One of the key issues IP aims to address is to explain how learners parse sentences in the L2 'when they do not have a fully developed parser as they do for L1 sentence processing?' (VanPatten 2015: 118). In other words, what happens when language learners first encounter a word order in a sentence that is different from the word order they would find in their L1? The learners' reliance on word order is posited in the following IP principle:

> P2 The First Noun Principle. Learners tend to process the first noun or pronoun they encounter in a sentence as the subject.

Research has shown that no matter what the word order in their L1 is (Subject-Verb-Object or Object-verb-Subject), learners would initially process the first noun in a sentence in an L2 as the subject. This explains why English learners of Spanish or German would misinterpret the following sentences (VanPatten 2012: 271):

> *Lo vio María.* (*Mary saw him.*)
> *Den Jungen küsst die Frau.* (*The girl kisses the boy.*)

According to Carroll's (2001) perspective on IP, which VanPatten (2009: 50) takes into account, 'acquisition occurs when there is a parsing failure that signals to the learner that something has gone wrong'. However, as VanPatten argues:

> [j]ust how much 'noise' can go by without the learner's parser detecting a failure? Learners can miss a lot of data in the input early on because their parser either cannot handle the information or merely do not process it.

The First Noun principle may be moderated when lexical semantics comes into play, as expressed by the following subprinciple:

P2 (a) The Lexical Semantics Principle. Learners may rely on lexical semantics, where possible, instead of on word order to interpret sentences.

Lexical semantics refers to how the meanings of verbs require particular nouns for an action or event to occur. For example, learners are less likely to misinterpret the sentence *The fence was kicked by the horse* compared with *The cow was kicked by the horse*: in the first sentence, the action expressed by the verb requires an animate subject/agent that can kick (*the horse*); in the second sentence, the action of 'kicking' might be performed by the two nouns (*the cow* or *the horse*) (VanPatten 2004: 16). It should thus be noted that this subprinciple accounts for the fact that 'sometimes learners step outside of the First Noun Principle and seemingly interpret sentences correctly not because they paid attention to grammatical cues but because they relied on non-grammatical information' (VanPatten 2012: 272).

In conclusion, the IP principles illustrated in this section aim to describe what L2 learners actually do when they attempt to process input while understanding a message; that is how they make form-meaning connections and what conditions affect their processing strategies. Meaning and form can be linked either at the morphological or at the sentence and discourse level. IP research has used different types of listening and reading tasks to investigate how learners understand sentences and what aspects they rely on to process new input. Empirical evidence for the IP principles served as the basis for Processing Instruction (PI), a pedagogical approach that will be presented in the following section (cf. Subsection 3.3.3).

3.3.3 Input Processing: Learning and teaching implications

The previous section examined the basic principles that explain how learners approach IP during comprehension. These principles have informed a type of instruction known as PI 'whose purpose is to affect the ways in which learners attend to input data' (VanPatten 1996: 2). As pointed out, the strategies that L2 learners use to process input are not always efficient and may sometimes be wrong. The aim of PI is to push learners away from these processing strategies towards better ones. As VanPatten (1996: 6) explains, in contrast to other approaches to grammar instruction (e.g. the PPP approach; cf. Chapter 4),

> [a]ppropriate processing instruction activities […] do not ask the learner to produce target grammatical items; instead, learners are pushed to attend to properties of the language *during activities in which they hear or see language that expresses some meaning*. These activities contain 'structured input' – purposefully manipulated sentences and discourse that carry meaning.

Moreover, what makes PI different from other 'focus on form' techniques (cf. Chapter 5) is that it first identifies the processing strategy that prevents learners from processing a particular form or structure correctly. Once the strategy has been identified, learners are involved in activities which help them process input more efficiently.

What kinds of procedures are involved in PI? This pedagogical approach consists of three main components (VanPatten 1996: 60):

> (1) explanation of the relationship between a given form and meaning it can convey; (2) information about processing strategies, showing learners how natural processing strategies may not work to their benefit and (3) 'structure input activities' in which learners are given the opportunity to process form in the input in a 'controlled' situation so that better form-meaning connections might happen.

While for the first component the information provided to learners may be similar to that in other approaches to grammar, the other two components pertain to PI. At first, learners are given explicit information about how the targeted linguistic form or structure works, focusing on one form or use at a time. What is important is that the explanation highlights the link between form and meaning. This type of information can be supplied in the L2 or in the L1, depending on the learners' language level and needs, and through examples (see Figure 3.1; bold is in the original).

The past simple tense is one of the tenses most used to talk about events in the past. It does refer to finished actions and events. Very often the English past simple tense ends in -*ed*:

Invited John for lunch.
I played tennis with Paula.

When you talk about a finished time in the past, the English past simple tense is often accompanied by a temporal adverb:

Yesterday I smoked 20 cigarettes.

Figure 3.1 Example of explicit information in PI (Benati 2005: 92).

Then, learners are informed of how to pay attention to particular formal features which may cause them possible processing problems, for example due to a particular word order in the sentence or the absence of adverbials that would provide a clue about the time of an action (see Figure 3.2).

DO NOT RELY ON THE TEMPORAL ADVERB TO UNDERSTAND WHEN THE ACTION TAKES PLACE AS SOMETIME YOU CAN HEAR A SENTENCE WITHOUT A TEMPORAL ADVERB.

YOU MUST PAY ATTENTION TO THE TENSE ENDING TO UNDERSTAND WHEN THE ACTION TAKES PLACE.

IN THE CASE OF DESCRIBING PAST EVENTS, PAY ATTENTION TO THE ENDING *-ED*.

Figure 3.2 Example of information about processing strategies in PI (Benati 2005: 92).

Finally, learners are involved in structured input (SI) activities; the term 'structured' refers to the fact that 'the input has been "manipulated" in particular ways; it is not free flowing communicative discourse, although it is meaning-bearing' (VanPatten 1996: 63–64). In these activities, learners are not involved in producing the target structure. Instead, they are made to pay attention to specific formal features while listening or reading so that they make appropriate form-meaning connections. The rest of the section will focus on these activities, as they are the most important feature of PI.

SI activities can be of two broad types: referential and affective. Each type is defined as follows:

> Referential activities require learners to pay attention to form in order to get meaning and have a right or wrong answer so the instructor can check whether or not the learner has actually made the proper form-meaning connection. Affective activities [...], instead require learners to express an opinion, belief or some other affective response as they are engaged in processing information about real world. (Wong 2004: 42)

Figure 3.3 supplies an example of referential activity in which learners must focus their attention on verb endings to comprehend the meaning related to the time when the actions happened. As Lee and VanPatten (2003: 143) explain, the purpose is to have learners 'circumvent' the strategy described in the P1b principle (cf. Subsection 3.3.1), by which learners will tend to rely on lexical items as opposed to grammatical forms to get meaning when both encode the same semantic information. After receiving an explanation of how past tense endings work, learners will practise matching the meaning of pastness to the *-ed* suffix.

Listen to each sentence. Indicate whether the action occurred last week or is part of a set of actions oriented toward the present.

	LAST WEEK	PRESENT
1	☐	☐
2	☐	☐
3	☐	☐
4	☐	☐
5	☐	☐

(Sentences read by instructor or heard on a recording)
1. John talked on the phone.
2. Mary helped her mother.
3. Robert studies for two hours.
4. Sam watched TV.
5. Lori visits her parents.

Figure 3.3 Example of referential SI activity (Lee and VanPatten 2003: 143).

Figure 3.4 illustrates an example of affective activity for the same target form and IP principle, which may follow in the teaching sequence. Using the model provided, learners will have to respond to what they hear according to their experience.

Listen to the speaker make a statement. Indicate whether you did that same thing last night.

(*you hear*) I studied for a test.

(*you say*) Me too.

or   I didn't.

Figure 3.4 Example of affective SI activity (Lee and VanPatten 2003: 143).

In the activities above, only the verb endings encode tense in the input sentence while 'lexical items and discourse that would convey the same meaning are excluded' (Lee and VanPatten 2003: 143). The input is thus contrived so that the grammatical form only carries meaning and learners must focus their attention on the form in order to carry out the task.

Normally, a sequence of SI activities would begin with two or three referential activities followed by affective activities. Referential and affective SI activities can be designed according to different response types: binary options, matching, supplying information, selecting alternatives, surveys, ordering and ranking. Each type may have variations in terms of content and technique (Lee and VanPatten 2003: 160–164). Examples of each type are described below.

(a) Binary options give learners two possible answers: true/false, yes/no/, agree/disagree, likely/unlikely or any other two-option answer (*Mum/Dad, teacher/student*) (Lee and VanPatten 2003: 157):

Read the following sentences. Are they true for a typical student at your school.

The typical student…	True	Not True
1. gets up at 6.30 a.m.	☐	☐
2. skips breakfast	☐	☐
etc.		

(b) In matching activities, learners indicate the correspondence between an input sentence and something else such as a picture, a name, an event, an activity and so forth. In the following example, learners have to match events to other events in order to make logical connections (Lee and VanPatten 2003: 161):

For each sentence in Column A, indicate to which activity in Column B it is the most logically connected.

Column A	Column B
Alice…	She…
1. gets good marks.	a. goes to the gym.
2. exercises five times a week.	b. studies every night.

(c) Learners may also be asked to supply missing information into given input sentences or discourse, but they are not required to produce the targeted form that has already been supplied (adapted from Lee and VanPatten 2003: 157):

Get into groups of three and listen to what John does every day. After listening, with your group members, complete these sentences with as many details you can remember. The group with most details wins.

1. John gets up at _____ .
2. He prefers not to _____ in the morning.
etc.

(d) Another way to expose learners to input is to give them a stimulus and ask them to select the correct response from three or more alternatives. As Lee and VanPatten (2003: 162) highlight, 'either the stimulus or the alternatives contain the targeted grammatical items being practised in the activity', as illustrated in the following example (VanPatten 2009: 57).

> Listen to each sentence and then select the word or phrase that goes with the sentence.
> 1. (*Learners hear*: John dropped the plate)
>   a. right now   b. last night   c. in two days
> 2. (*Learners hear*: Mary will eat in the cafeteria)
>   a. right now   b. last night   c. tomorrow

(e) Surveys can use a variety of response formats (binary options, supplying information, selecting from alternatives, matching). Learners find surveys engaging because they interact in the classroom (or outside) about interesting topics. Learners may be asked to respond to a survey item or elicit survey information from someone else. Typical survey tasks include the following: (1) indicating agreement with a statement, (2) indicating frequency of an activity, (3) answering 'yes' or 'no' to particular questions, (4) finding a certain number of people who respond to an item in the same way (Lee and VanPatten 2003: 162).

(f) In ordering and ranking activities, learners order items 'either in terms of importance or likelihood or in terms of chronology', as in the following example affective SI activity (adapted from Lee and VanPatten 2003: 164):

> 1. Following is a list of things your teacher might have done last night. Check off those that you think he or she did.
> Our teacher...
> _____ watched a TV soap opera.
> _____ walked the dog.
> _____ had a herbal tea.
> etc.
> 2. Listen to your teacher and check if you are right. Then put his or her activities in the order in which you think they happened.

SI activities, either referential or affective, have to work on particular processing problems. The processing problem may vary depending on the specific L2 features that learners might find difficult to process. For example, it may be word order, pronouns, relative clauses or morphological inflections. The selected examples above all target aspects of morphological inflections, which account for the processing problem posited in the Lexical Preference Principle (cf. Subsection 3.3.1). As VanPatten (2009: 57) argues, this principle is 'the problem': for example, while the progressive marker is easier to process because it generally does not have to agree with any lexical item, 'the past tense marker has to agree with something inside or outside the sentence'. He adds that 'until the lexicon is sufficiently built up such that there is easy lexical retrieval during processing, tense markers will be difficult to process (i.e. match to an adverbial phrase or time referent)'. The identification of a possible processing problem is thus crucial. The IP principles illustrated in the previous section (cf. Subsections 3.3.1 and 3.3.2) can help teachers understand what L2 learners actually do when they attempt to process input while understanding a message and what may affect their processing strategies. Once the processing problem has been identified, teachers will be in a better position to develop suitable SI activities.

A number of guidelines have also been suggested to help teachers implement appropriate SI activities (VanPatten 1996; Lee and VanPatten 2003; Wong 2004). These procedures are described below and further exemplified in the examples of teaching activities illustrated in the next section (cf. Section 3.4).

(1) Present one thing at a time.
    In order to facilitate the processing process, only one linguistic feature at a time should be the focus of the lesson or, more in general, of the teaching sequence. This is in contrast with what generally occurs in a traditional lesson or in most textbooks in which a whole set of rules pertaining to form and usage is provided before practice. Presenting one linguistic feature at a time has the advantage of keeping explicit presentation and explanation to a minimum and helps learners pay more focused attention to the targeted item. After introducing the linguistic feature, learners will be involved in the SI activities focusing on that particular feature.

(2) Keep meaning in focus.
    In SI activities, learners are led to make form-meaning connections. This implies that learners must process input for its meaning in order to successfully carry out the activities. For example, in the activity in Figure 3.3, learners have to say whether the action occurred last week or relates to the present; in order to do so they must pay attention to the meaning conveyed by the verb endings. As pointed out by VanPatten (1996: 68), 'if meaning is absent or if learners do not have to pay attention to meaning to complete the activity, then there is not enhancement of input processing'.

(3) Move from sentences to connected discourse.
Since learners have a limited capacity to process input, especially at early stages, it is preferable to involve them in activities at sentence level: 'short isolated sentences give learners processing time, whereas in longer stretches of speech, grammatical form can get lost if the demands to process meaning overwhelm the learner' (Lee and VanPatten 2003: 156).

(4) Use both oral and written input.
In order to account for individual differences, learners should be provided with both oral and written input in SI activities. As a matter of fact, some learners may respond better to one mode of input than to the other. A combination of oral and written input within a single activity is also suitable.

(5) Have learners do something with the input.
SI activities should not only be meaningful, but also be purposeful. The activities should provide learners with a specific reason for responding to the input in some way so that they are encouraged to make form-meaning connections. At this stage, learners will not respond by producing the target structure. They may simply be asked to agree or disagree, say *yes* or *no*, complete a survey, select alternatives, etc. In order to provide the requested information, they will have to attend to the meaning in the input sentence(s) and connect it to a particular form.

(6) Keep the learner's processing strategies in mind.

As pointed out, the goal of PI is to help learners use more efficient processing strategies. For this reason, the learners' natural processing strategies must be first identified in order to develop SI activities in which learners' reliance on the strategy is altered and their attention is appropriately guided to process a particular form to get meaning. As VanPatten (1996: 69) reports, this guideline was borne out of his work with trainee teachers:

some novice attempts to create structured input activities reflect an understanding that the activities should be input-based but do not reflect an understanding of what learners are doing when processing input.

So, for example, in the creation of past-tense activities they included an adverb or a time expression in each sentence, which actually detracts the learners' attention on the verbal tense marker.

Finally, it should be noted that besides the types of SI activities illustrated above, other teaching techniques may be used to help learners pay attention to grammatical forms (cf. Chapters 4 and 5). These techniques have been defined with the term of 'input enhancement' (Sharwood Smith 1993: 177) that refers to a deliberate attempt to make specific features of L2 input more salient in order to draw learners attention to these features.[2] Input enhancement may vary according to positive and negative type and degree of elaboration. While positive input enhancement is aimed at making certain correct forms in the input more salient, negative input enhancement 'would flag given forms as incorrect, thus signalling to the learners that they have violated the target norms'. Elaboration may also involve colour coding (e.g. for gender distinctions, tense marking, etc.), different types of textual enhancement such as boldfacing, underlining, capitalizing or, for oral input, using special stress and intonation and gestures (Wong 2005). However, as Sharwood Smith (1993: 176) cautions, 'input enhancement implies only that we can manipulate aspects of the input but make no further assumptions about the consequences of that input on the learner'. In this respect, the results of the research on textual enhancement are still 'quite mixed' yielding just 'small-size positive effect' on noticing, performance and development (Benati 2016: 74).

3.4 The principles in the classroom

This section aims to provide an example of the way PI (cf. Subsection 3.3.3) can actually work in a lesson. The SI activities presented below illustrate how a teacher 'structured' input to push learners to notice a particular lexicogrammatical feature and process it for meaning. The activities, which involve a group of young learners at an elementary level, target the processing problems posited in the Lexical Preference Principle and the Preference for Nonredundancy Principle (cf. Subsection 3.3.1).

3.4.1 Elena dealing with structured input activities

Video Extract 3

(a) As pointed out in the previous section, learners tend to process more redundant forms later than less redundant ones (cf. Subsection 3.3.1). For example, the third-person singular is a form that is acquired later than the *-ing* form. What type of techniques among those listed below do you use or would you use to have learners notice the third-person singular suffix in a spoken or written context? Which ones do you or would you consider particularly effective? Are there any other techniques you use or would use?

- repetition
- rephrase
- questions
- metalinguistic information
- intonation emphasis
- visual enhancement (bolding, underlining, highlighting)
- gap filling

(b) In PI, input structured activities are meant to have learners pay attention to specific formal features in the input while listening or reading so that learners make appropriate form-meaning connections. Watch the first part of Elena's lesson and summarize the main three steps of the activity.

(c) Input structured activities can be either referential or affective (cf. Subsection 3.3.3). What type of SI activity does Elena set up in the first part of her lesson?

3.4.2 Referential structured input activities

Referential SI activities make learners pay attention to grammatical features in order to get meaning. They have a right or wrong answer so that the teacher can check whether the learners have actually made the proper form-meaning connection. A sequence of SI activities may include two or three referential activities followed by affective activities (cf. Subsection 3.3.3).

(a) Look at an extract of the SI activity Elena uses in her first part of the lesson. The materials for the activities in this lesson were prepared by Elena Vergani under the authors' supervision. What type of SI activity is it (binary options, matching, selecting alternatives, etc.)? How is meaning kept in focus? How are learners led to notice the third-person singular suffix?

1. When Mr. Bean gets home he...
   a. says hello to Teddy.
   b. decorates the house.
   c. watches TV.

2. Mr. Bean closes the door and...
   a. goes into the kitchen.
   b. talks with Teddy.
   c. wears his party hat.

(b) Now, go through a short extract of the transcription related to this first activity. The teacher asks the students to read their sentences aloud before checking them with the information in the video. What kind of problems do some students seem to have in reading the sentences aloud?

T: *have you all finished?*
Ss: *yes*
T: *ok. Michele, finished? not yet? Francesco, have you finished? ok,*
    have you all finished?
Ss: *yes*
T: *so, let's read some of your sentences. Giulia sentence number*
    one: when Mr. Bean gets home he...
S1: *watch tv*
T: *he watches tv. ok. Stefano number two?*
S2: *two Mr. Bean closes the door and wear his party hat*
T: *wears his party hat. ok. someone else? over there? ok, Luca?*
    number three
S3: *when the doorbell rings, Mr. Bean goes and opens the door*
T: *and opens the door. [...]*

(c) In the second and third parts of her lesson, Elena uses the two SI activities below. The activities provide binary options and oral and written SI. Analyse each activity and answer these questions:

- Why are 'subjectless' sentences provided in the input?
- How is meaning kept in focus?
- How are learners led to notice the third-person singular suffix?
- What additional challenge does the listening activity provide?

Activity 1

LISTENING
Listen to ten sentences about Mr. Bean's party. Decide if they refer to Mr. Bean or to his friends.

	Mr. Bean	His friends
1.	☐	☐
2.	☐	☐
3.	☐	☐

(Sentences heard by students)

1. .... makes party hats.
2. .... meets a man.
3. .... sit down.

Activity 2

READING

Davide works at the university. Read the following sentences about Davide's routine and his parents' routine. Decide if the sentences are about Davide or his parents.

Davide   His parents

☐   ☐   1.........gets up early in the morning.

☐   ☐   2......... goes to work by car.

☐   ☐   3......... eat in a restaurant.

(d) Go through these two short extracts of the transcription of Elena's lesson. What types of techniques does she use to enhance the learners' noticing process in her interaction with them?

---

(1)
T: so, let's check together. sentence number one is makes party hats. who makes party hats Mr. Bean or his friends? Luca?
S1: Mr. Bean?
T: so, Mr. Bean makes party hats. meets a man. Giulia?
S2: friends?
T: listen carefully. meets a man. who meets a man? not his friends, but...
S2: Mr. Bean
T: Mr. Bean

(2)
T: ok. look at the white board. ok, so. gets up early. who? Davide or his parents? Davide. so, Davide gets up early. goes to work. Davide or his parents? [...]
Ss: Davide
T: ok, Davide, not his parents. ok. eat in a restaurant, who? Davide or his parents?
Ss: his parents
T: [...] ok. what do you notice? what do you see? what's the difference between this (writes on the board) and this? look at the verb. [...] do you remember the song Spiderman? catches thieves, just like arrives, comes, ok? so, the third-person singular is characterized by -s or -es. just the third-person singular. ok? is it clear? [...]

3.4.3 Affective structured input activities

As described in a previous section (cf. Subsection 3.3.2), affective SI activities require learners to express an opinion, belief or some other affective response as they are engaged in processing information. After carrying out a number of referential SI activities, Elena asks the students to compare Davide's routine with their own. Analyse these two short extracts of her interaction with the students. What does she do to trigger the students' response in relation to their experience? What types of techniques does she use to draw the students' attention on the third-person singular suffix?

---

(1)

T: *ok, just like Davide. Davide goes to work by car. what about you? do you go to work?*

S1: *I goes to school by car*

T: *sorry, can you repeat, please?*

S1: *I goes to school*

T: *I?*

S1: *I go to school by car*

T: *why not goes? you're not third-person singular. I is not third-person singular. so you go to school by car. but do you drive the car?*

S1: *no*

T: *no. and in your opinion, Davide?*

S2: *yes*

T: *tell me the sentence. The verb is drive*

S2: *yes, Davide drives the car*

T: *Davide drives his car*

(2)

T: *ok. Davide writes emails. do you write emails? Giulia?*

S3: *no*

T: *no? so, you don't write emails. who writes emails? only Stefano? Daniele, do you write emails? [...] your dad. so, your dad. my dad...*

S4: *my dad writes emails*

T: *ok, just like Davide. Davide writes email too*

3.5 Restructuring and planning

In this section you will be involved in the evaluation of examples of SI activities and asked to implement them according to the implications derived from the IP model (cf. Subsection 3.3.3).

(a) Look at the following two activities that aim to teach *-ing* complement with the verb 'enjoy'. Which of the two activities keeps meaning in focus? Which does not? In which activity are learners led to make form-meaning connections?

---

1. In the following paragraph circle all the uses of *-ing*. With what verb does it occur?

Barbard Smith is an instructor who enjoys only certain aspects of his job. On the one hand, he enjoys teaching. He especially likes to teach Portuguese 101. He really enjoys preparing new and innovative tasks for learners to do in class. On the other hand, he does not enjoy correcting essays. He finds it tedious.

2. Check off the statements you think are true based on what you know about your instructor.
He/She enjoys teaching.
He/She enjoys watching the news at night.
He/She enjoys preparing exams.
He/She enjoys correcting exams.
He/She does not enjoy reading student essays.

(From Lee and VanPatten 2003: 155)

(b) Look again at Task (b) presented in Section 3.2. Prepare a new listening task that will help learners optimize their processing strategies during comprehension. Design the task according to the following steps:

Step 1: Prepare a binary option SI activity so that learners are led to notice the lexicogrammatical feature targeted in the input. For example:

The student ...	True	False
1 **wanted** to see Buckingham Palace.	☐	☐
2 **showed** pictures of Hyde Park to his parents.	☐	☐
3 ...		

Step 2: Prepare an affective SI activity in which learners have to rank what the student did in London according to what they might have done.

(c) Analyse the following SI activity. How different is it from an activity based on a binary option? Use the grid provided below the activity to evaluate its effectiveness according to the criteria suggested for the construction of SI activities (cf. Subsection 3.3.3).

Would he or would he not?

Step 1
Break into two groups. Select someone from the class who you all think you know well. That person should sit by himself during the first part of the activity.

Step 2
Write that person's name in the blank as indicated. Then complete each statement with the information that you believe to be true.

Unless he had to, _____ (name)

1. would never eat _____
2. would never watch _____
3. would never go to _____
4. would never spend money on _____
5. would never _____

On the other hand, _____ (name)

6. would probably eat _____ without reservation.
7. would go to _____ on vacation.
8. would study _____, time permitting.
9. would gladly spend money on _____
10. would _____

Step 3
Each group should give its completed statements to the instructor who will read each statement aloud. If the selected person says that's true, then the group will receive a point. Which group knows him the best?

(From Lee and VanPatten 2003: 161–162)

Does the SI activity ...	Yes/No	Reasons
• present one thing at a time?	Yes	The focus is only on 'would'
• keep meaning in focus?		
• use both oral and written input?		
• have the learner do something with the input?		
• keep the learner's processing strategies in mind?		

3.6 Conclusions

In this chapter we have further explored the role of input in SLA through VanPatten's (1996, 2004, 2015) IP model. The model aims to explain how learners 'process' language input, that is how they make sense of the language they hear or read and how they connect (or do not connect) particular forms of a language with corresponding meanings. The model consists of two main principles that address different aspects of IP: the Primacy of Meaning Principle and the First Noun Principle. We have examined the implications for the model in relation to PI – a teaching approach that aims to optimize the ways in which learners make form-meaning connections and help them use appropriate processing strategies. We have also provided examples of the way SI activities and techniques suggested for PI can be used for classroom practice.

Three main points should further be stressed about IP. The first is that 'input processing is not a model per se or theory of acquisition' (VanPatten 2004: 5). Acquisition is a complex phenomenon consisting of multiple processes and IP is concerned with only the initial process involved in SLA. The second point is related to the misunderstanding that IP does exclude a role for production in acquisition. Given that input and output play complementary roles (cf. Chapters 5 and 6), IP aims to be a model 'of what happens during comprehension that may subsequently affect or interact with other processes' (VanPatten 2015: 113). Finally, IP is sometimes described as a pedagogical model. As VanPatten (2015: 126) clarifies, IP is not concerned about pedagogy: 'as a model of processing, it is meant to apply to all learners of all languages in all contexts (in and out of the classrooms)'.

IP has provided the theoretical underpinnings for PI: an approach to second language teaching aimed at altering learners' 'non-optimal processing' during comprehension. In this sense, PI is input- or comprehension-based. It can also be said to supply a form of 'receptive practice', that is, according to Leow (2007: 21–22) 'any exposure to manipulated L2 input that provides not only various exemplars of target L2 forms or structures [...] but also some form of opportunity to perform a limited productive or non productive task or activity'. As illustrated in the previous sections, during input structured activities learners are led to process a particular grammatical form to get the meaning. By pushing learners to make appropriate form-meaning connections during comprehension, PI will not only foster good comprehension but also promote acquisition.

In conclusion, compared to other types of input enhancement techniques used to help learners pay attention to grammatical forms, PI has shown that SI practice is more effective and its effects are consistent (Benati 2016).

Moreover, the findings from the large bulk of research on the effects of PI (cf. Lee and Benati 2009; Benati and Lee 2015 for full reviews) have highlighted the following positive advantages (Benati and Lee 2010: 93):

- PI is an effective pedagogic approach to lexicogrammar instruction for the acquisition of different languages and grammatical features.
- It is effective for learners with different language levels, of different age and L1 backgrounds.
- It is effective in diverting learners from inappropriate processing strategies during comprehension tasks.
- It helps learners make 'statistically significant' improvements in both sentence-level interpretation and production tasks.

These results may be insightful for teachers and provide further support for the introduction of PI into L2 classroom practice.

3.7 Notes

1 This principle is grounded in the notion of 'communicative value', which is defined as 'the relative contribution a form makes to the referential meaning of an utterance and is based on the presence or absence of two features: inherent semantic value and redundancy within the sentence-utterance' (VanPatten 1996: 24). If a grammatical form has inherent semantic value and is not redundant, it will tend to have high communicative value. This is a key factor in determining the learner's attention to this form during IP.
2 VanPatten (2009: 47) points out that, like PI, both input enhancement and focus on form techniques assume that 'work with formal properties of language for the purpose of fostering acquisition is best done if learner attention is simultaneously focused on meaning'.

3.8 Further reading

Benati, A. and J. Lee (2010), *Processing Instruction and Discourse*, London: Continuum.

Lee, J. and B. VanPatten (2003), *Making Communicative Language Teaching Happen*, 2nd edn, New York: McGraw-Hill.

VanPatten, B. (1996), *Input Processing and Grammar Instruction: Theory and Research*, Norwood, NJ: Ablex.

VanPatten, B. (2003), *From Input to Output. A Teacher's Guide to Second Language Acquisition*, New York: McGraw-Hill.

VanPatten, B. ed. (2004a), *Processing Instruction: Theory, Research, and Commentary*, Mahwah, NJ: Erlbaum.

VanPatten, B. (2004b), 'Input processing in SLA', in B. VanPatten (ed.), *Processing Instruction: Theory, Research, and Commentary*, 5–32, Mahwah, NJ: Erlbaum.

VanPatten, B. (2015), 'Input processing in Adult SLA', in B. VanPatten and J. Williams (eds), *Theories in Second Language Acquisition. An Introduction*, 113–134, New York: Routledge.

Wong, W. (2004), 'The nature of processing instruction', in B. VanPatten (ed.), *Processing Instruction: Theory, Research, and Commentary*, 33–63, Mahwah, NJ: Erlbaum.

Wong, W. (2005), *Input Enhancement: From Theory and Research to the Classroom*, New York: McGraw-Hill.

Chapter 4
Implicit and explicit knowledge

4.1 Key questions

No language teacher worth their salt would dispute the claim that the primary aim of language instruction is to enable students to acquire the ability to use a language spontaneously and effortlessly in spoken and/or written communication. On the other hand, many would probably also concede (Burgess and Etherington 2002) that the conscious study and the intensive practice of lexicogrammatical features help language learners along their way towards spontaneous language use, if only by speeding up the journey, particularly if the students are no longer children. Learners themselves often claim that the formal study of lexicogrammar is beneficial (Schulz 1996; Loewen et al. 2009). Within the SLA field, however, researchers seem to hold divergent views on the role of developing a conscious ('explicit') knowledge of a foreign language as a way towards acquiring a spontaneous ('implicit') mastery of it. Stephen Krashen (1981, 1982), for one, has been a highly vocal and influential supporter of the view that only subconscious acquisition really matters if a learner's ultimate aim is to become a natural communicator (cf. Chapter 2). This chapter will shed light on the concepts of implicit and explicit language knowledge and explore if and how the development of explicit knowledge can play a role in classroom-based language learning and teaching. The following key questions will be addressed:

- What does it mean to have implicit vs explicit knowledge of a second language?
- To what extent does explicit knowledge foster SLA?
- To what extent can explicit knowledge of a second language be learnt and how is it best taught in the classroom?

4.2 Experience

(a) Language teachers often hold different views about the value of learning a second language through conscious study. In the following extract, David, an EFL teacher, explains why he includes the explicit teaching of lexicogrammar (what he calls 'accuracy') in his lessons and what effect 'accuracy work' might have on his students' ability to communicate (what he calls 'fluency'). Read the extract and consider these questions:

- Why is David sceptical about the usefulness of explicit 'language focus' in classroom teaching?
- Based on your experience as a language learner and/or language teacher, would you agree with David's view about the effect of conscious language learning on the acquisition of the ability to communicate spontaneously?

> *I'm not entirely convinced that any focus on accuracy in the classroom has any effect on students' fluency in general. I'm trying not to exclude the possibility, perhaps the probability, that formal language focus at some point gets transferred into language which is acquired by the student. I wonder sometimes whether I'm also not covering myself with the students, by saying listen – if we do fluency activities all the time, I'm not sure how well that would go down with the students, basically. So, I feel that these are their expectations and I will do accuracy work.... I don't necessarily believe that it's going to help them. I've done this present perfect umpteen times with a million people. I still believe that nothing I've ever done in a classroom consciously with students, language focus, has actually helped them to acquire the present perfect, for example.*
>
> (Borg 1998: 27)

(b) Despite his scepticism about 'accuracy work' in the classroom, David believes that students should find out about 'language rules'. Read the following extract and consider these questions:

- What does David mean by the term 'language rules'?
- What kind of approach does he follow in teaching 'language rules' to his students?
- Can you think of possible advantages and disadvantages of David's approach?

> I find that when I learn languages I like finding out about rules myself. It
> helps me if I can perceive patterns, it really helps me. And I think that's
> true for many students, and I think it's part of their expectations too. And
> I see it as part of my role to help them to become aware of language
> rules, both grammatical and phonological and lexical, whenever possible,
> yes. And lying behind that is the rationale that if they can be guided
> towards a formulation of a rule through largely their own endeavours it is
> more likely to be internalised than if it was explained to them.
>
> (Borg 1998: 22)

(c) Language teachers are often called upon to 'explain' aspects of the language they teach, for example when students ask about mistakes they have made in their oral or written production. Each of the following sentences is ungrammatical. The part of the sentence containing the mistake is underlined. For each sentence, think of a possible 'explanation' about the mistake you might give to an EFL student. Which mistake did you find the hardest to explain?

1. I <u>must have to</u> wash my hands.
2. If Jane had asked, I <u>would give</u> her money.
3. His grades <u>were improved</u> last year.

(Ellis et al. 2009: 364–367)

4.3 The principle

Native speakers of a language are by definition those who are endowed with complete 'implicit' knowledge of their language. They can use their native language effortlessly and spontaneously in communication. Confronted with an utterance, they know whether it is grammatical in their native language from a formal, semantic and pragmatic perspective (cf. Chapter 1), often basing their judgement on 'feel' (Krashen 1981). On the other hand, only a few native speakers are able to provide justifications for their judgements on linguistic matters and explain 'why' things are the way they are in their L1. 'Explicit' knowledge of a language may be acquired through formal education and is possessed by individuals in different degrees. For example, language teachers are usually expected to have a high degree of both implicit and explicit knowledge of the language they teach (Leech 1994; Andrews 2007). The principle which will be explored in this chapter centres around the role played by explicit knowledge in the acquisition of implicit knowledge of a second language.

> **Explicit knowledge of lexicogrammar may assist the subsequent acquisition of implicit knowledge.** (Ellis 1994)

In learning a second language, a primary role is played by the input a learner receives. For language development to take place, the learner not only needs to be exposed to plenty of meaningful input that is made comprehensible for them (cf. Chapter 2) but also needs to process the input for 'learning'. In other words, learners need to be able to notice lexicogrammatical features in the input and to establish connections between the formal dimension of the noticed features and the semantic/pragmatic ones (cf. Chapters 1 and 3). This process may eventually lead to the development of the learners' interlanguage and thus to an increase in their implicit knowledge of the second language. To what extent does conscious awareness of lexicogrammar aid this process of language development? In other words, does explicit knowledge contribute to the development of implicit knowledge? If so, how? Among SLA researchers, three main positions on this issue have been taken. These are commonly referred to as the 'interface' positions, the term hinting at the fact that some sort of 'communication' may be hypothesized to take place between the implicit and explicit 'stores' of knowledge (Ellis 1997). These positions will be briefly illustrated below and further examined in the next part of the chapter (cf. Subsection 4.3.1).

The 'no-interface' position rules out any possible connection between explicit and implicit knowledge. Conscious study and awareness of lexicogrammar are thus said to play little or no role in the acquisition of the implicit knowledge that underpins our ability to use a language effortlessly and spontaneously. On the other hand, the 'strong interface' position claims that explicit knowledge directly turns into implicit knowledge under certain conditions. The 'weak interface' position, which is the view that is encapsulated in the principle targeted in this chapter, posits that explicit knowledge may play an indirect role in the acquisition of implicit knowledge. This view is consistent with the experience of many language learners and teachers who, while acknowledging that the conscious study of lexicogrammar is beneficial in language learning, have witnessed that what is known explicitly, even if it is the subject of targeted practice in the classroom, is hardly ever put into use straightaway in spontaneous communication outside the classroom. A major challenge for the language teacher is to devise teaching activities that enable learners to acquire the kind of explicit knowledge that may actually play such an indirect role in the acquisition of implicit knowledge. Examples of such pedagogical applications, which are seen as an important corollary of the principle, will also be explored in the chapter.

4.3.1 Implicit and explicit knowledge and the interface positions

Traditionally, within an educational context, knowledge has been viewed as the outcome of the process of formal learning, the latter resulting from – at least that is what teachers expect! – classroom teaching. The terms 'explicit' and 'implicit' have thus been used to refer to all three poles of the educational enterprise: knowledge, learning, teaching (Ellis 2009). Insights on the features of explicit and implicit knowledge of several areas of human experience have been provided by cognitive psychologists (Hulstijn 2005; Rebuschat 2015). SLA researchers have built on these insights to investigate the implicit and explicit knowledge of second languages and how these knowledge stores are learnt (DeKeyser 2003).

How does SLA research distinguish these two types of knowledge? Ellis (2004) has identified a number of characteristics associated with either type of knowledge (see Table 4.1).

Table 4.1 Implicit and explicit language knowledge (Ellis 2004).

Characteristics	Implicit knowledge	Explicit knowledge
Awareness	Learner is intuitively aware of linguistic norms	Learner is consciously aware of linguistic norms
Type of knowledge	Learner has procedural knowledge of grammatical rules and fragments	Learner has declaative knowledge of grammatical rules and fragments
Systematicity	Knowledge is variable but systematic	Knowledge is often anomalous and inconsistent
Accessibility	Knowledge is accessible by means of automatic processing	Knowledge is accessible only through controlled processing
Use of L2 knowledge	Knowledge is typically accessed when learner is performing fluently	Knowledge is typically accessed when learner experiences a planning difficulty
Self-report	Non-verbalizable	Verbalizable
Learnability	Potentially only learnable within the 'critical period'	Learnable at any age

When possessing explicit knowledge of a language speakers are consciously aware of features of that language (both systematic 'rules' and more or less fixed 'fragments'), they know them as 'facts' (as 'declarative' knowledge) and they may be able to talk about them (they are 'verbalizable'). As any other type of factual information, explicit knowledge of a language can potentially be learnt at any age (e.g. through a process of memorization, in the same way that we can memorize facts about history). On the other hand, explicit knowledge is often incomplete and applied inconsistently, requires a great deal of attention on the part of the learner to be accessed (through 'controlled processing') and seems to be engaged in language use only when speakers encounter some sort of difficulty in planning what to say.

Implicit knowledge is intuitive and can be accessed automatically and systematically in spontaneous language use. However, as it consists of 'procedures for action' (which become manifest only when we actually use the language) rather than declarative facts, it is usually non-verbalizable. It is also variable (this explains why we can be 'better' at speaking rather than writing) and at least some aspects of it cannot be learnt if individuals have reached a certain age (beyond the 'critical period').

Implicit and explicit knowledge can be viewed as the outcomes of respectively implicit and explicit learning. Although not all researchers would find this definition uncontroversial (see e.g. Schmidt 1990, 1994, 2001), implicit learning can be characterized as 'learning without awareness' (DeKeyser 2003). For example, language learners may learn aspects of a language without being aware of what exactly they are learning. The classic example of implicit language learning is children learning their L1. It is clear that implicit learning must also play a role in the acquisition of an L2, even when it mostly takes place in a classroom context, as Ellis (1997: 113) points out:

> The process of learning a language would become impossible if every
> rule out of the thousands that comprise the grammar of a language had
> to be first learnt as explicit knowledge.

As mentioned earlier, what remains a contentious issue in SLA is whether an interface, that is to say some sort of communication between the implicit and the explicit knowledge stores, can be hypothesized when learning a second language. We will now zero in on the three positions taken on the issue, labelled as 'no-interface', 'strong interface' and 'weak interface'.

The no-interface position

Supporters of the no-interface position claim that implicit and explicit knowledge are completely separate and independent language knowledge stores. Stephen Krashen (1981, 1982, 1985; cf. Chapter 2), to take a well-known example, has argued that implicit knowledge is 'acquired' and not 'learnt'. We can learn explicit knowledge through the conscious study of lexicogrammatical features, but that is claimed to play a very limited role in spontaneous language use as 'utterances are initiated by the acquired system – our fluency in production is based on what we have "picked up" through active communication' (Krashen 1981: 2). Explicit knowledge can only be relied upon – under specific constraints, e.g. if we have enough time to focus consciously on lexicogrammar – when, for example, we plan a prepared speech or we edit a written production. There is also hypothesized to be a wide range of abilities in making use of explicit knowledge even when the right conditions are present. Krashen labels 'monitor under-users' those who are prone to rely almost exclusively on their implicit knowledge while a very small percentage of highly academic 'super monitor users' are able to use their explicit knowledge to good effect even in spontaneous communication. More important, whatever explicit learned competence we develop is not amenable to turn into acquired competence (Krashen 1985). By the same token, what is acquired implicitly does not become explicit knowledge directly. As the two types of language knowledge are developed through two completely different psycholinguistic processes, they remain separate when they are stored and used. Three main arguments are put forward in support of this hypothesis.

In the first place, 'we often see acquisition in cases where learning never occurred' (Krashen 1982: 84). It is fairly common to come across (even highly) successful language learners who have acquired a foreign language by means of mere exposure to and interaction with proficient speakers, without any formal study of the language.

On the other hand, 'we also see learning that never seems to become acquisition' (Krashen 1982: 86). According to Krashen, this accounts for the language use of those learners who, despite having consciously studied and practised lexicogrammatical features (Krashen uses the familiar term 'rules'), use them incorrectly in spontaneous communication:

> This occurs when the performer has learned a rule, but has not acquired it. This happens typically with late-acquired items, such as the third person singular ending on regular verbs in English ('He goes to work every day'). What is particularly interesting is that these performers may have known the rule and have practised it for many years. Even after thousands of correct repetitions, and with a thorough understanding of the rule, such performers still make 'careless' mistakes on certain items. (Krashen 1982: 86)

Finally, it is pointed out that 'even the best learners master only a small subset of the rules of a language' (Krashen 1982: 86). Language professionals (academics/applied linguists, teachers, translators) usually succeed in developing a high degree of explicit knowledge of a language through conscious study, but this knowledge is still far from an accurate reflection of their overall linguistic competence. Indeed, descriptions of languages featured in reference books and academic articles reflect what linguistic science has uncovered at a certain stage in time, but there still exist several aspects of language knowledge and use that need to be accounted for and targeted by research. According to Krashen, the number of rules that are actually explicitly referred to by ordinary language learners in their most typical performance (spontaneous oral interaction rather than prepared speech or untimed writing) is – as shown by Figure 4.1 – much lower than the number of rules taught explicitly or learned by those students who have an analytical learning style and high motivation.

An important corollary of the no-interface view is that as no communication is hypothesized to occur between the implicit and the explicit knowledge stores, and it is implicit knowledge that drives language use, the primary target of language learning/teaching should indeed be implicit knowledge. According to this perspective, learning and teaching explicit knowledge would be 'at best a luxury' which 'does not lead in any meaningful way to the attainment of this ultimate goal' (Sharwood Smith 1981: 159).

Figure 4.1 Explicit knowledge of rules (Krashen 1982: 93–94).

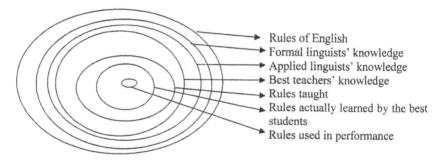

Rules of English
Formal linguists' knowledge
Applied linguists' knowledge
Best teachers' knowledge
Rules taught
Rules actually learned by the best students
Rules used in performance

The strong interface position

The strong interface position is premised on the assumption that communication between explicit and implicit knowledge occurs, and that explicit knowledge of a language plays 'a causal role' (DeKeyser 2015: 103) in the development of implicit knowledge underpinning the ability to use the language fluently in communication. In order for this to happen, targeted practice is required. As DeKeyser (2003: 328) explains, 'it is the role of practice to gradually bridge the gap between explicit knowledge and use'. This perspective is influenced by Skill Acquisition Theory originating in cognitive psychology, and in particular in the work of John Anderson (e.g. 1982, 2007). According to Anderson's framework, the acquisition of any skill (driving, learning to play a musical instrument, etc.) takes place in three stages: (a) a declarative stage, in which explicit knowledge is 'acquired through perceptive observation and analysis of others engaged in skilled behaviour' or 'transmitted in verbal form from one who knows to one who does not know' (DeKeyser 2015: 95); (b) a procedural stage, in which explicit knowledge becomes at least partly implicit, which translates into the 'smooth, rapid, procedural execution' (DeKeyser 2015: 95) of the skill and (c) an automatization stage, where fine-tuning of proceduralized knowledge takes place eventually leading to fluent, errorless performance of the skill.

As DeKeyser (2007: 49) points out, the key stage of 'proceduralization is achieved by engaging in the target behaviour – or procedure – while temporarily leaning on declarative crutches'. What does this mean for SLA? When a language learner engages in practice that mimics language use (hence it is meaningful, cf. Chapter 1) *and* that allows them to keep explicit knowledge of given lexicogrammatical features in working memory (hence it is not rushed), the development of procedural knowledge out of declarative knowledge takes place. Further, 'strengthening, fine-tuning and automatization of the newly acquired procedural knowledge' occur as 'a function of the amount of practice, which increases speed and reduces the error rate and the demand on cognitive resources' (DeKeyser 2007: 49).

Sharwood Smith (1981: 167) claims that the strong interface perspective fits in with the 'older, intuitively attractive' idea that 'practice makes perfect' and, to counter Krashen's no-interface hypothesis, argues that

> learners who cannot articulate rules may still have access to the relevant information in explicit knowledge; learners who do not have such access may well *at one time* have had access to such information when the relevant rule had not yet been automatised; learners who do not appear to automatise rules that they have had in explicit knowledge for long periods of time may simply not be disposed to spend the extra time and energy transferring the information to implicit knowledge: i.e. fossilisation has occurred in that part of their learning development where 'learning' has in fact preceded acquisition.

At the same time, he acknowledges that 'the exclusive use of explicit knowledge is inevitably going to be restricted, especially where "hard rules" are involved' (Sharwood Smith 1981: 166).

The weak interface position

Like the strong interface position, its 'weak' version claims that communication between the two knowledge stores can occur. As N. Ellis (2005: 307) sums up the relation between implicit and explicit knowledge, 'however unalike they are, these two types of knowledge interact'. While a strong interface entails that through practice explicit knowledge may become virtually indistinguishable from implicit knowledge, a weak interface assumes that in most cases explicit knowledge only exerts an indirect influence on the development of implicit knowledge. To investigate what this means in practice, we will refer to Ellis' (1994, 1997) conceptualization of the weak interface position. This is encapsulated in the following assumptions and represented visually in Figure 4.2.

1. Explicit knowledge can be converted into implicit knowledge in the case of non-developmental grammatical rules.
2. Explicit knowledge can be converted into implicit knowledge in the case of developmental rules, providing the learner has reached the stage of acquisition that allows for integration of the new rule into the interlanguage system.
3. Explicit knowledge cannot be converted into implicit knowledge in the case of developmental rules if the learner has not reached the requisite stage of acquisition.
4. Not all knowledge originates in an explicit form – more often than not L2 knowledge begins as implicit knowledge.
5. Formal instruction can help to automatize both explicit and implicit grammatical knowledge. (Ellis 1997: 115)

Ellis's weak interface proposal takes account of research (e.g. Meisel, Clahsen and Pienemann 1981) that has assigned either of two statuses to lexicogrammatical features from the perspective of their acquisition: developmental or non-developmental/variational. Developmental features are those lexicogrammatical features that are only acquired (as implicit knowledge) 'at a particular stage of learners' overall development' (Ellis 2008: 98). Such ordered stages are determined by psycholinguistic constraints inherent in the processes of development of learner interlanguage. It is, for

Figure 4.2 The weak interface position (Ellis 1997: 115).

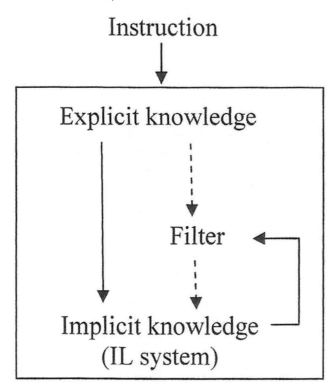

example, well known that the third-person singular present morpheme -*s* in English is one such feature, and is acquired late by language learners (although it may be quite easy to learn as explicit knowledge). Non-developmental/ variational features, on the other hand, are not subject to psycholinguistic constraints and can be acquired at any stage of development (if they are acquired at all), an example being the copula *be*.

According to Ellis, explicit knowledge may turn into implicit knowledge through instruction (meaningful practice, cf. above and Chapter 1) only when it targets non-developmental features. In this case, as is shown by the left-hand side of the figure, the interface between explicit and implicit knowledge is relatively direct. When developmental features are targeted, attempts at turning explicit into implicit knowledge are mediated by learners' existing implicit knowledge, which acts as a filter (right-hand side of the figure) 'that sifts explicit knowledge and lets through only that which they are ready to incorporate into the interlanguage system' (Ellis 1997: 115). Some explicit knowledge is hence screened out, and the conversion process does not take place. This may explain why what gets presented and practised in the classroom is not always available for use straightaway in spontaneous communication outside the classroom. In other words, in contrast to what the supporters of the strong interface position would claim, practice is not thought to be sufficient to overcome the constraints that are at work when developmental features are targeted (Fotos and Ellis 1991). The weak interface position also concedes that the explicit/implicit sequence is not the default learning condition, in that most knowledge is acquired as implicit knowledge (and only a small part of it eventually becomes explicit). Even if implicit and explicit knowledge remain separate, formal instruction can play an important role in language acquisition: it can make the access to whichever type of knowledge more rapid and efficient. We shall consider examples of instruction activities aimed at the development of explicit knowledge in the next sections (cf. Subsection 4.3.2 and Section 4.4).

Ellis's proposal has been supplemented over the years by a more fine-grained analysis of how explicit knowledge may help make the processes underpinning the development of implicit knowledge more efficient (cf. Figure 4.3). It appears to be uncontroversial that what as a rule kickstarts language acquisition is the conversion of input into intake (cf. Chapters 2 and 3). This process is mediated by the learner's 'noticing' 'elements of the surface structure of utterances in the input' (Schmidt 2001: 4). The more an element is communicatively redundant (hence it conveys very little semantic or pragmatic information within the message), such as the third-person singular present morpheme -s, the more likely it is that it will go unnoticed. Explicit knowledge of lexicogrammatical features may help make these features more 'conspicuous' in the input so that learners may be more likely to notice them and turn them into intake. While noticing is key to language acquisition, it is 'the first step in language building, not the end of the process' (Schmidt 2001: 41). As summarized by Ellis, 'new items and rules only become part of the developing interlanguage system if learners can establish how they differ from their existing interlanguage representation' (Ellis 1997: 121). In other words, learners must carry out a mental comparison between how given lexicogrammatical features are put to use in the L2 and how these are used (or fail to be used) in their interlanguage. Another type of noticing is hence required: 'noticing the gap' between target language use and learner interlanguage. Again, it is claimed that focused explicit knowledge may make the process of 'comparison of nontarget forms produced by the learner with

Figure 4.3 The role of explicit knowledge in L2 acquisition (Ellis 1997: 123).

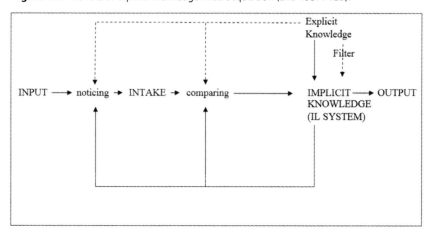

target forms that appear in input' (Schmidt and Frota 1986: 311) more likely to happen. What has been argued about the indirect influence of explicit knowledge sheds further light on the phenomenon of the delayed role of instruction – why the effect of learning explicit knowledge on the spontaneous use of the language often becomes manifest with a certain time lag rather than immediately.

A further possible indirect effect of explicit knowledge on implicit knowledge has been hypothesized (Schmidt and Frota 1986; Ellis 2005). This is related to the fact that the learning of explicit knowledge may occur through learners' output production (as in collaborative output tasks; see below). Such output may be used by learners as learner-produced input ('auto-input') to kickstart the process of implicit knowledge acquisition (cf. Chapter 6).

Drawing upon psycholinguistic and neurolinguistic research, N. Ellis (2005) provides further insights into the weak interface position. First language acquisition and cognitive research show that the interface between explicit and implicit knowledge is 'dynamic' (N. Ellis 2005: 325) and both implicit and explicit knowledge are involved whenever we process language. In first language use, we instinctively turn to our explicit knowledge store in search of help when we encounter a problem. In SLA, explicit knowledge plays an even more important role. N. Ellis (2007: 26) points out that 'the more novelty we encounter, the more the involvement of consciousness is needed for successful learning and problem solving'. What is more 'novel' than a second language? As we process second language input, we tend to rely on those automatic processing habits that we transfer from our first language (cf. Chapter 3). Explicit knowledge provides us with a way to deal with the novelty of second language processing – by helping us to minimize the effects of L1 automatic habits which prevent us from noticing how the L2 actually works.

We have already mentioned that the weak interface hypothesis seems to 'make sense' as it also chimes with the practical experience of many teachers and learners. That said, has it been empirically demonstrated that explicit knowledge actually helps the acquisition of implicit knowledge, and hence the full mastery of a second language? As Gutiérriez (2016: 42) comments in a recent article, 'the usefulness of explicit knowledge in the development and use of the L2 remains an unresolved issue in SLA'. There seem to persist problems in the way research studies are designed and explicit knowledge is measured that make giving an answer to this question harder than it might appear. However, it may be of interest to mention two research studies that have provided some evidence that time devoted to learning and teaching explicit knowledge may be time well spent.

The first one was carried out by Fotos (1993, 1994) and has played a trail-blazing role in the study of explicit second language knowledge. The study involved 160 Japanese university learners of English, divided into three groups. Two of the groups were taught explicit knowledge of three lexicogrammatical areas of English: adverb placement, direct object placement, relative clauses. The third group was only involved in communicative activities targeting implicit knowledge. Following each teaching session, each group was provided with two 'noticing' exercises: a story listening activity and a dictation. In both cases the students were asked to identify and underline any 'special uses of English' that they had noticed. The results showed a much higher level of noticing of the three target structures by the two groups who had received explicit knowledge compared to the group who had been engaged in communicative activities. This does not of course mean that the structures had been fully mastered by the students and were available for use in spontaneous communication but the study does provide evidence that the processes thought to underpin implicit knowledge acquisition had been kickstarted, thanks to explicit knowledge instruction.

The second study was carried out by Gutiérrez (2016) with forty-nine university students of Spanish in a Canadian university who had been taught explicit knowledge of several lexicogrammatical aspects during their university courses. This study was more ambitious in its aim than Fotos's study mentioned above as it sought to determine whether explicit knowledge might be related to proficiency in the second language. It started from the assumption that while having conscious awareness of a lexicogrammatical feature is evidence of possessing explicit knowledge of that feature, this awareness may or may not involve the knowledge of technical grammatical terminology. To couch this distinction in Ellis's (2006a) metalanguage (!), explicit knowledge may itself be viewed as consisting of two components: 'analysed knowledge' and 'metalinguistic explanation'. Hence, we may be aware of a lexicogrammatical feature consciously but may not necessarily be able to explain it using technical grammatical terms. The researcher started by testing students' explicit knowledge of sixteen lexicogrammatical areas of Spanish through two different tasks, aimed at bringing out each of the two components of explicit knowledge. The first was a grammaticality judgement test which consisted of sixty-four sentences the students were asked to judge as to their grammaticality. The second task was a metalinguistic knowledge test consisting of sixteen sentences, each with an underlined error (cf. Section 4.2.c). The students were asked to correct the errors and explain the lexicogrammatical phenomena related to the errors. The results of the students' tests of explicit knowledge were correlated with tests of the students' language proficiency in Spanish, spanning several aspects of language competence (oral/written, four skills, grammar/vocabulary). The outcome of this process is telling. The researcher found that a correlation did exist between explicit knowledge and second language proficiency. Second, explicit knowledge appeared to be more strongly correlated with written proficiency and grammar/vocabulary. Having explicit knowledge thus seems to help us to perform better in writing and in using lexicogrammar accurately, meaningfully and appropriately (cf. Chapter 1). Finally, the two components of explicit knowledge (analysed knowledge and metalinguistic explanation) did not seem to have the same strength of correlation with language proficiency. While having conscious awareness of lexicogrammar may have a strong impact on how we perform in a second language, being able to provide explanations using grammatical terminology may not be as crucial to our language proficiency.

4.3.2 Implicit and explicit knowledge: Learning and teaching implications

In this section, we will investigate what practical implications the implicit/explicit knowledge principle might have for learning and teaching second languages. In the previous section, we have established that while 'both explicit and implicit knowledge can be used in communication', 'effective participation in face-to-face conversation […] requires implicit knowledge' (Fotos and Ellis 1991: 606). Explicit knowledge may be employed 'in the formulation of sentences when there is no time pressure and also can be used to monitor output' (Ellis 2016: 134). We have also identified three positions put forward by SLA researchers on the interface between explicit and implicit knowledge when a second language is being learnt. In particular, if we assume that explicit knowledge has no role to play in the acquisition of implicit knowledge, the ultimate target of language acquisition (no-interface position), learning and teaching explicit knowledge is hardly time well spent. As summarized by De Graaff and Housen (2009: 734), according to this position, 'the role of L2 instruction is largely confined to providing adequate exposure and creating an appropriate affective climate for the operation of implicit acquisition processes'. If, on the other hand, the strong or weak interface positions are supported, it is vital to determine what kind of explicit knowledge of a foreign language is more beneficial for the subsequent acquisition of implicit knowledge, in what ways its learning can be achieved as well as what teaching procedures may be employed to foster explicit knowledge acquisition in the classroom. Although results from empirical research are still far from definitive (cf. Subsection 4.3.1), it seems likely that – in keeping with many teachers' and learners' experience – explicit knowledge does play at least an indirect effect on the acquisition of implicit knowledge. It is hence worthwhile to investigate what features of a second language can be learnt as explicit knowledge, how they are best learnt and how they can be taught most effectively. Three specific issues pertaining to the learning and teaching of explicit second language knowledge will be tackled in this section.

What features of lexicogrammar can be learnt as explicit knowledge?

Proponents of the no-interface position such as Krashen (1982) claim that only a very limited subset of the 'rules' of a language can be learnt as explicit knowledge. These are rules that are particularly 'simple', that is those 'easiest to describe and remember' (Krashen 1982: 97). Examples of such simple rules in English have to do with morphology (third-person present –s morpheme, -ed past tense morpheme) and punctuation (e.g. capitalizing the first letter of the word beginning a sentence). Syntactic rules are viewed as difficult to learn and hence attempts to learn or teach them as explicit knowledge as unwarranted.

A study carried out by Green and Hecht (1992) has, however, shown that learners can master a wider range of lexicogrammatical features as explicit knowledge. The study involved 300 German learners of English (both secondary school students and university students specializing in English language and literature) and 50 native English speakers (secondary school students). Both groups were asked to take the same test entailing the identification and correction of twelve lexicogrammatical errors in sentence exemplars and the formulation of a 'rule' accounting for each error. The errors concerned a range of morphosyntactic features involving mainly formal and semantic aspects (see Table 4.2).

All the features targeted in the study had been taught as explicit knowledge at some stage during the schooling of the German learners. The results of the study showed that explicit knowledge of a wide range of lexicogrammatical aspects (both morphological and syntactic) can be learnt and accessed by learners. Indeed, across the whole group of learners involved in the study, the success rate for the error correction task was 78 per cent. Green and Hecht's study also seems to suggest that, although all potentially 'learnable' as explicit knowledge, different aspects of lexicogrammar prove to be more or less difficult, which again confirms learners' and teachers' intuitions. This insight leads us to our next question.

Table 4.2 Features of explicit knowledge targeted in Green and Hecht's (1992) study (adapted from Green and Hecht 1992: 171).

- Subject-predicate order in declarative sentences
- Preterite (past tense) for focus on time of action in past
- Verb marked with *will* to show futurity
- *Do*-periphrasis with *not* in negative sentences
- Gerund for general liking (e.g. *I like going to the cinema*)
- Perfect to link past with present
- *Any* with negation
- Adverb form usually marked (*-ly*)
- Simple form for unmarked aspect
- Progressive form to mark aspect
- Relative *who* for persons
- *a*-form of indefinite article before consonants

What makes explicit knowledge more or less difficult to learn?

Even if we assume that virtually any aspect of lexicogrammar can be learnt as explicit knowledge, it begs the question of what makes some aspects more difficult to learn. SLA researchers have tried to establish criteria for the relative difficulty of items of lexicogrammar when learnt as explicit knowledge on the basis of features inherent in the lexicogrammatical items themselves. One of the criteria invoked (Ellis 2006b) is 'formal and functional complexity'. According to this criterion, a lexicogrammatical feature for which a one-to-one correspondence between form and meaning/use can be established should turn out to be relatively easy to learn as explicit knowledge. This is obviously the case of many items of vocabulary. It has, however, proved less straightforward to identity degrees of complexity inherent in grammatical items (De Graaff and Housen 2009).

Another approach to the issue has been to focus on how 'descriptions' of lexicogrammatical features are formulated and try to determine what it is that makes them easy or difficult to understand. Reference materials (grammar books, dictionaries, usage manuals), now available in paper and digital editions, aim to supply explicit knowledge of a language through more or less exhaustive descriptions of lexicogrammatical features, relying on terms ('metalanguage') of varying degrees of technicality. It goes without saying that if aimed at language learners ('pedagogical descriptions') lexicogrammatical descriptions should be not only quantitatively (amount of detail) but also qualitatively different from those aimed at specialist readers (students of linguistics, academics). What does this qualitative difference rest on? Michael Swan (1994: 45–55), an applied linguist and pedagogical grammarian, has singled out a much referred to set of 'design criteria' for 'pedagogical rules', encapsulated in the terms 'truth', 'demarcation', 'clarity', 'simplicity', 'conceptual parsimony' and 'relevance'. According to Swan, a pedagogical rule should be true to the way the language is actually used by its speakers; should 'show clearly what are the limits on the use of a given form'; should be clear and avoid the use of 'unsatisfactory terminology'; should be simple, hence with only the indispensable 'number of categories or subdivisions'; should be conceptually parsimonious, hence avoid the introduction of new conceptual frameworks if not absolutely necessary and should be relevant, hence 'should answer the question (and only the question) that the student's English is asking'. Obviously, a balancing act is required of materials writers and teachers as criteria such as truth and simplicity may be in conflict.

If we can hypothesize an order of 'understanding' of explicit knowledge based on the way it is couched in verbal descriptions, we still need to consider how this knowledge can be effectively learnt and taught in the classroom. Before we move on to explore this issue, it is useful to reiterate that even proponents of the weak interface position concede that not all knowledge of lexicogrammar starts as explicit knowledge. By the same token, not all aspects of lexicogrammar need to be taught and learnt as explicit knowledge in the classroom, as 'learners are clearly capable of learning a substantial amount of the L2 grammar without instruction' (Ellis 2006a: 88).

How can explicit knowledge be learnt and taught in the classroom?

As any type of explicit knowledge, L2 explicit knowledge can be learnt in the classroom through two main processes: straight memorization and problem-solving ('learners attempt to induce explicit information about the L2 from the input data they are exposed to or from their implicit knowledge', Ellis 1997: 117). In this section, we will focus in particular on how the latter can be engaged through two types of classroom teaching activities: consciousness-raising tasks and the dictogloss.

It should first be pointed out that the type of instruction we are going to explore here has also been dubbed 'explicit'. Unlike implicit instruction, which is 'directed at enabling learners to infer rules without awareness' (Ellis 2008: 17) (e.g. the Natural Approach; cf. Chapter 2), explicit instruction involves 'some sort of rule being thought about during the learning process' (DeKeyser 1995: 380). This means that, in one way or another, learners become explicitly aware of a language feature during instruction. It is customary to posit a distinction between explicit deductive and inductive teaching of lexicogrammatical features. In deductive teaching, a generalization about the language is presented first, followed by examples. In inductive teaching, learners induce generalizations from examples. While it is still the default mode of presentation in reference materials (Ellis 2002a), the deductive approach seems to be currently getting a bad press in language teacher training handbooks (Ellis and Shintani 2012), and some SLA researchers too acknowledge that there are 'sound educational reasons for not pursuing such an approach' in that 'it is based on a transmission model of education and, as such, may fail to engage some learners in taking active responsibility for their own learning' (Ellis 1997: 160).

Both Rutherford and Sharwood Smith (1985) and Ellis (1997, 2012) refer to explicit lexicogrammatical instruction with the term 'consciousness-raising'. Ellis posits that consciousness-raising can be accomplished in the classroom 'directly' (through the deductive approach mentioned above) or 'indirectly' (through 'consciousness-raising tasks').[1] As an extremely popular type (Nitta and Gardner 2005) of explicit inductive teaching activity, consciousness-raising tasks are, according to Ellis' (1997: 160) much quoted definition, pedagogic activities

> [...] where the learners are provided with L2 data in some form and required to perform some operation on and with it, the purpose of which is to arrive at an explicit understanding of some linguistic property or properties of the target language.

The keywords in the above definition are 'data' and 'operation'. To kickstart the process of induction, learners are provided with exemplars of the L2 and guided towards an understanding of targeted lexicogrammatical features through the analysis of these exemplars. Ellis (1997) provides a list of options of 'data' and 'operations' that may figure in consciousness-raising tasks, as illustrated in Table 4.3.

Table 4.3 Data and operations in consciousness-raising tasks (from Ellis 1997: 161–162).

Data	Operations
Authentic vs contrived (concocted by the material designer)	1. Identification ('the learners are invited to identify incidences of a specific feature in the data by, e.g., underlining it')
Oral vs written	2. Judgement ('the learners are invited to judge the correctness or appropriateness of features in the data')
Discrete sentences vs continuous text	3. Completion ('the learners are invited to complete a text, e.g., by filling in blanks as in a cloze passage or by selecting from choices supplied')
	4. Modification ('the learners are invited to modify a text in some way, e.g. by replacing one item with
Well formed vs deviant (containing mistakes)	another item, by reordering elements in the text, by inserting some additional item into the text or by rewriting part of it')
	5. Sorting ('the learners are invited to classify specific items present in the data by sorting them into defined categories')
Gap vs non-gap ('whether the data are distributed among the learners in such a way that the information contained in the data has to be shared or whether each learner has access to all the data')	6. Matching ('the learners are invited to match two sets of data according to some stated principle')
	7. Rule provision ('learners may or may not be asked to give a rule to account for the phenomena they have investigated; the rule can be presented verbally or non-verbally')

Consciousness-raising tasks may be performed by learners working individually, in pairs or in small groups; orally or in writing; in the L1 or the L2; 'in a straightforward manner' or with an element of 'competition' added in (Ellis 1997: 162).

If the task is performed in the L2 and the data are split between two or more learners working together, consciousness-raising tasks may involve an element of communicative information gap (cf. Chapter 6). Consciousness-raising tasks may thus also provide 'opportunities for interaction focused on exchange of information' (Fotos and Ellis 1991: 611) and based on 'serious content, in contrast to the trivial content of many information-gap activities' (Fotos and Ellis 1991: 623). They thus may be viewed as serving a 'dual purpose': stimulating 'meaning-centred interaction' as well as developing 'explicit knowledge of a predetermined linguistic feature' (Ellis 2012: 274–275).

While consciousness-raising tasks aim at the development of a mental representation of an L2 rule or generalization ('analysed knowledge'), its actual verbalization (the 'metalinguistic explanation' side of explicit knowledge, mentioned above) is not felt to be a compulsory element of this type of tasks. The development of sophisticated skills in metalinguistic explanation is normally required only of language professionals (teachers, academics) and particularly if the students are young, rule verbalization may be an unnecessary burden. Types of activities mainly or exclusively targeting the 'analysed knowledge' component of explicit knowledge are the input processing (IP) (referential/ affective) activities investigated in Chapter 2 (see also Ellis 1995).

Another optional element of a consciousness-raising task is a monitoring component. Following data analysis and (optional) rule verbalization, learners may be asked to use their explicit knowledge to edit some further language exemplars featuring the targeted lexicogrammatical features. As pointed out by Ellis (2016: 139), this activity 'provides an opportunity for the learners to apply the understanding they gained from the task and to refine it by working out how to correct errors they typically make. Such an activity also helps learners to refine their explicit knowledge'. Its aim is, however, not the proceduralization of explicit knowledge through productive use of the target features. According to supporters of the weak interface position, learners should indeed be left to 'make use of their explicit knowledge in their own way and in their own time' (Ellis 2016: 143).

Does empirical research support the preference that language teacher trainers and many teachers have for inductive ways of teaching explicit knowledge? The answer cannot again be conclusive but we can refer to Fotos's study mentioned above for some evidence. Three groups of learners were involved in the study – the first two were the 'treatment' groups (they received explicit knowledge instruction) while the third was the 'control' group (no explicit knowledge was taught to this group). Of the two treatment groups, the first was taught explicit knowledge through consciousness-raising tasks, while the second received traditional deductive grammar instruction. Tests were administered to the treatment students before and after the instruction. Among the results of the study, it emerged that consciousness-raising tasks were at least as effective a way of developing explicit knowledge as traditional deductive instruction (Fotos 1994).

Another type of teaching activity that may involve learners in the development of explicit knowledge through an inductive, problem-solving approach is the dictogloss. This is a collaborative output activity (cf. Chapter 5) in which learners are asked to write a text in pairs or small groups based on an input text that has been read to them by the teacher. Like the consciousness-raising tasks analysed above, the dictogloss is a language teaching activity which includes a communicative component, but in which 'communication is, in part at least, about language' (Swain 1998: 70). Ruth Wajnryb (1990: 6), an author of a well-known handbook on the dictogloss, summarizes the features and aims of this teaching activity as follows:

> Dictogloss is a task-based procedure designed to help language-learning students towards a better understanding of how grammar works on a text basis. It is designed to expose where their language-learner shortcomings and needs are so that teaching can be directed more precisely towards these areas.

The key stage of the dictogloss takes place when the students are left to try and reconstruct the input text from their notes in pairs or small groups. As they are instructed to produce a single version of the text for each pair or group, they engage in collaborative dialogue. What is 'collaborative dialogue'? Swain defines collaborative dialogue as 'dialogue in which speakers are engaged in problem solving and knowledge building' (Swain 2000: 102). Evidence from a series of studies the researcher conducted has shown that peer–peer interaction in which students carry out a collaborative task (e.g. the joint writing of a story, the preparation of a role play, strategic reading or listening) provides them with opportunities both to use language and to reflect on language use (cf. Chapter 6). Swain (2000: 113) posits that

> [a]s each participant speaks, their 'saying' becomes 'what they said', providing an object for reflection. Their 'saying' is cognitive activity, and 'what is said' is an outcome of that activity. Through saying and reflecting on what is said, new knowledge is constructed.

In the dictogloss task, in order to reconstruct the input text, students start from their skeletal notes, which usually consist of single words or short phrases, and first tap their L2 implicit knowledge. In so doing, they may come across a 'hole' in their knowledge – they may realize that they are not sure about the syntax of a lexicogrammatical construction, for example, or they may have doubts about the spelling of a word. Hence, they may 'notice what they do not know, or know only partially' (Swain 1995: 129). In order to try and tackle the problem 'caused by a "hole" in their interlanguage' (Swain 1998: 74), they use collaborative dialogue to reflect on language. The analysis of transcripts of examples of collaborative dialogue engaged in by groups of students pinpoints several instances of 'language-related episodes' ('any part of a dialogue in which the students talk about the language they are producing, question their language use, or other- or self-correct', Swain 1998: 70), where learners reflected consciously upon their language use and were thus led to 'deploy explicit knowledge' (Swain 1998: 74).

An example of a language-related episode occurring during collaborative dialogue is shown in the following extract where three university students of French are planning an activity by rehearsing the language they will need to carry out the activity.

---

1. Speaker 1: ... *and then I'll say* ... *tu as souvenu notre anniversaire de marriage* ... *or should I say mon anniversaire?*
2. Speaker 2: *Tu as* ...
3. Speaker 3: *Tu as* ...
4. Speaker 1: *Tu as souvenu* ... *'you remembered'?*
5. Speaker 3: *Yeah, but isn't that reflexive? Tu t'as* ...
6. Speaker 1: *Ah, tu t'as souvenu.*
7. Speaker 2: *Oh, it's tu es*
8. Speaker 1: *Tu es*
9. Speaker 3: *tu es, tu es, tu* ...
10. Speaker 1: *t'es, tu t'es*
11. Speaker 3: *tu t'es*
12. Speaker 2: *Tu t'es souvenu*

Speaker 2 notices (2) that something is amiss in the output provided by speaker 1 (1). Speaker 3 also seems to detect a possible problem (3) and eventually Speaker 1 too is led to question their lexicogrammatical knowledge (4). To tackle the problem, speaker 3 resorts to their explicit knowledge (5), which is further developed by speaker 2 (7). This enables speaker 1 to reach a new understanding of the concept of 'reflexive' in French (8) – reflexive verbs need the auxiliary *être*. Finally, the correct form is arrived at thanks to the shared resources of the three speakers (12).

(From Donato 1994: 44, quoted in Swain 1995: 138)

The above extract shows how collaborative dialogue has enabled the three students to 'negotiate about form' (Swain 1995), thereby developing their explicit knowledge about reflexive verbs in French and succeeding in producing the reflexive verb construction correctly (*tu t'es souvenu*).

Although in this example a metalinguistic term was used by one of the students ('reflexive'), metalanguage is not held to be essential to the development of explicit knowledge in collaborative dialogues (Swain 1998).

In order to more accurately keep track of the development of explicit knowledge emerging in collaborative dialogues, researchers have devised ways of categorizing the precise focuses of language-related episodes. For example, in a study that aimed at determining the effectiveness of pair vis-à-vis individual work in carrying out a 'text-editing task' (a variation of the dictogloss task, cf. 4.5.d), Storch (2007) distinguished three types of language-related episodes emerging in the collaborative dialogue engaged in by pairs of students: those focusing on morphology and syntax (F-LRE), those targeting lexis (L-LRE) and those dealing with mechanics (punctuation, spelling and pronunciation – M-LRE). Most of the language-related episodes in Storch's study were about morphosyntax, in keeping with the overall focus of the text chosen as input for the task. However, students often deviated from the main focus envisaged by the researcher in that, as confirmed by several other studies (Swain 1998), in collaborative dialogue 'the learners talk about what they need to talk about, that is, those aspects of language about which they are not sure' (Swain 1998: 73).

To what extent does the dictogloss lead to learners' development of explicit knowledge? The dictogloss study reported on in Swain (1998), which was preceded by a number of similar studies, has provided some evidence that the dictogloss fosters explicit knowledge and overall language development. The researchers found that each pair of students who had engaged in collaborative dialogue during the reconstruction phase of a dictogloss generated language-related episodes and in the majority of cases (54.7 per cent) the problems discussed were solved correctly. Specially designed post-tests targeting the lexicogrammatical features that had arisen in the language-related episodes also showed that the knowledge – whether correct or incorrect – developed through the collaborative dialogues 'stuck'. Both pairs who had reached correct solutions and those who had reached incorrect solutions mostly provided the same solutions in the post-tests that they had arrived at in their collaborative dialogues. It would thus appear that language teaching tasks such as the dictogloss which have collaborative dialogue as an essential design feature provide a highly effective way for learners to develop new explicit linguistic knowledge or consolidate already existing knowledge by reflecting on their implicit knowledge. This is done while carrying out a communicative task (cf. Chapter 6), hence 'in a highly context-sensitive situation' (Swain 1998: 68).

As a final caveat, it is important not to underestimate the teacher's role in the implementation of the dictogloss. Swain's (1998) study mentioned above, while highlighting that most of the problems worked out by the students led to correct solutions, also acknowledged that in a limited number of cases the outcome of the students' discussions was incorrect knowledge. Worse, this knowledge appeared to 'stick'. For this reason, the teacher has an essential role during the implementation of the dictogloss. To ensure thorough student learning, they need to address problems of incorrect knowledge and provide targeted feedback on the final outcome of the students' reconstruction phase.

4.4 The principle in the classroom

According to the principle we have been exploring in this chapter, explicit L2 knowledge may play a role – albeit indirect – in the acquisition of implicit knowledge. It follows that activities aiming to develop learners' explicit knowledge should have a place in a language teaching curriculum. In this section, examples of materials and activities designed to raise learners' conscious awareness of lexicogrammatical features of English will be provided.

(a) Language teaching and reference materials often feature pedagogical descriptions. These are aimed at helping learners acquire explicit language knowledge and are also often used by teachers to provide corrective feedback (cf. Chapter 5) and to answer students' queries. Below you will find examples of three pedagogical descriptions of English lexicogrammar. Read each description and evaluate it according to a selection of Michael Swan's criteria (cf. Section 4.3).

---

1. The present perfect progressive is used to talk about an action or a state that started in the past and continues at the time of speaking.
2. We use *for* and *since* with the present or the past perfect. They are used to express duration.
3. In the first conditional you replace the future simple in the *if* clause with the present simple, the future progressive with the present progressive and the future perfect with the present perfect.

	Truth	Demarcation	Clarity	Simplicity
	Is the description an accurate reflection of how English is actually used?	Does the description enable the learner to tell apart the targeted lexicogrammatical feature from a similar one?	Does the description avoid the use of ambiguous or overly technical terminology?	Does the description provide just the right amount of information and avoid the use of too many categories and subcategories?
Description no. 1				
Description no. 2				
Description no. 3				

4.4.1 Developing explicit knowledge through guided induction: Consciousness-raising tasks

Besides acquiring explicit knowledge deductively, through pedagogical descriptions provided by a coursebook or reference material, or through teacher explanation, students can be led to develop conscious knowledge in an inductive way. Consciousness-raising tasks (cf. Section 4.3) can be used to implement this process of guided induction in the classroom.

(a) The following consciousness-raising task is made up of three steps (A, B, C).

Go over step A below. What is the lexicogrammatical focus of the task?

A. In the following sentences, why does *give* have two grammatical patterns whereas *explain* has only one?

She gave a book to her father. (grammatical)
She gave her father a book. (grammatical)
The policeman explained the law to Mary. (grammatical)
The policeman explained Mary the law. (ungrammatical)

Steps B and C of the task are provided below.

B. Say whether each of these sentences is grammatical or ungrammatical. Your teacher will check your answers.

1. They saved Mark a seat.
2. His father read Kim a story.
3. They donated the hospital some money.
4. They suggested Mary a trip on the river.
5. They reported the police the accident.
6. They threw Mary a party.
7. The bank lent Mr. Thatcher some money.
8. He indicated Mary the right turning.
9. The festival generated the college a lot of money.
10. He cooked his girlfriend a cake.

C. Work out a rule for verbs like 'give' and 'explain'.
1. List the verbs in part B that are like *give* (i.e. permit both sentence patterns) and those that are like *explain* (i.e. allow only one sentence pattern).
2. What is the difference between the verbs in your two lists?

(Ellis 2016: 136)

(b) A consciousness-raising task engages students in the analysis of exemplars of L2 'data' with a view to leading them to reach a generalization about the form, meaning and/or use of targeted lexicogrammatical feature(s) through specific data analysis 'operations'. With regard to the consciousness-raising task provided above, consider the following questions:

– In which step(s) of the task are the data provided?

– What types of data were chosen by the material writer? Complete the following chart by putting a tick in the appropriate columns.

Consciousness-Raising Task Data									
Authentic	Contrived	Oral	Written	Discrete sentences	Continuous text	Well formed	Deviant	Gap	Non-gap

– What kinds of operations are students required to carry out in order to analyse the data? Complete the following chart by putting a tick in the appropriate columns.

Consciousness-Raising Task Operations						
Identification	Judgement	Completion	Modification	Sorting	Matching	Rule provision

(c) Below you will see another example of a consciousness-raising task. The steps (A–D) which make up the task are in the wrong order. Can you reconstruct the original sequence of steps? Compared to the task in section (a) above, this consciousness-raising task has an extra step. What do you think is this extra step aimed at?

A. Study these sentences about these people. When is 'for' used and when is 'since' used?

Mr Reagan has been working for his company for most of his life.
Mr Bush has been working for his company since 1997.
Ms Cameron has been working for her company for 13 months.
Ms Thatcher has been working for her company since January.

B. Make up one sentence about when you started to learn English and one sentence about how long you have been studying English. Use 'for' and 'since'.

C. Here is the information about when four people joined the company they now work for and how long they have been working there.

Name	Date joined	Length of time
Mr Reagan	1978	39 years
Mr Bush	1997	20 years
Ms Cameron	2016	13 months
Ms Thatcher	2017 (January)	20 days

D. Which of the following sentences are ungrammatical? Why?

Mr Reagan has been working for his company for 1978.
Mr Bush has been working for his company for 20 years.
Ms Cameron has been working for her company since 2016.
Ms Thatcher has been working for her company since 20 days
Try and make up a rule for when 'for' and 'since' are used.

(Adapted from Ellis 2002b: 173)

(d) It has been hypothesized (cf. Subsection 4.3.1) that 'analysed knowledge' and 'metalinguistic explanation' are two distinct components of explicit knowledge. Students may develop conscious awareness of a lexicogrammatical feature ('analysed knowledge') without necessarily needing to acquire the ability to provide a description of that feature using grammatical metalanguage ('metalinguistic explanation'). To what extent do the two consciousness-raising tasks (a and c above) succeed in developing L2 analysed knowledge without requiring the deployment of complex technical terminology?

4.4.2 Developing explicit knowledge through language-related episodes: Alessandro dealing with a dictogloss

Video Extract 4

A dictogloss is a collaborative output task which can help students develop explicit knowledge by having them notice and reflect on 'gaps' in their interlanguage (cf. Subsection 4.3.2). In this section, we will explore how Alessandro, a secondary school EFL teacher, has implemented a dictogloss with his intermediate level students.

(a) Watch an extract in which Alessandro introduces a dictogloss to his class. Reorder the steps of the activity according to the teacher's instructions. How does a dictogloss differ from a traditional dictation?

A. The teacher introduces the context and the topic of the text that will be read out.
B. The teacher tells the students to work in groups of three. They have about 10 minutes to reconstruct the text. The reconstructed text must be as close as possible to the original text.
C. The teacher reads the text at normal speed while the students listen without writing down anything.
D. The teacher writes a few words/expressions on the board and asks the students if they know what they mean.
E. The teacher explains how the activity works. He says it is a special kind of dictation…
F. The teacher reads the text a second time and asks the students to note down words/expressions.

(b) Look at the input text the teacher has used for the dictogloss. What is the lexicogrammatical focus of the dictogloss? Consider in particular the parts underlined in the text.

> Our work at the quarry <u>was meant to</u> show us that we were no different from the other prisoners.
>
> However, the authorities still <u>treated us like</u> the lepers who once populated the island.
>
> Sometimes we saw a group of common law prisoners working <u>by the side of</u> the road.
>
> Their warders ordered them into the bushes so they would not see us as we marched past.
>
> <u>It was as if</u> the sight of us might somehow affect their discipline.
>
> Sometimes, <u>out of the corner of an eye</u> we could see a prisoner raise his fist in the African National Congress salute.
>
> (Adapted from Boers and Lindstromberg 2008: 31)

(c) Go through the notes taken by two students as the teacher read the text aloud. What kind of words and expressions did they manage to write? What other kinds of words do they need to reconstruct the text?

Student 1	Student 2
work quarry	*work at quarry*
no different from prisoners	*no different from others prisoners*
authorities→ lepers treated	*authorities*
group of common law prisoners	*↓*
hide in the bushes	*lepers*
site of us	*sometimes common law prisoners*
affect their disciplines	*not see us*
race	*discipline*
african national congress saluts	*1 prisioner raise his face?!*

(d) Analyse the collaborative dialogue of a group of students who are reconstructing their version of the first part of the dictogloss text. Refer back to the input text of the dictogloss. Does their negotiation lead to a successful outcome?

> S1: *allora {so} our work at the quarry was meant to*
> S2: *was meant to show us that there was no different with the other prisoner*
> S1: *we were no different from*
> S2: *we were no different*
> S1: *from the other prisoners*
> S2: *were no different from the other prisoners.*
> S3: *mm. but the warders*
> S1: *but the warders treated us like lepers*
> S2: *no io ho scritto {no I wrote} however the authorities*
> S1: *va be' è uguale {yeah it's the same}*
> S2: *è {it's} however*
> S3: *however the authorities*
> S2: *um treated u*
> S3: *treated*
> S1: *us*
> S2: *us as the lepers*
> S1: *who once*
> S2: *populated the island. however the authorities treated us treated us as the lepers*
> S1: *as lepers anche senza {also without}*

(In the transcripts, translations into English of the original words spoken by the students in Italian are provided in curly brackets)

(e) Analyse these examples of language-related episodes drawn from the students' collaborative dialogues. For each episode, consider the following questions:

– What kind of language problems are the students trying to sort out in the episode? Decide if the episode targets morphosyntax (F-LRE), lexis (L-LRE) or spelling/pronunciation (M-LRE).
– Can you detect evidence of explicit knowledge of the language being developed by the students?
– How do they convey this knowledge to each other?
– To what extent do the students use technical terminology (metalanguage)?

1.
S3: *the sight of us or our sight?*
S4: *the sight of us.*
S3: *sight non si scrive così si scrive {it's not written like that it is}*
     s i g h t
S4: *sì ho capito. {yeah I got it}*

2.
S4: *and there were*
S3: *and there were*
S4: *no different*
S3: *no*
S4: *differen-*
S3: *there <u>was</u> no difference*
S4: *yes.* [...]
S3: *we were no different*
S4: *mm*
S3: *from the other prisoners.* [...]

3.
S3: *that the sight of us*
S4: *could affect*
S3: *could affect*
S4: *their disciplines.*
S3: *their disc- discipline /diʃʃipline/ dot.*
S4: */plines /*
S3: */pline/ (raises one finger to indicate 'just one')*

(f) Go through one of the reconstructed texts written by the students. Compare it to the original dictogloss text. Did the students succeed in using correctly the lexicogrammatical items that were the main target of the dictogloss? To which language features would you draw the students' attention in the feedback phase?

We were working at the quarry and we were no different from other prisoners. However the authorities treated us like if we were lepers that once used to populate the land. One day we saw a group of common law prisoners working on the side of the street. The warders told them to hide into the bushes in order not to see us because they believed that the sight of us could affect their discipline. Out of the corner of an eye a man raised his fist in order to show the South African National Congress salute.

(g) During the final stage of the activity the teacher provides feedback on the students' reconstructed texts. Analyse the following extracts in which he interacts with the class about one of the students' texts (cf. f) comparing it to the original.

- Which features does he target? Are they the same as those you selected?
- Why do you think he targeted these features in particular?
- Do you think he was effective in helping the students notice any 'holes' they had in their knowledge of these features?
- To what extent did he succeed in developing the students' explicit knowledge about these features?

1.

> T: *the second text said we were working at the quarry and we were no different from other prisoners. however the authorities treated us like if we were lepers that once used to populate the land. the original text as you can see here says our work at the quarry was* <u>*meant*</u> *to show us that we were no different from other prisoners. so our work there at the quarry was* <u>*meant*</u> *to show us that we were no different. was meant to. what does it mean? was meant to. can you use another expression? another word to say that? was meant to show us*
> S: *was intended for*

2.

> T: *in your text? ok. the authorities treated us* <u>*like*</u> *ok if we were lepers. very good. ok. would you say they treated us* <u>*as*</u> *or* <u>*like*</u>*? which one would you use? both?*
> Ss: *like*

3.

> T: *out of the corner of an eye a man raised his fist in order to show the south African national congress salute. m? and we said that the meaning is more or less the same. m? but let's see the original text. as you can see here it was* <u>*as*</u> *if the sight of us might somehow affect their discipline. sometimes out of the corner of an eye we could see a prisoner raise his fist in the African national congress salute. so it was as if. it was as if. m? what's he doing? he's?*

> S: *imagining*
> T: *i- he's?*
> S: *imagining*
> T: *imagining. right. ok. he's making a hypothesis. eh? ok?*

4.5 Restructuring and planning

In this section, you will be asked to evaluate and/or adapt materials aimed at developing students' explicit knowledge of several commonly taught lexicogrammatical areas of English.

(a) Go back to the pedagogical descriptions in Section 4.4.a and review your evaluation of them on the basis of Swan's criteria. Try and improve each description so that they can be of help to intermediate level EFL students.

(b) The following consciousness-raising task (Steps 1–3) is meant to raise students' awareness of the use of the English present perfect vis-à-vis the simple past. What types of data are students asked to analyse? What is the purpose of the listening activity? Why does it feature a gapped text? How are students guided to analyse the data? The final step in the task is the verbalization of the 'rules'. Design a further step enabling students to check their understanding of the use of the present perfect.

---

1. Listen to the following interviews. Mr Naraporn is being interviewed for a job as an airport baggage handler and Ms Adams is being interviewed for a job as an aerobics instructor.
While you are listening, fill in the blanks with the word or words in parentheses ()

Interview with Mr Naraporn:
Interviewer: _____ this kind of job before, Mr Naraporn?
1 (Did you do/Have you done)
Mr Naraporn: *Not exactly.*
Interviewer: *But you* _____ jobs like this before?
2 (had/have had)
Mr Naraporn: *Yes, from 1990 until 1995 I* _____ in a Nike shoe factory.

---

3 (worked/have worked)

Interviewer: *And what was that like?*

Mr Naraporn: *It _____ very noisy. I _____ the same thing over and over.*

4 (was/has been)   5 (did/have done)

Interview with Ms Adams:

Interviewer: *Ms Adams, I _____ at your CV. All your previous jobs at health clubs were part-time positions.*

6 (looked/have looked)

Ms Adams: *Yes, that's right.*

Interviewer: *You _____ a full-time job?*

7 (didn't want/haven't wanted)

Ms Adams: *Well, from 1993 until 1997 I _____ a student.*

8 (was/has been)

Interviewer: *I see. But you _____ with people of different ages?*

9 (worked/have worked)

Ms Adams: *Oh yes: children, adults, senior citizens. And last year I _____some seminars on sports medicine.*

10 (took/have taken)

2. Work with a partner. Look at the verbs listed in the box. Find these verbs in the interviews. Write the verb as it is written in the interviews.

Verb	Simple past	Present perfect
1. do		*Have you done*
2. have		
3. work	*worked*	
4. be		
5. do		
6. look		
7. want		
8. be		
9. work		
10. take		

3. Complete the following statements:

- We use the _____ tense to describe an action in the past that took place at a specific time.
- We use the _____ tense to describe an action that was completed during a specific period of time in the past.
- We use the _____ tense to describe an action that took place at some indefinite time in the past, when no specific time is mentioned.
(Adapted from Ellis and Gaies 1998: 18–19)

(c) Language teaching coursebooks often feature consciousness-raising tasks. The example you will see below has been drawn from a popular EFL coursebook and is aimed at developing students' explicit knowledge of the use of *will* versus *be going to*. Identify the types of data provided and the operations students are asked to carry out to analyse the data. Do the data provide enough examples of the targeted lexicogrammatical features? What kinds of clues are students given to enable them to work out the semantic difference between *will* and *be going to*? Do you think they are effective to guide the students' inductive process?

Peter: *I'm just going to the shops. Do you want anything?*
Anne: *No, I don't think so. Oh hang on. We haven't got any sugar left.*
Peter: *It's all right. It's on the list. I'm going to buy some.*
Anne: *What about bread?*
Peter: *Ok. I'll go to the baker and buy a loaf.*

Shopping list
sugar
tea
coffee
cheese
biscuits
cornflakes
tins of beans
yoghurt

Grammar questions
Why does Peter say: *I'm going to buy some (sugar)* but *I'll go to the baker?*
What's the difference between 'will' and 'going to' to express a future intention?
        (Soars and Soars 1986, quoted in Batstone and Ellis 2009: 195–196)

(d) Several variations of the classic dictogloss task have been devised. The following activity is called 'text-editing' task and, like the dictogloss, involves students in collaborative dialogue with a view to developing their explicit knowledge of targeted lexicogrammatical features. What is the lexicogrammatical focus of this task? How does it differ from a classic dictogloss? What advantages/disadvantages do you think a text-editing task might have vis-à-vis a dictogloss?

Text-editing task
The task includes two versions of a text: a correct version (version A) and a version with errors (version B).

1. The teacher reads the original text (version A) at a normal pace while students listen for meaning.
2. Students receive version B, and try to make any changes needed to the text based on what they just heard. (They try to make version B as grammatically accurate as possible.)
3. Students form groups of two and then compare their responses and try to justify their choices.
4. Students compare their edited versions with the original version. The teacher provides feedback or explanations as needed.

Original text (version A)
There was a little girl who used to go camping with her parents every summer. They would travel by car for hours and reach a cabin just as the sun was going down. Before they even unpacked their belongings, her parents started a fire and roasted hot dogs and marshmallows. The girl used to go swimming with her mom every morning, and her dad would play with her until it was dark outside. When she wasn't playing she was chasing her pet dog around the cabin for hours. She never wanted to go away when camping was over, but always remembered that they would come back the next summer, and this made her very happy.

Original text (version B)
There was a little girl who use to go camping with her parents every summer. They would travel with car for hours and reach a cabin just as the sun was going down. Before they even unpack their belongings, her parents started fire and roast hot dogs and marshmallows. The girl used to go swimming with her mom every morning, and her dad will play with her until it was dark outside. When she wasn't playing she was chasing his pet dog around the cabin for hours. She never wanted to go away when camping was over, but always remembered that they would come back next summer, and this made her very happy.
(Adapted from Fotos and Nassaji 2011: 114–115)

4.6 Conclusions

In this chapter, we have tried to 'unpack' the concepts of explicit and implicit knowledge of a second language. We have seen that what underlies the ability to use a language effortlessly in natural communication is implicit knowledge. Nevertheless, many SLA research studies seem to suggest that explicit knowledge may have an important role to play in second language learning and teaching in that it is thought to facilitate the acquisition of implicit knowledge. Likewise, if it has been recently argued that 'the bulk of language acquisition is implicit learning through usage' (N. Ellis 2005: 306), it also seems likely that 'many aspects of a second language are unlearnable — or at best are acquired very slowly — from implicit processes alone' (N. Ellis 2005: 307). Explicit knowledge and learning seem to be particularly beneficial in the case of learners who experience 'fossilization', i.e. lack of development, in some areas of their L2 language system (Ellis 2005).

In the language classroom, it is customary to oppose two ways of providing explicit knowledge: a deductive approach and a discovery-based inductive approach. In actual fact, this distinction may be an oversimplification. Sharwood Smith (1981) suggests that what he dubs 'language consciousness-raising' may be implemented in several different ways, depending on 'the degree of elaboration or conciseness with which it is presented, as well as the degree of explicitness or intensity in the way attention is drawn to the relevant regularities' (Sharwood Smith 1981: 160). He identifies two main dimensions ('elaborateness' and 'explicitness') along which the provision of explicit knowledge may vary. Pedagogical descriptions found in reference materials represent an explicit but less elaborate way of language consciousness-raising, while the use of 'brief, indirect "clues"', such as the technique of input enhancement (cf. Chapter 3), is a less explicit and less elaborate way. An example of a more explicit and more elaborate approach is currently favoured by proponents of Sociocultural Theory (cf. Chapter 5). Researchers such as James Lantolf start from the premise that 'neither the strong nor the weak SLA position has given sufficient attention to the quality of the explicit knowledge made available through intentional instruction' (Lantolf 2007: 52). It is claimed that pedagogical descriptions, which are referred to as 'rules of thumb', are not the ideal incarnation of explicit knowledge in that they at best offer simplified half-truths which are often interpreted as inflexible injunctions by learners, thus eventually hampering language use and development. Lantolf suggests replacing 'rules of thumb' with 'scientific concepts', 'systematically organized in accordance with the findings of linguistic theory and related research' (Lantolf 2007: 38). It remains to be empirically verified to what kinds of learners this latter type of more explicit and more elaborate descriptions can be of use. What seems likely, as pointed out by Ellis (2016: 135), is that 'explicit knowledge of grammatical rules is itself a "developmental" phenomenon. Learners may commence with some oversimplified rule but gradually refine this over time'. It also seems clear that, on the whole, mastery of metalanguage is independent from explicit knowledge (Ellis 2009), although it is also likely that 'learners with highly developed analysed knowledge will also possess extensive metalinguistic knowledge' (Ellis 2006a: 436).

Two specific types of teaching activities aiming at developing learners' lexicogrammatical awareness, consciousness-raising tasks and the dictogloss, have been presented in the chapter. Both kinds of activities rely on learners' analytical skills and require intellectual effort to be completed and thus may not be particularly suitable for younger learners (Ellis 1997). With regard to the dictogloss more specifically, whether it succeeds in eliciting the type of collaborative dialogue that is thought to favour the emergence of explicit knowledge rests on 'the level of learners' proficiency, the age of the learners, and any of a host of other factors' (Swain 1998: 79). For example, results of Leeser's study (2004) point to the fact that higher proficiency students produce more language-related episodes in their collaborative dialogues and hence more opportunities to develop explicit knowledge. The implementation of the dictogloss makes heavy demands on the teacher, who needs to be able to handle the feedback stage for it to foster learners' emerging explicit knowledge. This is by no means an easy enterprise, as the 'Principle in the classroom' section has shown (cf. Subsection 4.4.2.g). While it is down to the teacher to design effective materials targeting the development of explicit knowledge, whether and how an actual interface is implemented between explicit and implicit knowledge 'is in the hands of the learner, not in those of the teacher' (Ellis 2016: 145).

4.7 Note

1 Rutherford (1987) does not view the direct provision of explicit knowledge ('grammar teaching') as an instantiation of consciousness-raising.

4.8 Further reading

DeKeyser, R. (2003), 'Implicit and explicit learning', in C. J. Doughty and M. H. Long (eds), *The Handbook of Second Language Acquisition*, 313–348, Oxford: Blackwell.

Ellis, N. C. (2005), 'At the interface: dynamic interactions of explicit and implicit language knowledge', *Studies in Second Language Acquisition*, 27 (2): 305–352.

Ellis, R. (1994), 'Explicit/implicit knowledge and language pedagogy', *TESOL Quarterly*, 28 (1): 166–172.

Ellis, R. (1997), *SLA Research and Language Teaching*, Oxford: Oxford University Press.

Ellis, R. (2004), 'The definition and measurement of L2 explicit knowledge', *Language Learning*, 54 (2): 227–275.

Ellis, R. (2006), 'Current issues in the teaching of grammar. An SLA perspective', *TESOL Quarterly*, 40 (1): 83–107.

Ellis, R. (2016), 'Grammar teaching as consciousness raising', in E. Hinkel (ed.), *Teaching Grammar to Speakers of Other Languages*, 128–150, London: Routledge.

Ellis, R. and S. Gaies (1998), *Impact Grammar*, Hong Kong: Longman.

Ellis, R., S. Loewen, C. Elder, H. Reinders, R. Erlam and J. Philp, eds (2009), *Implicit and Explicit Knowledge in Second Language Learning, Testing and Teaching*, Bristol: Multilingual Matters.

Fotos, S. (1994), 'Integrating grammar instruction and communicative language use through grammar consciousness-raising tasks', *TESOL Quarterly*, 28 (3): 323–351.

Fotos, S. and R. Ellis (1991), 'Communicating about grammar. A task-based approach', *TESOL Quarterly*, 25 (3): 605–628.

Swain, M. (1998), 'Focus on form through conscious reflection', in C. Doughty and J. Williams (eds), *Focus on Form in Classroom Second Language Acquisition*, 64–82, Cambridge: Cambridge University Press.

Swan, M. (1994), 'Design criteria for pedagogic language rules', in M. Bygate, A. Tonkyn and E. Williams (eds), *Grammar and the Language Teacher*, 45–55, Harlow: Prentice Hall.

Wajnryb, R. (1990), *Grammar Dictation*, Oxford: Oxford University Press.

Chapter 5
Interaction and corrective feedback

5.1 Key questions

In the previous chapters (cf. Chapters 2 and 3), we analysed the role of one of the main components in second language learning: input. As pointed out, input is the language to which learners are exposed and is available to them in different forms and through a variety of sources. Researchers have investigated how input can be made comprehensible to serve as the basis for acquisition (cf. Chapter 2). However, a good deal of acquisition is also dependent on the way learners use strategies to interpret or process what they hear or read, that is, how they make appropriate form-meaning connections during comprehension (cf. Chapter 3). For this reason, teachers need to optimize the ways in which input is made comprehensible helping learners use appropriate processing strategies to attend to input.

Comprehensible input, though, is not assumed to be sufficient for language acquisition on its own. Research has shown that learners also need opportunities to produce and use the language to progress in their language development (cf. Chapter 6). In particular, the production of 'pushed' output through feedback stimulates learners to reflect on the language they use and produce more accurate and comprehensible language. As Mackey (2012: 17) highlights, 'output has benefits regardless of whether it is more, less, or equally as target-like as a learner's original utterance', that is to say, 'the process of modifying one's output is as important as the ultimate product'.

This chapter aims to illustrate the processes involved 'when learners encounter input, [...] receive feedback and produce output' (Gass and Mackey 2015: 181) and how these processes foster language acquisition. We will also consider how these interactional processes can be affected by cognitive factors such as attention and memory. We will then examine the mechanisms of 'scaffolded' help, which arise from collaborative dialogue in both learner–teacher and learner–learner interactions, and how these mechanisms can mediate language development. The theoretical background for the principles and constructs presented in the chapter is supplied by two main lines of research: the Interaction Hypothesis (Long 1983, 1996), which found a following expansion within the more comprehensive framework of the Interaction Approach (Mackey 1999, 2007, 2012; Gass 2003; Gass and Mackey 2015), and the Sociocultural Theory (Aljaafreh and Lantolf 1994; Donato 1994; Lantolf 2000; Lantolf and Thorne 2006). The implications of these principles for teaching will be examined in relation to a number of options aimed at exploiting the learning potential of interaction activities in second language classrooms.

The following questions will be addressed in the chapter:

- What types of 'interactional adjustments' can facilitate comprehension and foster language learning?
- How can 'scaffolding' taking place during verbal interaction mediate language learning?
- What can teachers do to help learners notice problematic aspects of their production during interaction?
- How can collaborative dialogue between teacher and students be enhanced to support language learning?

5.2 Experience

(a) Read this transcription of a short interaction between a non-native speaker (NNS), presumably a learner, and a native speaker (NS) interlocutor. What is the problem involved in this interaction? Do you think that the NNS speaker eventually understands the word 'vase' or is she/he simply repeating what the NS said?

NNS: *There's a basen of flowers on the bookshelf*
NS: *a basin?*
NNS: *base*
NS: *a base?*
NNS: *a base*
NS: *oh, a vase*
NNS: *vase*

(From Mackey et al. 2000: 473)

(b) Most teachers and students assume that corrective feedback by the teacher is a necessary component of the language teaching/learning process. A great deal of corrective feedback takes place during interactions. In what ways should corrective feedback be provided? Complete the statements below with your suggestions.

---

1. Teachers should interrupt learners when they make an error when…
2. Teachers can give delayed feedback in the following situation(s)…
3. Teachers can help learners to self-correct or to correct each other's errors by…
4. Three ways of giving feedback on spoken errors are…
5. Some errors should remain uncorrected by the teacher because…
6. Corrective feedback should be carried out paying attention to students' sensitivity not to…

(Adapted from Tanner and Green 1998: 95)

(c) The choice of specific corrective feedback strategies during classroom interaction may be related to a number of factors; for example, the type of task in which students are involved, the need to make what is said comprehensible, the need to draw learner's attention on a particular language feature and so on. Consider the case described below. Which corrective feedback strategy or strategies would you choose to respond to the learner's utterance? Provide reasons for your choice.

A student is in front of the class and she is giving an oral report about her family. She says:
'My brothers, he always teased me.'
Possible teacher's corrective feedback options:
1. *There is a mistake in your sentence.*
2. *My brothers…*
3. *He always teased me or they always teased me?*
4. *Try again please.*
5. *They always made fun of me.*
6. *The pronoun has to reflect the same number as the noun.*
7. *My brothers, he always teased me. No!*

(Adapted from Nunan and Lamb 1996: 70)

5.3 The principles

Interaction has traditionally received a great amount of attention in second language teaching and is considered one of the priorities in most learning syllabuses. As Ellis and Shintani (2014: 194) highlight, most guides for second and foreign language teaching 'include an entry for "interaction" in their indexes and in some cases deal with it at considerable length'. As it turns out, the role of interaction is often discussed in relation to four main aspects of teaching:

– how to develop students' conversational skills and help them achieve a balance between accuracy and fluency;
– how to facilitate learners' participation in interaction activities in order to help them control factors that may inhibit or increase it; these factors may be self-confidence and willingness to communicate, anxiety, relationships with other students and so on;
– how to set up group work in order to allow greater student talk-time, independence and collaboration;
– how to select the most appropriate participatory structure for a particular interaction activity (e.g. teacher–class interaction for a general discussion or a dialogue in pairs for an information-gap task).

However, as Ellis and Shintani (2014: 202) argue, what is not tackled in teacher guides is the crucial issue of 'how language learning arises out of interaction'. This section aims to illustrate how research has addressed this issue. It will focus on two principles that account for the role of interaction in SLA from two different theoretical perspectives: the first is provided by the Interaction Hypothesis (cf. Subsection 5.3.1) and the second by the Sociocultural Theory (cf. Subsection 5.3.2). The teaching implications for each principle will be discussed through the presentation of specific options and techniques (cf. Subsection 5.3.3) and through the analysis of actual examples from classroom practice (cf. Section 5.4).

5.3.1 The Interaction Hypothesis

Early research into the interactions between second language learners and their interlocutors dates back to the late 1970s. Krashen's Input Hypothesis (cf. Chapter 2) suggested ways in which proficient speakers can modify their speech when interacting with learners in order to make input more comprehensible. Building on Krashen's hypothesis and research investigating the role of interactional skills for second language development (e.g. Hatch

1978), Long (1983) argues that there are other ways in which input is made comprehensible than modifying the input itself. In particular, he draws the attention on the modifications not of the input per se, but of 'the interactional structure of conversation through such devices as self- and other-repetition, confirmation and comprehension checks and clarification requests'. Examples of these modifications are provided below (Long 1983):

(a) comprehension checks are used to find out whether the interlocutor understands something:

T: *Do you understand?*

(b) confirmation checks are used to find out whether the speaker has heard or understood something the interlocutor has said:

S: *I wan one job.*
T: *You're looking for work?*

(c) clarification requests are used when the speaker (teacher or NS) needs to understand something the interlocutor (a student) has said:

T: *What do you mean?*

These modifications are likely to occur during interactions when the interlocutors need to sort out a communication problem. According to Long, comprehension checks and clarification requests will be more frequent when the flow of information is from teacher to student; confirmation checks will be more frequent when information is also conveyed in the other direction.

Long's (1983, 1996) pioneering research eventually substantiated in his Interaction Hypothesis, which provides the theoretical underpinnings for the first principle that will be explored in this part:

> **Interactional feedback is key to the learning of lexicogrammar.**

Central to this principle is the general claim that the negotiation for meaning taking place in oral interaction facilitates the development of a second language (Long 1996: 418):

> It appears that the informational structure of two-way tasks obliges
> NSs and NNSs to negotiate for meaning, and through the negotiation
> process, to make what they say comprehensible to their interlocutors.
> Negotiation for meaning is the process in which, in an effort to
> communicate, learners and competent speakers provide and interpret

signals of their own and their interlocutor's perceived comprehension, thus provoking adjustments to linguistic form, conversational structure, message content, or all three, until an acceptable level of understanding is achieved.

The example below (Mackey 1999: 559) shows how the interactional modifications occurring during the negotiation of meaning help comprehension:

> NS: There's there's a a pair of reading glasses above the plant.
> NNS: A what?
> NS: Glasses reading glasses to see the newspaper?
> NNS: Glassi?
> NS: You wear them to see with, if you can't see. Reading glasses.
> NNS: Ahh ahh glasses glasses to read you say reading glasses.
> NS: Yeah.

In the example, a NS and a NNS are involved in the interaction. The NNS does not understand the word 'glasses' used by the NS. The NNS asks for clarification and the word is repeated. Then the original phrase is extended and rephrased and a synonym is provided. This eventually seems to help the NNS understand the word.

However, although comprehension is consistently improved by interactional modifications and by a combination of simplification and elaboration,[1] Long (1996: 424) posits that comprehensible input alone is insufficient for acquisition to occur. In effect, even many quite advanced learners, who have been exposed to great amounts of comprehensible input, do not seem to incorporate into their interlanguage lexical items, grammatical constructions and other specific features that are successfully learned by NSs at an early stage. In contrast to his first version of the Interaction Hypothesis, which simply highlights the role of the negotiation process in making input comprehensible, Long's later version affords a deeper analysis of the way negotiation can support acquisition:

> [n]egotiation for meaning, and especially negotiation work that triggers interactional adjustments by the NS or more competent interlocutor, facilitates acquisition because it connects input, internal learner capacities, particularly selective attention, and output in productive ways. (Long 1996: 451–452)

How are then input, learner attention and output connected through negotiation for meaning during interaction and how does this support acquisition? According to Long (1996: 452), negotiation work can indeed afford denser semantically related talk, which assists acquisition in a number of ways:

- A higher frequency of target forms in the reformulations tends to increase the saliency of these forms and the likelihood of their being noticed by the learner.
- Input modifications (e.g. stress of keywords and pauses before and after them, partial repetition, lexical switches) involved in some reformulations likewise make target forms salient.
- Reformulations also often involve rearrangements of adjacent utterances, which show learners how their constituents should be segmented and help them notice the communicative value of linguistic forms.

As Long concludes, 'the increased comprehensibility that negotiation brings helps reveal the meaning of new forms and so makes the forms themselves acquirable'. Once the intended message is made clear through the negotiation process, learners can thus devote their attention to the linguistic forms in the input:

> Although there is no guarantee that the spare attentional resources will be allocated to form, of course, the chances that the learner will detect the changes, understand them, and incorporate them is likely to be higher than when both form and meaning are opaque. (Long 1996: 452)

Learners' enhanced attention to new linguistic features in the input will also help them notice a possible 'mismatch' between input and output, that is, their production during interaction. Such mismatches, as Long (1996: 453) argues, 'may also provide at least some of the information a learner needs about what is not permissible in a language' and this information may eventually lead them to modify their utterances. For example, in the following interaction (Mackey et al. 2003: 37), a NS reformulates a learner's utterance providing both the correct form of 'shelf' and the missing article:

> NNS: And in the er kitchen er cupboard no no shef.
> NS: On the shelf. I have it on the shelf.
> NNS: In the shelf, yes OK.

This helps the learner (NNS) notice that what he or she said was not correct and leads him or her to reformulate his or her previous utterance modifying 'shef' into 'shelf' including the correct article, although the correct preposition is not preserved. It should be noted, though, that despite getting opportunities to modify their output through interactional feedback, learners do not always reformulate their ungrammatical forms correctly: 'they may repeat their original utterances, modify grammatical features in the direction of the target or not, or not respond to the feedback at all' (Mackey 2007: 94).

Negotiation during second language interactions is accomplished by means of a variety of feedback strategies, which have been described and compared with each other. While much of early research aimed to identify all the options available to the teacher in order to capture the decision-making process prior to the feedback move, later studies identified a smaller set of corrective strategies that provided the basis for both experimental and classroom-based research. In their seminal study investigating teacher–student interaction in French immersion classrooms in Canada, Lyster and Ranta (1997: 46–49) identified six different types of teacher corrective feedback strategies which are described in Table 5.1.

Ellis (2012: 139) argues that these types of strategies can be applied to both feedback which is 'didactic', that is, directed purely at linguistic correctness, and 'communicative', that is directed at resolving a communication problem. Lyster and Ranta's investigation was motivated by the fact that the language used to convey subject matter needs to be highlighted through specific feedback strategies that make certain features more salient for L2 learners. This 'didactic' use of feedback is posited to aid language acquisition.

Drawing on their previous individual research, Sheen and Ellis (2011: 593) classify teachers' oral feedback strategies according to four broad types, as specified in the last column in Table 5.1:

- implicit (clarification is requested in response to the learner's erroneous utterance but without directly signalling that a correction is being undertaken);
- explicit (the error is corrected and/or some kind of metalinguistic explanation of the error is provided);
- input-providing (the correct form is provided to the learner);
- output-prompting (the correction of the form is elicited from the learner).

The distinction between input-providing and output-providing strategies is, according to Ellis (2008: 227), 'of theoretical importance because it is related to the nature of the data that learners obtain, that is, whether the data afford both positive and negative evidence or just negative evidence'. As Long (1996: 413) points out, positive evidence is supplied by 'models of what is grammatical and acceptable (not necessarily the same) in the L2'; this occurs with recasts in a more or less explicit way (Table 5.1, example b); negative evidence, instead, is provided by 'direct or indirect information about what is ungrammatical' (Table 5.1, examples d and f).

As for implicit and explicit feedback strategies, these two types should be considered more as poles on a continuum rather than a dichotomy, with recasts and clarification requests as being more implicit (Table 5.1, examples b and c) and explicit correction and metalinguistic feedback as being more explicit (Table 5.1, examples a and d). It should also be noted that strategies can be combined; for example, explicit correction can be followed by a metalinguistic comment or elicitation. Moreover, the degree of explicitness

Table 5.1 Types of teacher corrective feedback strategies.

Feedback strategies	Description	Examples	Types
a. Explicit correction	The explicit provision of the correct form indicating that what the student had said was incorrect.	S: *They're their.* T: *Theirs. Theirs.*	Explicit; output-prompting
b. Recast	The reformulation of all or part of a student's utterance, replacing the error with the correct language form.	S: *Because he needs some warms clothes.* T: *Because he needs some warm clothes.*	Implicit; input-providing
c. Clarification requests	These requests indicate to students either that their utterance has been misunderstood or that the utterance is ill-formed in some way.	S: *Did you ever been to London?* T: *Sorry, can you repeat please?*	Implicit; output-prompting
d. Metalinguistic feedback	Comments, information or questions related to the well-formedness of the student's utterance, without explicitly providing the correct form.	S: *While I was there we went at the Yellowstone National Park.* T: *While I was there we went, pay attention to the preposition.*	Explicit; output-prompting
e. Elicitation	It is aimed at eliciting the correct form from the student through: (a) the completion of the teacher's own utterance; (b) the use of questions to elicit correct forms; (c) the reformulation of the students' utterance.	S: *How much are...no...how much much* T: *How much ...?*	Explicit; output-prompting
f. Repetition	An utterance that repeats the student's erroneous utterance with or without emphasis on the erroneous part.	S: *She always study English.* T: *She always study?*	Implicit; output-prompting

The underlined text in the table provides examples of types of feedback strategies.
These examples of feedback strategies are from interactional data collected in two Italian lower-intermediate EFL classes (Pedrazzini 2017).

Figure 5.1 Examples of implicit/explicit recasts.

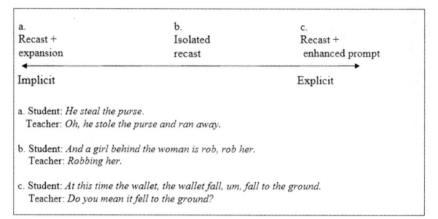

a.
Recast +
expansion

b.
Isolated
recast

c.
Recast +
enhanced prompt

Implicit   Explicit

a. Student: *He steal the purse.*
   Teacher: *Oh, he stole the purse and ran away.*

b. Student: *And a girl behind the woman is rob, rob her.*
   Teacher: *Robbing her.*

c. Student: *At this time the wallet, the wallet fall, um, fall to the ground.*
   Teacher: *Do you mean it fell to the ground?*

may also vary within each feedback type. For example, according to Nassaji (2015: 57–61) recasts may vary from being implicit to explicit, as shown through the examples in Figure 5.1. However, as Sarandi (2016: 236) points out, 'explicitness' is not only a matter of teachers' intentions but it should also be investigated from a learners' perspective in order to understand the extent to which corrective moves are perceived as 'salient'.

There are now a very large number of studies that have looked into the effectiveness of different types of oral corrective feedback strategies on SLA. The first response to teacher corrective feedback can be observed through learner uptake, that is,

> a student's utterance that immediately follows the teacher's feedback and that constitutes a reaction in some way to the teacher's intention to draw attention to some aspect of the student's initial utterance. (Lyster and Ranta 1997: 49)

An example of the way uptake moves may occur is illustrated in the extract below (Ellis 2012: 178), in which the learner mispronounces the word 'alibi' (1):

1. S: I have an ali[bi].
2. T: you have what?
3. S: an ali [bi].
4. T: an ali-? An alib [ay].
5. S: ali [bay].
6. T: okay, listen, listen, alibi.
7: SS: alibi.

The learner responds to the teacher's request for clarification (2) with a first uptake move but fails to repair the pronunciation (3). After the teacher's explicit correction (4), a further uptake move occurs (5) but the learner again fails to repair the error. More explicit correction by the teacher is needed (6) and the class as a whole pronounces 'alibi' correctly in a final uptake. This example shows that student uptake can be of two main types and take place at different stages during interaction: (a) utterances with 'repair' of the error on which the feedback focused and (b) utterances that still 'need repair'. Learner repair can be either a repetition or self-repair or may include simple acknowledgement, the repetition of the initial error, a different error, hesitation or a partial repair. Repair can be followed by teacher's 'reinforcement' through short statements of approval or by repeating students' corrected utterance.

Lyster and Saito's (2010) meta-analysis of the pedagogical effectiveness of oral corrective feedback in classroom settings has revealed three patterns in terms of overall effectiveness of corrective feedback types:

a. Recasts, prompts (elicitation, metalinguistic feedback, clarification requests and repetition) and explicit correction all are significantly effective.
b. Prompts proved significantly more effective than recasts.
c. Effects of explicit correction were not significantly different from those of recasts or prompts.

The analysis of outcomes has shown that effects of oral corrective feedback are larger when students' improvement is measured through tasks in which they produce free-constructed responses. It is also worth noting that young learners appear particularly sensitive to prompts but not so receptive when recasts are used. This may be due to young learners' difficulty in noticing linguistic features in the input without guided support; by contrast, 'older learners with substantial analytical abilities might be able to make the most of different corrective feedback types' (Lyster et al. 2013: 27). However, Ellis (2010: 344) cautions that it should be made clear which meaning is attached to the term 'acquisition' when gauging the impact of corrective feedback on learning outcomes: does it imply the acquisition of a new linguistic feature or does it denote an increase in the accuracy with which partially acquired features are used? Research into oral corrective feedback has typically addressed the effects on acquisition in terms of accuracy (cf. Chapter 6).

Moreover, the effects of feedback may vary according to the target grammatical feature. For example, in Ellis's study (2007), metalinguistic explanations were found to be more effective than recasts in improving learners' use of the comparative -er. Although morphosyntactic errors seem to be the most targeted, learners end up noticing and/or repairing lexical and phonological errors more successfully. For example, Egi (2007) reports that noticing a particular target-like form in recasts led to substantially greater improvement in vocabulary knowledge. Similarly, studies on the acquisition of phonological features (e.g. Saito and Lyster 2012) suggest that recasts with a focus on pronunciation provide students with opportunities to notice their errors and to practise the correct form in response to their teachers' model of pronunciation.

Finally, interactional processes can also be affected by factors such as attention and working memory. As mentioned, it is through interaction that learners are led to notice specific language forms and the mismatch between these forms and the forms available in the learners' interlanguage. The extent to which learners are able to notice new forms will lead them to modify their utterances during interaction more or less successfully. Interaction research has also sought to investigate the relationship between output and memory after interactional feedback. For example, findings from studies addressing this issue (Mackey 2012: 106) have highlighted that learners with higher working memory capacity are more likely to notice recasts, modify their production and eventually show more lasting benefits than peers with lower memory capacity who, instead, seem to be better equipped to simply engage in immediate modifications.

In conclusion, interaction studies have emphasized the crucial role of interaction in second language development. We have illustrated how interaction not only exposes learners to input but, through negotiation, also induces their attention to linguistic forms, and provides them with opportunities to modify their own production. Findings from interactional research can help teachers become more aware of the way interactional processes take place and which corrective strategies best support these processes and favour acquisition (cf. Subsection 5.3.3 and Section 5.4).

5.3.2 Interaction: The sociocultural perspective

In the previous part, we focused on the role of interactional feedback as being responsible for the activation of cognitive processes. According to this perspective, acquisition thus results from the interaction of input with the learner's mental knowledge and capacities. In this part of the chapter, we will examine the role of interaction in SLA from a different perspective that was inspired by the Sociocultural Theory (Aljaafreh and Lantolf 1994; Donato 1994; Lantolf 2000; Lantolf and Thorne 2006). It should be clarified that despite the label 'sociocultural', the theory does not aim to provide an explanation of the social or cultural aspects involved in second language learning. It is rather 'a theory of mind' that recognizes the central role of experiences of a sociocultural nature in the development of cognitive processes:

> Participation in culturally organized practices, life-long involvement in a variety of institutions, and humans' ubiquitous use of tools and artifacts (including language) strongly and qualitatively impact cognitive development and functioning. (Lantolf and Thorne 2006: 1)

The theory underpins the principle that will be explored here:

Collaborative dialogue between teacher and students facilitates acquisition.

As Ellis (2012: 238) highlights, implicit in the sociocultural view is that 'when two or more people are speaking they create their own linguistic resources [...] and in so doing demonstrate acquisition taking place in flight'. In contrast with an interactionist perspective, language learning occurs 'in' rather than 'as a result of' the participation in dialogic interaction. Use and acquisition do therefore overlap. Collaborative interaction in the classroom between teacher and students or students and students is thus considered to provide a facilitating condition for acquisition to take place.

The Sociocultural Theory was mainly inspired by the work of Vygotsky (1987), which offered a framework for explaining how second and foreign language processes develop. Within this framework, language is primarily viewed for its semantic potential and properties. It follows that

> [l]earning a new language is about much more than acquiring new signifiers for already given signifieds (for example, the Spanish word for 'fork' is *tenedor*). It is about acquiring new conceptual knowledge and/ or modifying already existing knowledge as a way of mediating one's interaction with the world and with one's psychological functioning. (Lantolf and Thorne 2006: 5)

The theory is informed by a number of interrelated constructs. We will focus on two in particular – mediation and the zone of proximal development (ZPD) and explain how they may impact second language learning processes.

Mediation is the central concept in the theoretical framework provided by Sociocultural Theory. Lantolf and Thorne (2006: 79) define mediation as

[t]he process through which humans deploy culturally constructed artifacts, concepts and activities to regulate (i.e. gain voluntary control over and transform) the material world or their own and each other's social and mental activity.

Learning is not only something that takes place only inside the head of the learner but is mediated by his or her participation in cultural activities (e.g. playing, reading, writing, etc.) in which cultural artefacts (books, paper, toys, etc.) and cultural concepts (e.g. person, family, etc.) interact in complex dynamic ways with each other and with the learner's psychological or mental activity (Lantolf and Thorne 2006: 59). Artefacts can be concrete, for example physical objects, or symbolic such as language, which is the most powerful artefact used for mediation. Symbolic mediation includes not only speaking, but also writing and gestures.

How does language mediate the learning process? Language can be used as a tool of both social interaction and thinking. The use of language to regulate mental (and possibly physical) activity is called private speech. As Lantolf and Thorne (2006: 75) explain, 'private speech may be fully externalized to the extent that is audible [...] or it may be whispered or even subvocal, audible only to the speaker'. It can be used, for example, to maintain the speaker's attention on specific features of a task, orient oneself to a task, support memory-related tasks or facilitate internalization of new or difficult information (language forms, sequences of numbers). This use of language shows features such as 'lowered speech volume, altered prosody, abbreviated syntax, and multiple repetitions' (Lantolf et al. 2015: 211).

Ellis (2008: 531) argues that it is necessary to distinguish the use of private speech 'for the purpose of practicing/learning the L2 and the purpose of self-regulating mental activity'. We will focus on the latter. When L2 learners use private speech, they may resort to their L1 or the L2; however, when they use the L2, they may not employ target-like language forms. In a study of private speech in Japanese as a foreign language, Ohta (2001) describes three types of L2 private speech, which can be summarized as follows (Ellis 2008: 531):

- vicarious response: the learner covertly answers a questions addressed to another student, completes the utterance of another or repairs another's error;
- repetition: the learner repeats words, part of or whole phrases or sentences;
- manipulation: the learner manipulates sentence structure, words or sounds.

Each type may assist learning in different ways: vicarious response helps learners test hypotheses about the L2; repetition is used to gain control over

Table 5.2 Types of use of private speech.

T: *Were you taking a nap, a little nap? [directed at another student]* L: *nap, I take nap... ing*	L vicariously answers a question that teacher asked another student. L first repeats the noun 'nap'. L uses the word with 'I' in the full phrase and changes the progressive of the verb 'take' into the simple present form (the pause after the second instance of 'nap' may be interpreted as L's attempt to reproduce the teacher's utterance after realizing that had been omitted).

new words or phrases and help retention; manipulation serves as a means for analysing language. An example of the use of private speech according to these functions is analysed in Table 5.2 (Lantolf and Thorne 2006: 201–202).

Researchers have also investigated the extent to which learners are able to deploy L2 forms to regulate themselves in challenging tasks. For example, McCafferty (1994) examines the use of private speech by students of different language proficiency ranging from low-intermediate to advanced and native proficiency levels. Participants were asked to construct a story based on a series of six consecutive drawings presented one at a time in sequence. One of the most striking differences between the narratives produced refers to the relative degree of control that each learner was able to exercise over the task. As illustrated in the examples in Table 5.3, the lower proficiency student produced a greater frequency of private speech utterances. The learner attempts to divide each picture into its component parts and seems to be 'regulated' by each part he attempts to describe. The NS, by contrast, gradually gains full control of the task, focusing on the events in the story and producing a narrative that is both coherent and cohesive. McCafferty also found that advanced learners used the past tense significantly more often than lower proficiency learners. This allowed them to structure temporal relationships cohesively in the narrative. In the example, the NS used the historical present tense to convey a sense of immediacy to events and at the same time to provide coherence.

Moreover, data from sociocultural research have highlighted how the interaction between learners and concrete tasks determines the extent to which learners use their linguistic resources to mediate their activity:

[T]his is in keeping with Vygotsky's argument that people make sense out of what they are doing not in advance of their activity but in their very engagement in, and reflection on, practical-critical activity itself. (Lantolf and Thorne 2006: 89)

Table 5.3 Use of private speech in a retelling task (from McCafferty 1994: 426).

Low-intermediate L2 subject	Adult NS
(1) *I see a man on... in the picture. He's looking at some monkeys – the monkeys are in the tree. Monkeys are playing in the tree. There is a house next to the tree. There are some hats in baskets ...two baskets. Maybe the man is thinking about how happy are the monkeys? Maybe he's looking at the sky.* (2) *What do I see? There is another basket of hats. Now, the monkeys look at the man. The man is sleeping. Now, because the man is sleeping the monkeys are playing with the hats.*	(1) *The man's watching the monkeys playing... and the monkeys want to get all his hats – I guess.* (2) *And when he falls asleep the monkeys come down, get his hats and put them on back in the tree.*

Teachers should then reflect on the opportunity to observe learners when they are engaged in self-regulatory private speech during a particular task. If a student is in the process of supplying a response, he or she should not therefore be immediately 'corrected' but given enough time to formulate his or her utterance. The way learners use private speech does indeed provide teachers with a 'glimpse of the learning process as it unfolds in real time' (Lantolf and Thorne 2006: 184).

Another means to mediate SLA is through social interaction. This leads us to introduce another construct in Sociocultural Theory: the Zone of Proximal Development (ZPD). The ZPD is defined (Vygotsky 1987: 86, cited in Lantolf and Thorne 2006: 266) as follows:

> The distance between the actual development level as determined by independent problem solving and the level of potential development as determined through problem solving under adult guidance or in collaboration with more capable peers.

Vygotsky's definition assumes that cognitive development results from social and interpersonal activity. The ZPD can thus be considered 'a conceptual tool that educators can use to understand aspects of students' emerging capacities that are in the early stages of maturation' (Lantolf and Thorne 2006: 267). This concept has been appropriated by L2 researcher and teachers according to different uptakes or interpretations (Kinginger 2002). We will focus here on a 'scaffolding and feedback' interpretation (e.g. Aljaafreh and Lantolf 1994; Donato 1994).[2] The teaching implications of this interpretation will be addressed in later sections (cf. Subsection 5.3.3 and Section 5.4).

ZPD has been associated with the construct of 'scaffolding'. This concept, which derives from cognitive psychology and L1 research, refers to the dialogic process by which one expert speaker (a teacher or another learner) assists another speaker (a learner) to perform a task that he or she is unable to carry out alone. The process implies continual revisions of the help provided by the expert speaker according to the less expert's response. Scaffolding is aimed at promoting the learner's internalization of 'co-constructed' knowledge during a shared activity. Compared to negotiation of meaning (cf. Subsection 5.3.1), scaffolding 'addresses both the cognitive demands of a learning goal and the affective states of the learners attempting to achieve the goal' (Ellis 2008: 527). This implies that corrective feedback and negotiation are approached from a different and broader perspective:

> Corrective feedback and negotiation are contextualized as a collaborative process where the dynamics of the interaction itself shape the nature of the feedback and inform its usefulness to the learner (or learners in the case of more symmetrical peer-interaction). (Lantolf and Thorne 2006: 276)

Participation in interaction thus provides affordances for learning that need to be tailored to individual learners' actual level of development.

Aljaafreh and Lantolf (1994) used the ZPD concept to investigate the relationship between corrective feedback and language learning. Their seminal study analysed the interactions arising between a tutor and three L2 learners enrolled in an early intermediate ESL writing and reading course. The analysis aimed to describe the quantity and quality of scaffolding provided by the tutor and its correlation to the learner performance. Two criteria were used to determine the development of the learners' interlanguage: the first was to look for signs of improvement in the use of the relevant linguistic features; the second was to search for signs of the learner's attempt to move away from the tutor's help ('other-regulation') to reliance on personal resources ('self-reliance'). Through the analysis of the interactions during the tutorial sessions, Aljaafreh and Lantolf (1994: 471) identified different levels of help that were further arranged in a 0–12 regulatory scale modelling the tutor's feedback from implicit ('Tutor asks the learner to read, find the errors, and correct them independently, prior to the tutorial') to explicit ('Tutor provides examples of the correct pattern when other forms of help fail to produce an appropriate responsive response'). The scale, which can be used as a tool to operationalize the quality and quantity of scaffolded assistance, will be reported and analysed in more detail in the following section (cf. Subsection 5.3.3). The methodology adopted by sociocultural researchers to illustrate the stages learners go through to achieve self-regulation is referred to as the 'genetic method'. As Ellis (2008: 521) underlines, this method 'focuses on the situations and discoursal contexts in which learner utterances are found rather than on learner language in isolation'; moreover, 'emphasis is placed on examining the process by which new functions emerge rather than on the products of learning'.

Collaborative work involving learners provides similar opportunities for scaffolding as in teacher-learner relationships. As Donato (1994: 42) suggests, 'during open-ended collaborative tasks, second language learners mutually construct a scaffold out of the discursive process of negotiating contexts of shared understanding or [...] intersubjectivity'. The aim of Donato's study, which involved L2 learners of French working together on the preparation of a scenario they were asked to act out, was twofold: (a) illustrate 'how students co-construct language learning experiences in the classroom setting' and (b) uncover 'how L2 development is brought about on the social plane', that is, 'how social interactions result in the appropriation of linguistic knowledge by the individual' (Donato 1994: 39). The analysis of the students' interactions has shown that the three learners were able to construct a 'scaffold' for each other by jointly managing aspects of the problem, identifying critical features of differences between what had been produced and the ideal solution, thus reducing frustration and risk. According to Donato (1994: 46) 'their collectivity is also exhibited by their ability to establish intersubjectivity': affective markers appeared to 'converge' at critical points in the interaction, when incomplete or incorrect knowledge is transformed into positive knowledge. This, in Donato's view, indicated a 'point of development for the participants'. The implication for these findings is that 'the obdurate nature of some language tasks inhibit learners from engaging in dialogically constituted guided support, or collective scaffolding' (Donato 1994: 53). This conclusion has relevant implications for teaching in that group work activities should not simply provide opportunities to exchange linguistic information but enhance forms of collective and shared language acquisition.

Insights from sociocultural research presented in this section have highlighted the role of situated interaction as the source for learning. Scaffolding and collaborative dialogue arising in expert-learner (as in learner-learner interactions) enable learners to produce and learn linguistic features that they would not be able to use independently. In the following part, we will consider the possible implications of these insights for the implementation of interaction strategies and collaborative activities in second language classroom practice.

5.3.3 Interaction and corrective feedback: Learning and teaching implications

In the previous sections, we focused on two principles that account for the role of interaction in second language learning from the theoretical perspectives of the Interaction Hypothesis (cf. Subsection 5.3.1) and the Sociocultural Theory (cf. Subsection 5.3.2). In this section, the teaching implications for each principle will be considered. In particular, we will illustrate how teachers can employ two types of methodological options aimed at exploiting the processes involved in interaction in view to enhancing language learning. The first type of option aims to draw learners' attention to formal features of the language when they are engaged in communicative language use (cf. 'Focus-on-form options'); the second type is meant to supply scaffolded help during teacher–learner interactions (cf. 'Scaffolded help').

Focus-on-form options

'Focus on form' is a term first introduced by Long (1991: 45–46) to define a type of teaching option that 'overtly draws students' attention to linguistic elements as they arise incidentally in lessons whose overriding focus is on meaning or communication'. It should be noted that the term 'form' may refer to any aspect of linguistic form: phonological, graphological, lexical or grammatical. Moreover, the focus on a particular form does not exclude any attention to the meaning or function that is being conveyed. Originally, Long (1991) distinguished between two types of methodological options aimed at highlighting formal language features: focus on forms and focus on form. The former involves the pre-selection of specific features that are first taught and subsequently practised in exercises and activities. In focus on form, instead, the attention to form arises out an act of communication in which students are engaged, such as listening, conversing, reporting and so on. The focus on a particular language item should thus be 'triggered' incidentally by a problem that may arise during communication:

> [D]uring an otherwise meaning-focused classroom lesson, focus on
> form often consists of an occasional shift of attention to linguistic code
> features – by the teacher and/or one or more students – triggered by
> perceived problems with comprehension or production. (Long and
> Robinson 1998: 23)

It is thus assumed that meaning and use must already be evident to the learner when attention is drawn to the linguistic features and that 'teachers should wait for issues to emerge and respond to them as needed' (Williams 2005: 672). Ellis (2001, 2012) uses the term 'form-focused instruction' to incorporate both 'focus-on-form' and 'focus-on-forms' options, which, however, require different instructional processes. Corrective feedback strategies previously illustrated in Table 5.1 are common to both options.

Why should teachers incorporate focus-on-form options into their teaching? The theoretical rationale for a focus-on-form approach rests on a number of premises (Ellis et al. 2002: 422):

a. To acquire the ability to use new linguistic forms in communication, learners need to engage in similar activities in which the primary focus is on 'meaning' (e.g. when they need to convey or exchange information, express an opinion, etc.).

b. Learners will acquire new linguistic forms if they also have the opportunity to pay attention to form while they are engaged in meaning-focused activities.

c. Given that learners have difficulty in simultaneously attending to form and meaning, they are likely to process meaning over form (cf. Chapter 3). It is thus necessary to draw their attention to form when they are engaged in a communicative activity.

A variety of techniques have been suggested to implement a focus on formal aspects of the language during classroom activities. Two broad types of options can be distinguished: planned focus on form and incidental focus on form (Ellis et al. 2002). It should be noted that both types of focus on form assume the use of communicative tasks (cf. Chapter 6). The main features of each type are highlighted in Table 5.4. Planned focus on form tends to be more intensive as it is concentrated on specific linguistic features which are targeted in the task. Incidental focus on form, on the other hand, is typically extensive as it needs to address a wide range of linguistic features that may arise during the performance of the task.

Table 5.4 Planned and incidental focus-on-form options (from Ellis et al. 2002: 420–421).

Type of focus on form	Type of task	How the focus on form occurs
Planned focus on form	'Focused' tasks: communicative tasks designed to elicit the use of a specific linguistic form in the context of a meaning-focused activity.	In a 'same-or-different task' using pairs of pictures, learners have to use 'at' and 'in' to decide whether the pictures are the same or different. The attention to form occurs in interaction. Learners are not made aware that a specific form is being targeted.
Incidental focus on form	'Unfocused' tasks: communicative tasks designed to elicit general samples of the language rather than specific forms.	In an opinion-gap task, learners might make a number of errors which the teacher corrects, or they might need to ask the teacher how to say something.

These two main types of focus-on-form options can be accomplished through a number of techniques or strategies available to teachers and students alike (cf. Table 5.5). They can be described according to (1) reactive focus on form (negotiation and feedback), which involves the treatment of learner errors by the teacher or another student, and (2) pre-emptive focus on form (student or teacher initiated), that is when the teacher or a student makes a linguistic form the topic of the conversation even though no error has been made.

Given that a 'didactic' and more explicit focus on form tends to be far more common in foreign language classrooms (cf. e.g. Pedrazzini 2017), the distinction between 'conversational' and 'didactic' negotiation strategies can help teachers become more aware of the potential provided by conversation strategies. In effect, through the negotiation of meaning arising from a communication problem, these strategies shift learners' attention on formal features that otherwise would go unnoticed. As Ellis et al. (2002: 425) underline, 'salience and communicative need, both evident in conversational focus on form, constitute the ideal conditions for noticing and acquisition to take place'.

Table 5.5 Focus-on-form options and techniques (adapted from Ellis et al. 2002: 429).

Options and techniques	Description
1. Reactive focus on form	
→ Negotiation	
a. Conversational	The response to the error is triggered by a failure to understand what the student meant ('negotiation of meaning') by means of a request for confirmation or clarification.
b. Didactic	The response occurs even though no breakdown in communication has occurred ('negotiation of form').
→ Feedback	
a. Implicit feedback	The teacher or another student responds to a student's error without directly indicating an error has been made (e.g. by means of a recast).
b. Explicit feedback	The teacher or another student responds to a student's error directly indicating an error has been made (by correcting the error or by using metalanguage to draw attention to it).
2. Pre-emptive focus on form	
→ Student initiated	A student asks a question about a linguistic form.
→ Teacher initiated	The teacher gives advice about a linguistic form which is thought to be problematic or asks a question about the form.

Similarly, the distinction between implicit and explicit corrective feedback will help teachers reflect on the 'obtrusiveness' of their intervention (Doughty and Williams 1998), that is, on the degree to which a technique interrupts the flow of communication and possibly the processing of meaning. As argued, teachers may vary their choice of a feedback strategy 'depending on their assessment of the student' ability to attend to form being corrected' (Ellis et al. 2002: 426).[3]

Finally, both teachers and students have an option of using pre-emptive focus-on-form strategies to raise a specific form to attention. For example, students may ask the teacher a question about a specific lexicogrammatical feature, which he or she may choose to answer, not to answer or redirect at the class or another student. Teachers may likewise interrupt the flow of a communicative activity to draw the students' attention to a specific form by asking a question or providing an 'advisory statement'. However, according to Ellis et al. (2002: 428), teacher-initiated pre-emptive focus on form may be problematic because teachers 'cannot know for sure whether the gaps they assume to exist in the students' knowledge are actual gaps. [...] In this respect, student-initiated preemptive focus on form is to be preferred'.

In conclusion, the teacher has a key role in facilitating the focus on lexicogrammatical features during language use in interactional and communicative activities. One of the main reasons for employing focus on form is 'to make learners aware of specific forms at the time they need to use them' (Ellis et al. 2002: 428).[4] Through the teacher's (and learner's) use of negotiation and feedback strategies, focus on form is crucial in facilitating the acquisition of lexicogrammatical features and increasing control at different stages of development (Williams 2005: 686). We have illustrated a number of focus-on-form options that can be implemented in the second language classroom either in a planned or incidental way. Reactive focus on form provides the teacher with a wider variety of options – ranging from conversational to didactic and from implicit to explicit. As Ellis et al. (2002: 429–430) point out, these techniques should not be considered 'either-ors' but may occur either alone or in combination in any single lesson, according to the type of activity and whether the activity is performed in a whole-class context or is carried out in groups.

Scaffolded help

Insights from sociocultural research (cf. Subsection 5.3.2) have highlighted the role of scaffolding and collaborative dialogue during both expert–learner and learner–learner interactions. As Donato (1994: 41) maintains 'scaffolded performance' is built through dialogue that 'promotes the learner's internalization of knowledge co-constructed in shared activity'. In this part of the chapter, we will consider the possible implications of these insights for the implementation of interaction strategies and collaborative activities through scaffolding and collaborative dialogue in second language classroom practice.

Wood et al. (1976, cited in Donato 1994: 41) identified six features characterizing 'scaffolded help' which teachers need to take into account when they plan, set up and monitor interaction activities:

a. recruiting interest in the task
b. simplifying the task
c. maintaining pursuit of the goal
d. marking critical features and discrepancies between what has been produced and the ideal solution
e. controlling frustration during problem-solving
f. demonstrating an idealized version of the act to be performed

These features, which are described at a general level, can apply to the scaffolding in different interactional tasks. They also imply that the teacher or the expert speaker will have an active role in progressively adapting his or her scaffolded help in response to the learner's needs and skills. A number of these features are illustrated in the analysis of a short interaction between a teacher and a beginner learner (Ellis 2008: 235) (Table 5.6). As shown in the example, the teacher's feedback is adapted to the learner's problems arising during the task and is thus shaped by the dynamics of the interaction itself. As

Table 5.6 Features of scaffolded help 'in action'.

1. T: *I want you to tell me what you can see in the picture or what's wrong with the picture.*	After stating the aim of the task (1), the teacher gradually simplifies it and maintains pursuit of the goal through the use of prompts and repetition (3–5).
2. L: *A /paik/ (bike)*	
3. T: *A cycle, yes. But's what's wrong?*	
4. L: */ret/ (red)*	The teacher controls frustration by accepting the learner's contribution and providing a better version through recast (5–7).
5. T: *It's red yes. What's wrong with it?*	
6. L: *Black.*	
7. T: *Black. Good. Black what?*	
8. L: *Black /taes/ (tyres).*	

Ellis (2008: 235) points out, 'the learner's final utterance ('black/taes') […] is constructed with assistance from the teacher'.

A tool which can help teachers and tutors 'operationalize' the quantity and quality of scaffolded help during interactional activities is a scale that was developed by Aljaafreh and Lantolf (1994) after examining the one-to-one interactions between learners and a tutor (cf. Subsection 5.3.2). The 13-point regulatory scale describes the levels of help during the tutorial sessions following a writing task (Table 5.7).

Table 5.7 Levels of help in tutor–learner interaction during a task (Aljaafreh and Lantolf 1994: 471).

0	Tutor asks the learner to read, find the errors, and correct them independently, prior to the tutorial.
1	Construction of a 'collaborative frame' prompted by the presence of the tutor as a potential dialogic partner.
2	Prompted or focused reading of the sentence that contains the error by the learner or the tutor.
3	Tutor indicates that something may be wrong in a segment (e.g., sentence, clause, line) – 'Is there anything wrong in this sentence?'
4	Tutor rejects unsuccessful attempts at recognizing the error.
5	Tutor narrows down the location of the error (e.g., tutor repeats or points to the specific segment which contains the error).
6	Tutor indicates the nature of the error, but does not identify the error (e.g., 'There is something wrong with the tense marking here').
7	Tutor identifies the error ('You can't use an auxiliary here').
8	Tutor rejects learner's unsuccessful attempts at correcting the error.
9	Tutor provides clues to help the learner arrive at the correct form (e.g., 'It is not really past but something that is still going on').
10	Tutor provides the correct form.
11	Tutor provides some explanation for use of the correct form.
12	Tutor provides examples of the correct pattern when other forms of help fail to produce an appropriate responsive action.

The levels in the scale are graduated from the most indirect or implicit (low numbers) to the most direct or explicit (high numbers). However, they are not expected to be followed 'rigidly'. Teachers and tutors need to evaluate which forms of feedback are going to be more relevant and adapt them to the degree of assistance to be provided. Aljaafreh and Lantolf (1994: 471) indeed argue that

> the collaborative work of both participants determines the level of assistance to be invoked, if one or more levels will be skipped, where to stop and allow the learner to assume responsibility, and when to withhold assistance.

This is in keeping with three main mechanisms for effective help within ZPD by which the teacher or expert intervention should be graduated (affording the appropriate level of assistance), contingent (it should be offered only when needed) and dialogic (involving a collaborative interaction of the 'expert' and the 'novice'). We will further show how an adapted version of the scale can be used to analyse examples of teacher–learner interactions during a collaborative group work task (cf. Subsection 5.4.3).

However, as Donato (2004: 287) claims, not all interactional activities that are set up in the classroom involve sharing and collaboration. For an interaction to be called collaborative, it will involve:

- a meaningful interaction activity with a defined outcome, such as in information/opinion gap activities and group decision activities;
- the contributions of each individual for the goal of the activity to be achieved;
- the building of coherence in terms of social relations and knowledge among the members of the group.

Two examples of activities that may qualify as 'collaborative' according to the features described above are illustrated in Table 5.8 (cf. Subsection 5.4.3 for another example of collaborative task).

Table 5.8 Examples of collaborative interaction activities (adapted from Lee and VanPatten 2003: 65; 66–67).

1. Information-gap activity	'Comparing provinces' 1. Each person in the group reads a different short text produced by the national travel bureau. Each text describes the desirable features of a province in order to generate tourism to that region. [...] As you read your own text, think about how you might describe or explain the content of the reading to the other members of your group. 2. Working together, the group completes a chart with the information about each province as regards terrain, festivals, sporting, climate. 3. Weighing all the information, the group must plan a travel itinerary to visit each of the three provinces. First, plan one for a two-week stay and then one for a one-week stay.
2. Group decision activity	'The Time Capsule' 1. Your university/school/town wants to place a time capsule in the new library being constructed. The capsule will be opened in the year 2030, and in it there will be ten items that represent the last part of the twentieth century. What will those items be? [...] Anything you choose must be small. 2. Work in groups of four or five to come to a consensus about the contents of the time capsule. 3. Present and explain your list to the rest of the class. Listen and take notes as the other groups present and explain their lists. Finally, as a class, come to a consensus on what to include in the capsule.

In these types of activities, learners need to communicate as well as to work collaboratively to achieve a specific goal. Each person contributes in a different way and after negotiating various proposals, the group must reach a consensus and take final decisions. In this way, as Donato (2004: 287) underlines, 'collaboration co-constructs new knowledge that goes beyond any knowledge possessed by a single member in isolation'.

5.4 The principles in the classroom

In this section we will consider how interactional processes actually take place in a classroom during two activities involving a group of university students at an upper intermediate level: a discussion led by the teacher and a group work task. By taking into account the principles explored in the previous sections (cf. Subsections 5.3.1 and 5.3.2) and the teaching implications related to each principle (cf. Subsection 5.3.3), we aim to illustrate how the teacher involved implemented his use of negotiation and feedback strategies and provided scaffolded help during his interaction with the students and during student–student interaction.

5.4.1 Tim dealing with corrective feedback in a whole class discussion and in a group work task

Video Extract 5

(a) Central to the principle 'Interactional feedback is key to the learning of lexicogrammar' (cf. Subsection 5.3.1) is the general claim that the negotiation work taking place in oral interaction facilitates language learning. In particular, negotiation can help comprehension and draw learners' attention to linguistic forms. Which techniques or strategies among those listed below do you use or would you use to have learners interact on a topic during a class discussion? Which do you think would best support negotiation work during interaction and draw the students' attention to specific language features?
 1. eliciting opinions/suggestions/examples/experiences
 2. questioning about experiences
 3. giving examples of experiences
 4. repeating students' opinions/suggestions/examples/experiences
 5. rephrasing students' opinions/suggestions/examples/experiences
 6. feeding with words/expressions
 7. asking students to rephrase their opinions/suggestions/examples/ experiences

(b) Watch the beginning of Tim's lesson and refer to the techniques listed above. Which techniques does he use to deal with his class discussion on taboo conversation topics? Which techniques are particular effective to enhance negotiation work with the students? Which techniques does he use to draw the students' attention to specific linguistic features?

5.4.2 Corrective feedback strategies in teacher–student interaction

As illustrated, negotiation during second language interactions is accomplished by means of a variety of corrective feedback strategies (see Table 5.1). They can be used in isolation or in a combined way. They may be implicit or explicit; input-providing (the correct form is provided to the learner) or output-prompting (the correction of the form is elicited from the learner); conversational or didactic. They may or may not lead to the learner uptake (cf. Subsection 5.3.1).

(a) Look at the extracts 1–5 from the class discussion on taboo conversation topics between Tim and his students. Which feedback strategy does he use at the different stages of the discussion? Explicit correction, recast, clarification requests, metalinguistic feedback, elicitation, repetition? You may refer to Table 5.1 to identify the type of feedback strategy. Say whether each strategy is implicit or explicit, input-providing or output-prompting.

---

1.   S2: *the behavior could be inappropriate*
       T: *behavior could be inappropriate yeah or…*

2.   T: *[…] can you think of a person that you could ask a question like how much do you earn? yeah?*
       S3: *my parents*
       T: *your parents?*
       S3: *yeah*
       T: *because you have a vested interest in knowing how much they earn yeah?*

3.   S4: *a question could be he left you or you left him?*
       T: *ok so it's a question go back and rephrase those as a question. imagine you're asking the question directly. how would you ask it?*
       S4: *ok, like someone sees that you are sad*

---

4.   S4: *something is wrong with my boyfriend. so ehm... he left you?*
     T: *ok but rephrase that as a question. rephrase that as a direct question if you're asking somebody that question with he leave you, ask it as a question in the past. what's the question?*
     S4: *ah... oh my god, ehm...*

5.   T: *[...] what's the question?*
     S4: *ah... oh my god, ehm...*
     T: *do...does...did ... remember?*
     S4: *did... did you... did he leave you?*
     T: *good. or?*
     S4: *or?*
     T: *the other way round? did he leave you or ...?*
     S4: *did you...did you leave him?*
     T: *perfect. fantastic, there you go. did he leave you or did you leave him? [...]*

(b) Findings from interaction research have shown that feedback strategies can also be combined. For example, explicit correction can be followed by a metalinguistic comment or preceded by elicitation. The combined use of different strategies is thought to enhance the effectiveness of the teacher's feedback move. Analyse extract 6 of the class discussion involving Tim and his students. Which feedback strategies does he use here? In what way are they combined?

6.   T: *[...] ok, what about the questions? tell me the question you got. let's write them up. direct questions, anybody. did you hear the actual examples of specific questions? anyone? yep*
     S5: *how much do you make?*
     T: *ok that's what he says how much do you make?. did we do that question before? or do we ask it in a different way?*
     S5: *we asked how much money do you make?*
     T: *ok. how... much... do... you... make? ok? sorry about my writing. ok, so make instead of earn, you can use both, ok? how much do you make, what else? yeah, just shout out*

(c) As pointed out, negotiation and feedback strategies may have either a 'conversational' or 'didactic' focus (see Table 5.5). Teachers have therefore the option of overtly drawing students' attention to linguistic elements through the negotiation of meaning arising from a communication problem. Go over the interactions between Tim and his students in extracts 1–6. Decide whether in each interaction the strategy he uses is:

- 'conversational', that is focused on meaning (e.g. trying to ask for clarification or confirming his understanding);
- 'didactic', that is focused on form (correcting the student's error or asking the student to correct his error).

(d) The first response to teacher corrective feedback can be observed through learner uptake. Go through extracts 1–6 again. In which interactional exchange does the teacher's use of a particular strategy lead to the learner uptake?

5.4.3 Scaffolded help to facilitate student–student dialogue

Findings from sociocultural research have highlighted the key role of scaffolding and collaborative dialogue for second language learning (cf. 5.3.2). In this section, we will analyse how the use of scaffolding and collaborative dialogue is implemented through teacher–learner and learner–learner interactions during a cooperative group work task.

(a) In the second part of the lesson, Tim engaged his students in a group work task. The task involves a practical outcome after following the guidelines provided in the task card below.

You are the members of the marketing department of a company that produces a famous brand of cornflakes. Your boss is very worried about competition from other companies in the same market sector and is determined to increase sales. She can't change the product itself so she decides to change the packaging.

YOUR TASK: Design an object for the back of the packet which the buyer can cut out and use at home.

1. Decide on the object.
2. Make a note on the reason for the choice of the object.
3. Design the object on a piece of paper.
4. Invent a name for the product.
5. Write a text for the packet to describe the object.

During the group work task, the teacher monitors and enters a 'collaborative dialogue' with the students in each group to help them complete the task successfully. Go through the interaction arising between the teacher and a group of students. Focus on the teacher's turns and analyse how 'scaffolded help' is provided. Answer the questions below quoting instances from the extract.

Second Language Acquisition in Action

- How does the teacher raise interest in the task?
- Does he simplify the task?
- How does he maintain pursuit of the goal?
- How does he mark critical features and discrepancies between what has been produced and the 'ideal' solution?
- How does he monitor frustration during the task?
- Does he suggest an optimal version of what students are expected to produce?

T: *ok? how do we do with the phrases there? what have you got?*
S3: *buy me. have a funny breakfast with us*
T: *ok*
S2: *[writing] have a funny breakfast with...*
T: *with us. I thought that what you would have is fun. (...) funny fun cause funny is aha aha you know but fun is enjoyable yeah? (...) what about something like are you selling it to them? what about something like breakfast has never been so much fun just to start you off, ok?*
S2: *breakfast. ok. so, breakfast has never been so fun*
S1: *so fun*
S2: *so... never been...*
S1: *never been so fun*
T: *ok, so this is breakfast, singular? have a look at that again, yeah? (...) [...]*
S2: *have a fun breakfast [...] have. is this correct have fun or have a fun?*
T: *breakfast has never been...*
S1: *no, in the first sentence*
T: *the first sentence. which one then? have a fun breakfast. [...]*
Ss 1–2: *have a fun?*
T: *yeah, cause it's a breakfast and fun it's like an adjective, ok? (...)*
S1: *yeah, è vero. [it's true]. have fun? have fun?*
T: *have fun, without a, because fun there is a noun. have fun. if you say a fun breakfast it becomes an adjective. (...) ok? good question. I was thinking of the second phrase, the second phrase you got there. breakfast has never been so much fun*
S1: *so much fun?*
T: *to replace the first sentence. but it's ok, they can both be on different parts of the packet. that's good*
S2: *yeah*
Prof: *ok?*

(b) Focus on the teacher's turns underlined in the extract and identify the levels of scaffolding provided using the scale below. The levels of help/ assistance are arranged from what we consider to be the most indirect, or implicit (lower numbers), to the most direct, or explicit (the higher numbers). How do the levels of assistance change during the interaction? Is the teacher's help more implicit or explicit? Why?

---

1. Teacher/Tutor indicates that something may be wrong in a segment (e.g. sentence, clause, line) – "Is there anything wrong in this sentence?"
2. Teacher/Tutor narrows down the location of the error (e.g. tutor repeats or points to the specific segment which contains the error).
3. Teacher/Tutor indicates the nature of the error, but does not identify the error (e.g. "There is something wrong with the tense marking here").
4. Teacher/Tutor identifies the error ("You can't use an auxiliary here").
5. Teacher/Tutor provides clues to help the learner arrive at the correct form (e.g. "It is not really past but something that is still going on").
6. Teacher/Tutor provides the correct form.
7. Teacher/Tutor provides some explanation for use of the correct form.

(Adapted from Aljaafreh and Lantolf 1994: 471)

5.5 Restructuring and planning

In this section you will be involved in the analysis of examples of interactions and interactive tasks from different second language teaching contexts. You will be asked to evaluate key aspects related to the use of corrective feedback strategies and scaffolded help and their overall effectiveness with a view to implementing these options in actual teaching practice.

(a) Analyse two classroom extracts in which the teacher provides corrective feedback. For each extract, consider the following questions:

 – What type of corrective feedback strategy is employed?
 – Do students show awareness of being corrected?
 – Do students uptake the corrections?
 – Does the teacher allow time for this to happen?

(1)

T: *Do you remember this guy? [points to a picture in the book]*
Ss: *Alan!*
T: *Alan, yeah!*
S: *He's more older.*
T: *He's older. Do you think? I don't think so.*
S: *A little bit.*
T: *A little bit. So. OK.*

(2)

S: *When I opened the door, the cat run out.*
T: *Ran out.*
S: *Ran out.*
T: *Ran.*
S: *Ran.*
T: *Run, ran, run.*
S: *She run downstairs to open the door.*
T: *She ...?*
S: *Ran. She ran downstairs to open the door, but it was too late. The postman had gone.*
T: *Yes!*

(From Nunan and Lamb 1996: 79)

(b) Identify the instances of elicitation in the following feedback episode.

- How do students respond to the elicitations?
- How successful are the elicitations?
- Do you feel the elicitation is overdone or not?
- What other feedback strategy/strategies could the teacher have used?

T: *OK. Give me a sentence. For example, tell me something about her, in the present.*
S: *She is... [one-second pause]*
[...]
T: *OK, not with the verb to be. Sorry. Except with the verb to be.*
S: *She work in ...*
T: *She...?*
S: *... works ...*
T: *... works – it's very important. She works at home. Now put the same sentence, Tati, in the negative.*
S: *She don't work.*
T: *She...?*
S: *... doesn't...*
T: *doesn't. very important. She doesn't work at home. And the question?*
S: *Does she...?*
T: *Very good.*
(From Nunan and Lamb 1996: 94)

(c) Analyse a new extract in which Tim provides assistance to a different group of students. Focus on the teacher's turns and analyse how feedback strategies and scaffolded help are provided. Consider the questions below quoting instances from the interaction:

- Are the teacher's feedback strategies more conversational or didactic?
- Which feedback strategies does he use to mark critical features in the learners' written work?
- How successful are his feedback strategies in terms of students' uptake?
- What other feedback strategy/strategies could he have used?
- What levels of assistance does he provide during the interaction? Refer to the levels of the scale in 5.4.3. Is his help more implicit or explicit?

S2: *we have to say what we wrote?*
T: *well, let's have a look I can see it. so ok that's good. have a look at the spelling. a few spelling mistakes there. ok*
S2: *where?*
T: *the children probably won't noticet but*
S2: *the spelling mistakes?*
T: *that's not the point you see we'd like them to learn to read and write. ok, ok, all right. Football fans! it's time to buy ok that's good maybe we need that in a sort of colloquial form this is where we use all of our contractions ok?*
S3: *I change it?*
T: *yeah. just you know this is informal it's for kids. you're selling it to the kids. that's great. find out things about your favorite player on the end, yeah? have fun trading*
S3: *where where where?*
T: *favourite with an e on the end. ok, your friends, for an exciting and complete breakfast eat uniflakes! oh, that's interesting. ok, that's pretty good*

5.6 Conclusions

In this chapter we have explored the relationship between interaction and second language learning. While there is considerable variation regarding how interaction is dealt with in actual teaching practice, research has investigated the main interactional processes involved and how they affect acquisition. In particular, studies have shown how negotiation facilitates comprehension and what types of corrective feedback strategies are more effective in helping learners focus on formal features thus providing them with opportunities for language development. We have also examined the mechanisms of 'scaffolded' help, which arise from the collaborative dialogue between teacher–learner interactions, and how these mechanisms mediate language learning.

The principles and constructs presented in the chapter originate from the cognitive interactionist and the sociocultural frameworks. As illustrated, each theoretical framework assumes a different perspective on second language learning, and therefore investigates interactional processes in different ways thus supplying different insights into these processes. On the one hand, the Interaction Hypothesis emphasizes the role of negotiation during interaction, which connects input, internal learner capacities (especially selective attention) and output in productive ways. Negotiation work, which can be accomplished by means of a variety of corrective feedback strategies, can increase comprehensibility and draw the learners' attention to the formal features of the language and facilitate their acquisition. Ellis (2008: 257), though, highlights a number of caveats related to this hypothesis. The main one is that a theory of language acquisition based on a single type of interaction (negotiation) cannot account for the different types of interaction that a learner may experience. Moreover, it should be considered that 'negotiation may work best with intermediate learners; beginner learners lack the resources to negotiate effectively' and it has been shown to be more effective in targeting lexical and syntactic features. Therefore, the Interaction Hypothesis 'may not be able to explain how learners acquire all aspects of linguistic competence' (Ellis 2008: 260).

On the other hand, Sociocultural Theory views language learning occurring during dialogic interaction but affordances provided through interaction need to be suited to the individual learners' actual level of development. The aim of interaction, including corrective feedback, is therefore to help learners move towards 'self-regulation' in order to be able to use language without assistance. In contrast to a cognitive interactionist perspective, the sociocultural approach rejects the idea that it is possible to identify specific corrective strategies *a priori*. Corrective feedback needs to be 'graduated' and supply the minimal level of assistance required to achieve self-correction. In particular, among the sociocultural constructs, the ZPD has been captivating for researchers and teachers as it came to be linked to the notion of 'assisted performance' and more precisely of scaffolding or scaffolded dialogue. According to Ellis (2008: 533), this construct 'explains a number of important phenomena about learning', for example, why learners are able to perform some structures with assistance but not alone, or why 'they come to internalize new structures'.

In the last two sections of the chapter, we have also illustrated a number of research-based methodological options – focus on form and scaffolded help – that teachers can use to 'exploit' the learning potential arising from teacher–student interaction in communicative tasks. Insights from interactional research presented in the chapter can help teachers become more aware of the corrective nature of feedback and the strategies to be implemented in the classroom practice.

However, despite the general finding that interactional feedback facilitates learning, a number of questions still remain unanswered (for researchers and teachers alike); for example, how do learners' cognitive processes mediate the relationship between interaction and learning? What is the role of selective attention and working memory? What aspects of language and type of knowledge (implicit vs explicit, controlled vs automatic) does interaction impact and under what conditions? (Mackey 2012: 8–9). The answers to these questions will contribute to gaining a better understanding of the interactional processes themselves and their impact on second language learning.

5.7 Notes

1 According to Long (1996: 422) 'interactional adjustments compensate for linguistic complexity by elaboration (i.e., adding redundancy to discourse through the use of repetition, paraphrases and appositionals) and by making semantic structure more explicit', as shown in these examples:
   a. NS version: *Because he had to work at night to support his family, Paco often fell asleep in class.*
   b. Simplified version: *Paco had to make money for his family. Paco worked at night. He often went to sleep in class.*
   c. Elaborated version: *Paco had to work at night to earn money to support his family, so he often fell asleep in class next day during his teacher's lesson.*
2 For a 'metalinguistic' 'interpretation' of scaffolding and the use of peer–peer 'collaborative dialogue' cf. Swain 2000 (cf. Subsection 4.3.2).
3 Examples of negotiation and feedback strategies have been illustrated in Table 5.1 and Figure 5.1.
4 This is in contrast with the suggestion commonly found in teaching guides that teachers should not interrupt and correct students when they are involved in communication activities but rather address the language problem when the activity is over.

5.8 Further reading

Aljaafreh, A. and J. Lantolf (1994), 'Negative feedback as regulation and second language learning in the zone of proximal development', *The Modern Language Journal*, 78 (4): 465–483.

Donato, R. (1994), 'Collective scaffolding in second language learning', in J. P. Lantolf and G. Appel (eds), *Vygotskian Approaches to Second Language Research*, 33–56, Norwood, NJ: Ablex.

Donato, R. (2004), 'Aspects of collaboration in pedagogical discourse', *Annual Review of Applied Linguistics*, 24 (1): 284–302.

Ellis, R. (2001), 'Investigating form-focused instruction', in R. Ellis (ed.), *Form-Focused Instruction and Second Language Learning*, 1–47 Malden, MA: Blackwell.

Ellis, R., H. Basturkmen and S. Loewen (2002), 'Doing focus on form', *System*, 30 (4): 419–432.

Lantolf, J., ed. (2000), *Sociocultural Theory and Second Language Learning*, Oxford: Oxford University Press.

Lantolf, J. and S. Thorne (2006), *Sociocultural Theory and the Genesis of Second Language Development*. Oxford: Oxford University Press.

Long, M. (1983), 'Native speaker/non-native speaker conversation and the negotiation of comprehensible input', *Applied Linguistics*, 4 (2): 126–141.

Long, M. (1991), 'Focus on form: a design feature in language teaching methodology', in K. de Bot, R. Ginsberg and C. Kramsch (eds), *Foreign Language Research in Cross-Cultural Perspective*, 39–52, Amsterdam: John Benjamins.

Long, M. H. (1996), 'The role of the linguistic environment in second language acquisition', in W. C. Ritchie and T. K. Bahtia (eds), *Handbook of Second Language Acquisition*, 413–468, New York: Academic Press.

Lyster, R. and L. Ranta (1997). 'Corrective feedback and learner uptake: negotiation of form in communicative classrooms', *Studies in Second Language Acquisition*, 19 (1): 37–66.

Mackey, A. 2012. *Input, Interaction and Corrective Feedback in L2 Learning*. Oxford: Oxford University Press.

McCafferty, S. G. (1994), 'Adult second language learners' use of private speech: a review of studies', *The Modern Language Journal*, 78 (4): 421–436.

Nassaji, H. (2015), *Interactional Feedback Dimension in Instructed Second Language Learning*, London: Bloomsbury.

Chapter 6
Output production

Output production has traditionally been the Cinderella of language teaching. In the mainstream Present–Practice–Produce (PPP) Approach (Byrne 1986), for example, the last 'P' is the one that is usually sacrificed (East 2017), often on account of the challenges that teachers experience in setting up and implementing production activities. In SLA research, however, increasing evidence has accrued that producing output, and not only comprehending input, plays a number of key roles in language development (e.g. Izumi et al. 1999; Izumi and Bigelow 2000; Toth 2006; Song and Suh 2008; Russell 2014). This chapter will shed some light on the reasons why output production is thought to be a key element in the process of acquisition of a second language. First, we will explore Swain's (e.g. 1985) Output Hypothesis and show how it has led to a reappraisal of the role of output production in SLA. We will then zero in on the concept of fluency, which is held to be one of the main contributors to learners' automatization of linguistic knowledge. Finally, we will explore 'tasks' as language learning and teaching tools for eliciting learners' 'pushed output' as well as techniques and tasks for fostering fluency. The following key questions will be addressed in the chapter:

- How does output production support the process of learning another language?
- What can teachers do to help learners develop their language knowledge through output production?
- How does fluency impact on output production?
- What can teachers do to help learners become more automatic and fluent in their output production?

6.2 Experience

(a) Read these two extracts of classroom lessons in which students are involved in spoken activities. Analyse the two extracts and answer these questions for each activity:

  – Who is talking?
  – What is the aim of the activity?
  – How long does each student talk?
  – How guided is each student's production?

1.

T: *Okay. Listen. Where d'you live? Where d'you live? Where d'you live? Where do you live? Everyone.*
S: *Where do you live?*
T: *Okay. Victor, please ask Roberto.*
S: *Where do you live?*
T: *Where do you live?*
S: *I live ... in Smithfield.*
T: *Okay, fine. What was number five – the question – 'languages'?*
S: *What, er, what ... what ... what ... languages ...*
T: *What languages...*
S: *What ... languages ... do...*
T: *do*
S: *...you ... speak.*
T: *Yes. What languages do you speak? [...] Okay, Daniel, ask Pia.*
(Nunan 1991: 164)

2.

S. *I see a man on ... in the picture. He's looking at some monkeys – the monkeys are in the tree. Monkeys are playing in the tree. There is a house next to the tree. There are some hats in baskets ... two baskets. Maybe the man is thinking about how happy are the monkeys? What do I see? There is another basket of hats ...*
(McCafferty 1994: 426)

(b) Read this extract from an interview with a young native English speaking woman who is talking about her experiences of learning and using French in Canada. How did she learn French at school? What was 'missing' in her school learning of French? Why does she feel that 'having a conversation' is not enough in order to develop her knowledge of French?

Student: *Well, we did a lot of reading and a lot that is done on your own. You go off and read, and that was about it. We read. That's all I can remember, is reading.*

Researcher: *Do you think you would have profited if you had more opportunities to speak in class or to speak in small groups?*

Student: *I think so. I wouldn't mind being able to sit down with someone and have a conversation, but just don't let me go when I say the odd word in English. I add them in, and that's perfectly acceptable to my teachers, but usually they don't hit me back with 'This is the word in French. This is how you say this'.*

Researcher: *In other words, you feel that a person in the stores you were in in Montreal would be a much harsher critic than your teachers?*

Student: *I think so.*
(Swain 1993: 158–159)

(c) Fluency is an important feature of L2 spoken production. How would you rate these features of speech according to your idea of fluency? 1= least relevant; 5= most relevant. Are there any other features you would consider relevant for rating L2 speech fluency?

Amount of speaking time	1 2 3 4 5
Number of pauses	1 2 3 4 5
Length of pauses	1 2 3 4 5
Repetitions	1 2 3 4 5
Restarts	1 2 3 4 5
Self-repairs	1 2 3 4 5
Reformulations	1 2 3 4 5

(d) An English language teacher has carried out the following activity with her intermediate level class. Most pairs ended up completing it in less than a minute. Why do you think the activity did not work very well? Have you ever experienced a similar situation when using spoken production activities?

> ## Career moves
>
> What are your opinions about working in a family business, or working freelance from home? Tell your partner.
> (Adapted from Willis and Willis 2007: 154)

6.3 The principle

Krashen's Comprehensible Input Hypothesis (cf. Chapter 2) posits that all it takes to develop proficiency in a second language is to be exposed to massive amounts of comprehensible input roughly tuned to a learner's competence. An important corollary of this hypothesis is that speaking and writing may be evidence of language acquisition, but do not in themselves cause acquisition. The principle that will be explored in this chapter challenges Krashen's Comprehensible Input Hypothesis and is premised on Swain's Output Hypothesis (cf. Section 6.3.1).

> **Comprehension by itself is not sufficient for language acquisition. Output production is also necessary.**
>
> (Swain 1985)

While exposure to input that is made comprehensible for a learner is a needed starting point for SLA, it is in itself insufficient to satisfy all the demands of acquisition. Engaging in second language production, through both speaking and writing, is thus held to be crucial for acquisition, particularly if a learner wishes to increase their proficiency towards more native-like accuracy. The principle posits that output production plays a variety of key roles in SLA – from the automatization of existing linguistic knowledge to the development of new knowledge.

6.3.1 The Output Hypothesis

The Output Hypothesis emerged in the mid-1980s, as a result of studies (e.g. Harley and Swain 1978) carried out with learners who had undergone immersion education in Canada, having been taught, that is, the whole or part of their curriculum in a second language for part of their schooling.[1] Despite having received vast amounts of comprehensible input through content classes taught in a second language, immersion students were found to fall short of NSs in some areas of their linguistic competence. In particular, shortcomings appeared 'to be particularly evident in those aspects of communicative performance which demand the use of grammatical knowledge' (Swain 1985: 244–245). Something seemed to be amiss in the theory that comprehensible input equals language acquisition.

Merrill Swain and colleagues at the Ontario Institute for Studies in Education found that although students were required to speak and write in a second language in their immersion classes, their production was not as elaborate as might have been expected.[2] They hence argued that what hampered immersion students' language development was the fact that in most cases learners were not 'pushed' to produce output consisting of 'a message that is not only conveyed, but that is conveyed precisely, coherently and appropriately' (Swain 1985: 249). Being 'pushed' to produce output with the above characteristics was hypothesized to lead to stretching one's second language competence and develop native-like accuracy, the missing element in immersion students' otherwise relatively fluent language production.

Why did the Canadian researchers argue that comprehensible input was not sufficient to drive language development forward? It was pointed out that comprehension usually entails only semantic processing of a language (we can get away by focusing on 'lexical information plus extra-linguistic information', Krashen 1982: 66). On the other hand, to engage syntactic processing, we need to *produce* language, as language production entails that attention is paid to lexicogrammatical features. As Swain (1995: 127) put it, 'learners (as well as native speakers, of course) can fake it, so to speak, in comprehension, but they cannot do so in the same way in production'. As an essential ingredient to SLA, 'pushed output' was hence thought to be 'a concept parallel to that of the "i+1" of comprehensible input' (Swain 1985: 249).

How does SLA come about through pushed output? Swain attempted to explore this question by singling out 'functions' that output may play in second language development. As any language teacher and learner is well aware, output fosters fluency. By speaking or writing with a meaningful purpose we exercise our 'linguistic resources', get increasingly more adroit at accessing our stored language knowledge and thereby eventually automatize its use (cf. Section 6.3.2). Yet this is only part of the story: 'just speaking and writing are not enough' (Swain 1993: 160). In order to develop accuracy as well as fluency, learners need to be 'pushed' to make *full* use of their linguistic resources. According to Swain, being pushed to produce output plays three specific roles that are thought to account not only for the consolidation and automatization of previous language knowledge but also for the development of new knowledge.

The first of such roles is a 'noticing' (or 'consciousness raising', cf. Chapter 4) function, which consists in learners noticing a 'hole' in their interlanguage ('learners may notice that they do not know how to express precisely the meaning they wish to convey *at the very moment of attempting to produce it*' – emphasis in the original, Swain 2000: 100). In other words, as they struggle to make their message accurate, meaningful and appropriate (cf. Chapter 1), learners may notice a gap 'between what they want to say and what they can say, leading them to recognize what they do not know, or know only partially' (Swain 1995: 125–126). This is a key aspect of the Output Hypothesis – noticing a shortcoming in one's language knowledge need not be brought about by what Swain and Lapkin call 'external feedback', i.e. by a listener asking for clarification, but may be initiated by a student through the very act of producing output (cf. Figure 6.1). As a result of this awareness, students may analyse their interlanguage, tap into their linguistic resources and try and find a solution to the problem. If they can't find a solution, they may seek targeted input (e.g. from their teacher or a more proficient speaker), which they are ready to analyse with 'more focused attention'. If they do find a solution, the outcome is 'new, reprocessed', modified output (Swain and Lapkin 1995: 386).

'Hypothesis testing' represents, according to Swain, the second main function played by output in language development: 'to test a hypothesis, learners need to do something, and one way of doing this is to say or write something' (Swain 1995: 131). Being pushed to produce output may enable learners to try out their own hypotheses about the 'comprehensibility or linguistic well-formedness' (Swain 1995: 126) of the meanings they wish to express and, if needed, lead them to revise such hypotheses. The outcome of this process is the development of new linguistic knowledge. The following extract of two adult learners of English interacting (Hiroko is describing a

Figure 6.1 Output and second language learning (adapted from Swain and Lapkin 1995: 388).

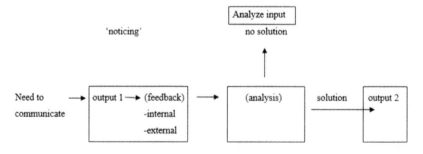

picture and Izumi is drawing it) shows how output can be used to notice a hole in one's interlanguage and to test a hypothesis.

---

1. Hiroko: *A man is uh drinking c-coffee or tea uh with the saucer of the uh uh coffee set is uh in his uh knee*
2. Izumi: *in him knee*
3. Hiroko: *uh on his knee*
4. Izumi: *yeah*
5. Hiroko: *on his knee*
6. Izumi: *so sorry. On his knee*
(Gass and Varonis 1989: 81, quoted in Swain 1995: 136)

During the interaction, Hiroko notices a problem in her output ('uh in his uh knee') (1), which she seems to resolve by relying on her own linguistic resources (3). On the other hand, Izumi is led to produce modified output (6) after having tested a hypothesis (2).

Finally, output may also provide learners with an opportunity to 'not only reveal their hypotheses but reflect on them, using language to do so' (Swain 1995: 132). This 'metalinguistic' function (or 'reflective' role) of output is involved when learners engage in 'metatalk' – they 'talk about language', and this very often occurs through collaborative dialogue during a language teaching activity they carry out in pairs or groups (cf. Chapter 4). As a result of this reflective process, which may (but need not) involve the deployment of metalinguistic terminology, learners are led to consolidate or develop both implicit and explicit linguistic knowledge (cf. Chapter 4).

Building on Swain's work, Skehan (1998) drew up another possible taxonomy of functions that output may play in the development of second language competence (see Table 6.1).

Skehan's functions can be classified according to whether they play an indirect or a direct role on language acquisition (Ellis 2008). Functions a,

Table 6.1 Six functions of output (Skehan 1998: 16–19).

a. To generate better input
b. To force syntactic processing
c. To test hypotheses
d. To develop automaticity
e. To develop discourse skills
f. To develop a personal voice

c, e, f seem to impinge on second language development indirectly. Hence, output can help learners to obtain higher quality comprehensible input, through feedback that is 'more finely tuned' to their current competence (function a), often as a result of testing hypotheses (function c); through the development of 'discourse management', 'turn-taking skills' and 'a range of similar capacities which regulate the negotiation of meaning in ongoing discourse' (function e), and by providing 'the opportunity to steer conversations along routes of interest to the speaker, and to find ways of expressing individual meanings' (function f) (Skehan 1998: 16–19). On the other hand, as has been argued above, output can impact more directly on acquisition by leading to learners' automatization of their linguistic knowledge (function d) and by engaging syntactic processing (function b).

Recent developments of the Output Hypothesis have been influenced by new insights on language and language learning afforded by the Sociocultural Approach to SLA (cf. Chapter 5). To counter the fact that the Output Hypothesis had often been taken as entailing a view of output merely as a 'product', a 'thing', the outcome of the process of learning, Swain (2005, 2006) suggested considering output as 'languaging'. What is involved in 'languaging'? First, 'languaging' entails a 'process', a 'verb', a dynamic activity. In keeping with the Sociocultural Approach, producing language is believed to have an important cognitive function in the development of new knowledge in any area of human thought. By languaging we not merely turn a 'ready-made' thought into words but we often come to develop new understandings *as we are involved in the process of languaging*. Hence, according to the 'languaging' perspective, language is not only a vehicle, 'a conveyer of meaning' but also 'an agent in the making of meaning' (Swain 2006: 96). We naturally 'language' to learn – to better understand new concepts and to appropriate knowledge. The concept of 'languaging about language', which is central to Swain's reinterpretation of the Output Hypothesis through the lens of Sociocultural Theory, takes up and expands the earlier characterization of a metalinguistic function of output. By 'talking about language', either privately or in collaboration, we learn 'both through and about language' (Swain 2006: 106), thereby developing both implicit and explicit knowledge (Chapter 4) – in any domain of language.

An example which showcases the power of languaging at work is offered by Watanabe's (2004) study (mentioned in Swain 2006). Two Japanese learners of English are shown working through the second draft of a composition after their teacher has read and commented on it. In particular, the teacher has suggested reformulations of two noun phrases written by the students ('in nineteenth century of Japan' reformulated as 'in nineteenth-century Japan' and 'people in nineteenth century' reformulated as 'people in the nineteenth century'). At first, one of the students, Ken, appears to reject the teacher's suggestions. The feedback provided just does not seem to make sense to him as it does not match what he knows of the language. As is shown in the following extract, it is only when Ken 'talks through' the feedback that he eventually comes to accept the teacher's reformulations, having developed new insights into the language.

Yoji: *'People in the' ... [reading]*

Ken: *in the, in the, in the, in THE nineteenth century.*

Yoji: *Here, 'in nineteenth-century Japan' [referring to the first reformulation]*

Ken: *Ahhh! [the moment of insight]*

Yoji: *So this is different ... so if we put 'the'.*

Ken: *Yes, it sh-, it should be noun, noun. [= we should put 'the' if 'nineteenth century' is a noun]*

Yoji: *In the nineteenth century.*

Ken: *If we, if we, if we want to use 'nineteenth century' as a noun...*

Yoji: *Mm.*

Ken: *... maybe we need article.*

Yoji: *Article. If we don't put articles ...*

Ken: *We don't have to put in article for 'in nineteenth-century Japan' because this 'nineteenth-century' is adjective ... difference. Okay.*

(Watanabe 2004, quoted in Swain 2006: 101)

In this section, we have seen that Swain's Output Hypothesis challenges Krashen's contention that output is at best an unnecessary luxury for acquisition. It has been shown that as well as playing an indirect role in acquisition, output may impinge on language development directly. This can result not only in fostering the automatization of existing language knowledge but also in the development of new knowledge, a process that can be powerfully engaged by 'languaging'.

6.3.2 Automaticity and fluency in output production

As pointed out, production plays several roles in SLA. In this section, we will examine fluency in more detail as one of the aspects of learners' automatization or 'automaticity' of their linguistic knowledge. As Segalowitz (2003: 383) points out, a task is carried out 'automatically' when we perform it 'without experiencing the need to invest additional effort and attention'. In this way, our performance appears to be 'more efficient, faster, more accurate, and more stable'. We will deal here more specifically with those aspects of automaticity that contribute to speech fluency in second language output production.

Automaticity has been described and operationalized in different ways in the research literature. DeKeyser (2001) presents a number of criteria for automaticity used in cognitive psychology. What is 'automatic' is defined as fast, effortless, unaffected by memory set size (i.e. the number of elements to be kept in the working memory at the same time), hard to control/alter/suppress, the result of large amounts of practice, having little interference from/with other factors/processes, unconscious (no attention or monitoring is required), requiring constant memory retrieval. This variety of criteria reflects 'the inability of the field to agree on a definition applicable to all tasks' (DeKeyser 2001: 129). Segalowitz (2003) singles out a number of characteristics that are most frequently associated with automaticity in the research literature. Each characteristic refers to the type of processing involved while performing a task in an automatic way. We will focus on four main characteristics here which will be further analysed (cf. Table 6.2).

Table 6.2 Automaticity and type of processing (Segalowitz 2003).

a. Speed of processing	b. Ballistic or unstoppable processing	c. Load-independent processing	d. Effortless processing

First of all, automaticity is often associated with speed (a). It is common to think that once a mechanism has become automatic, it will operate faster. For example, readers are supposed to read faster in their L1 than in a language they have acquired later. However, as Segalowitz (2003: 385) argues, 'while automatic processing may entail fast processing, it does not follow that all fast processing is automatic'. This raises the question whether automaticity simply refers to a quantitative ('faster processing'), or also a qualitative change of performance involving a 'restructuring' of the underlying processes. Second, automaticity is also characterized by 'ballistic' or unstoppable processing (b). For example, this was observed with readers in their L1 in the process of comprehending word meaning, while only the very highly fluent readers showed unstoppable processing in the L2 (Favreau and Segalowitz 1983, cited in Segalowitz 2007: 182–183). This explains that when automatic processes are activated, they are unconscious and prevail over non-automatic or controlled processes, which require more time to occur. It was also found that an automatic process is load independent (c); that is, it operates 'without regard to how much information' has to be processed provided that a particular stimulus-response experience requires the same type of operation and occurs under the same conditions (Segalowitz 2003: 390). This also means that 'the automatized behavior that results from consistent practice is highly specific' (DeKeyser 2001: 131). An important pedagogical implication is that, for example, what has been practised in one language skill (fast reading and understanding) cannot be 'transferred' to another language skill (fast speaking). Finally, automatic processing has proven to be 'effortless' (d). As Segalowitz (2003: 390) points out, effort refers here 'to the expenditure of a limited attentional resource'. Normally, performing a task that is itself effortful interferes with the performance of a simultaneous effortful task. By contrast, if the primary task is largely automatic (resulting from a highly practised skill), it will not require redirecting attention or effort away from a secondary task. It can thus be concluded that the type of processing involved in the performance of an automatic task implies 'greater efficiency'. There are thus several reasons for promoting automaticity in second language learning.

We have pointed out that one of the roles for output in second language learning is to help learners develop automaticity and fluency in their use of linguistic knowledge (cf. Section 6.3.1). In broader terms, language fluency refers to 'those aspects of productive and receptive language ability characterized by fluidity (smoothness) of performance' (Segalowitz 2007: 181). As argued,

> successful second language (L2) mastery requires more than knowledge of phonology, vocabulary, syntax, semantics, pragmatics, sociolinguistic conventions, and sensitivity to cultural norms. The successful L2 user must also be able to implement that knowledge in an appropriately fluent manner. (Segalowitz 2007: 181–182)

Automaticity thus allows learners to 'go beyond constructed sentences and achieve some level of natural speed and rhythm' (Skehan 1998: 18).

As one of the aspects that characterize L2 production, fluency has also been used as a benchmark for second language development descriptors and assessment scales (Segalowitz 2010: 77). For example, it is one of the categories in the descriptors of the six levels of speaking ability ranging from A1 (the lowest level) to C1 (the highest level) provided by the Common

European Framework (Council of Europe 2001), as illustrated in the examples of the descriptors for levels A2, B1, B2 in Table 6.3.

Table 6.3 Fluency aspects of spoken production in the Common Reference Levels (Council of Europe 2001: 28–29).

A2	Can make him/herself understood in very short utterances, even though pauses, false starts and reformulation are very evident.
B1	Can keep going comprehensibly, even though pausing for grammatical and lexical planning and repair is very evident, especially in longer stretches of free production.
B2	Can produce stretches of language with a fairly even tempo; although he/she can be hesitant as he/she searches for patterns and expressions. There are few notably long pauses.

This provides an additional reason for focusing on fluency, not only in terms of 'performance' but also in relation to the underlying cognitive processes involved.

Segalowitz (2010: 48–51) identifies three meanings or dimensions of fluency that pertain to oral performance and are relevant to L2 output production: cognitive fluency, utterance fluency and perceived fluency. Each dimension including the mechanisms involved will be illustrated in Table 6.4.

Table 6.4 Fluency in oral production (from Segalowitz 2010: 6; 48–51).

Cognitive fluency	The speaker's ability to efficiently activate and integrate the cognitive processes required for producing an utterance.	Planning the utterance, lexical search, packaging the information into grammatically appropriate form, generating an 'articulatory script' for speaking the utterance, reducing sources of interference.
Utterance fluency	Features of an utterance: temporal characteristics, pausing, hesitation, repair.	Speech rate (syllable/minute including pauses), articulation rate (syllable/minute excluding pauses), speaking time, number and length of pauses, dysfluencies (repetitions, restarts, repairs), pace (stressed word/minute).
Perceived fluency	The listener's inference/judgement about the speaker's fluency based on perceptions/impressions of the speech samples produced by the speaker.	

As Segalowitz (2010: 49) highlights, in terms of cognitive fluency, the planning and the assembling of an utterance 'need to be integrated temporally for utterances to be executed with the desired characteristics of timing, pausing and hesitation, and repair features'. This calls for specific attention to the efficiency by which these operations take place and the features of oral performance that reflect cognitive fluency. As regards utterance fluency, Skehan (2003) and Tavakoli and Skehan (2005) suggest a further distinction between breakdown fluency, repair fluency and speech rate. Breakdown fluency is evidenced by the number and length of filled and unfilled pauses in the ongoing flow of speech; repair fluency has to do with the frequency of reformulation, replacement, false starts and repetition; speech rate is evidenced by the number of words/syllables in a given time. Ellis (2008: 492) argues that, although it is not easy to separate the various constructs related to utterance fluency, this distinction can be useful to highlight the difference between repair fluency and breakdown fluency, and between these and other linguistic features of speech production such as complexity and accuracy (cf. Subsection 6.3.3, 'Output production tasks')

Given the key role of cognitive fluency for efficient oral performance, two features will be considered in more detail: access fluidity and attention control (Segalowitz 2007: 182). Access fluidity, also defined as lexical access, refers to 'the process of connecting words and expressions to their meanings'. It is important to note that fluidity does not simply mean 'speed' of processing, but rather 'the smoothness' by which the process takes place. Attention control refers to 'the process by which a language user focuses and refocuses attention in real time as the message being communicated unfolds'. According to Segalowitz (2010: 92), two types of attention are involved here: attention-to-language and language-directed attention. Table 6.5 illustrates the situations in which the first type of attention is addressed to specific language features.

Table 6.5 Examples of attention-to-language in L2 cognitive fluency (adapted from Segalowitz 2010: 93).

- Selective attention to details of linguistic form as opposed to meaning
- Attention to the feedback received
- Selection of appropriate words from among similar alternatives
- Self-monitoring (checking one's own speech for errors in real time and making corrections as necessary)
- Using communicative strategies to deal with word finding or grammatical complexity problems
- Attention to sociolinguistic features that serve as social cues to politeness, emotion, register shifts, irony, turn-taking, etc.
- Focusing on the speech stream under noisy conditions and ignoring competing sounds

In language-directed attention, instead, 'the control of attention originates from within the linguistic message itself, and is directed back toward the mental representation that is associated with the meaning of the message' (Segalowitz 2010: 95). Devices such as the use of stress patterns, the foregrounding and backgrounding of various types of information by word order or through specific lexicogrammatical features and the use of spatial prepositions ('over' vs 'above') imply differences in terms of the speaker's perspective of what he or she considers more important to underline in the message.[3] Having to deal with these devices during online communication may indeed place a special burden on learners' attention and ultimately reduce their control on utterance fluency.

After analysing the main features of fluency in output production, we will turn our attention to the possible challenges learners may face to perform in a fluent way. Kormos (2006: xxv) claims that 'whereas lexical, syntactic, morphological and phonological encoding is almost automatic in the L1 speech production, these mechanisms are only partially automatic even in case of advanced L2 learners'. Segalowitz (2010: 9) then identifies possible 'fluency vulnerability points', that is, 'critical points where underlying processing difficulties could result in L2 speech dysfluencies'.[4] Seven fluency vulnerability points (f) are proposed at the different stages of the speech production cycle, from conceptual preparation to the actual speech production: microplanning (f1), grammatical encoding (f2), lemma retrieval (f3), morpho-phonological encoding (f4), phonetic encoding (f5), articulation (f6) and self-perception (f7). We will illustrate each fluency vulnerability in Table 6.6.

Research has shown that these potential fluency difficulties can affect learners' production in different ways. For example, the participants in Tavakoli's study (2011) were found to pause more repeatedly and to have longer periods of silence than L1 speakers. Some of their pauses were associated with processes such as replacement, reformulation and online planning. In Kahng's study (2014: 845), lower proficiency learners claimed that during oral production they almost always relied on their L2 explicit knowledge, especially when deciding on function words such as articles and prepositions, and putting words together to construct a sentence. This had the effect of slowing down their performance. However, not all aspects of fluency in L2 speech can be directly related to L2 proficiency. For example, by looking at the separate facets of utterance fluency (speech rate and pausing), De Jong et al. (2013) found that whereas linguistic skills were most strongly related to average syllable duration, average pausing duration was also affected by the learners' personal speaking style or personality traits. On account of the complex and multifaceted nature of L2 oral fluency (Skehan 2003), what has been highlighted by research can help teachers become more

Table 6.6 Fluency vulnerability points in L2 speech production (from Segalowitz 2010: 8–17).

Stages of speech production	The L2 speaker has difficulty
f1 Microplanning	turning a concept into a preverbal message, for example he is not sure how to convey a particular meaning because he may not know the lexical items or grammatical forms needed
f2 Grammatical encoding	encoding a preverbal message into a grammatical structure, for example how to express spatial locations, countability of nouns, etc.
f3 Lemma retrieval	retrieving a lemma (families of related words, including idioms and fixed expressions), for example distinguishing between synonyms and related words
f4 Morpho-phonological encoding	encoding the message into a morpho-phonological form that can be associated with it. This process is based on syllable distinction rather than individual phonemes. For example, this implies being able to look at the word ahead and shift the stress of the previous word accordingly (<u>six</u>teen dollars and not six<u>teen</u>)
f5–f6 Phonetic encoding and articulation	encoding the phonological form into the required phonemes needed to articulate speech
f7 Self-perception	monitoring his/her own speech in order to catch errors and reformulate the message

aware of the possible challenges fluency development may pose to learners and take a more suitable approach to promoting fluency in the classroom.

6.3.3 The Output Hypothesis: Learning and teaching implications

In the first part of the chapter, we have explored how, according to the Output Hypothesis, output can play several functions in second language acquisition. In the second part, we will shift our focus to the main learning and teaching implications of this hypothesis. We will kick off by exploring the concept of 'task', which represents the main 'instrument' that researchers have relied on to investigate pushed output. Next, we will zero in on specific techniques and tasks which research has found to be effective in learning and teaching fluency in output production.

Output production tasks

The word 'task' is sometimes used by language teachers to refer generically to a teaching activity associated with communicative language teaching (CLT) (Howatt 2004). Skehan (2003: 1) notes that it was in the 1980s that the term 'task' started to gradually replace the term 'activity' (as in the phrase 'communicative activity/task'). In SLA 'task' has, however, taken on a distinctive meaning. This has not prevented – as is often the case – the proliferation of several slightly different interpretations of the construct (cf. Long 1983; Prabhu 1987; Skehan 1998; Ellis 2003, 2012; Long 2015). Ellis (2009: 227) acknowledges this state of affairs when remarking that 'the definition of a task has proved problematic'. For the sake of clarity, we will refer to Ellis's (e.g. 2012) definition as a baseline. According to Ells (2012: 19), the defining criteria of a task are the following:

1. The primary focus should be on 'meaning' (by which I mean learners should be mainly concerned with processing the semantic and pragmatic meaning of utterances).
2. There should be some kind of 'gap' (i.e. a need to convey information, to express an opinion or to infer meaning).
3. Learners should largely have to rely on their own resources (linguistic and non-linguistic) in order to complete the activity.
4. There is a clearly defined outcome other than the use of language (i.e. the language serves as the means for achieving the outcome, not as an end in its own right).

A 'task' is often opposed to a language teaching 'exercise'. To better appreciate the distinctive features of a task as couched in Ellis's quotation, we shall analyse a sample task ('What can you buy?') vis-à-vis an exercise ('Going shopping') (cf. Table 6.7).

In the 'What can you buy?' task, students are required to formulate and process utterances focusing on the semantic meanings conveyed (the food items in the two lists). At the same time, they are required to identify the most appropriate way(s) of formulating an inquiry and replying to it (hence engaging pragmatic meanings, cf. Chapter 1). The task includes a communication gap: Student A, who plays the role of the customer, does not know at the outset what products Student B, who plays the role of the shopkeeper, has in stock. The only way to 'close' this gap in information

Table 6.7 Task versus exercise (Ellis 2012: 199).

What can you buy?	Going shopping
Student A You are going shopping at Student B's store. Here is your shopping list. Find out which items on your list you can buy. Mary's Shopping List 1. oranges 4. powdered milk 2. eggs 5. biscuits 3. flour 6. jam *Student B* You own a store. Here is a list of items for sale in your store. Make a list of the items that Student A asks for that you do not stock. 1. bread 7. mealie meal flour 2. salt 8. sugar 3. apples 9. curry powder 4. tins of fish 10. biscuits 5. coca cola 11. powdered milk 6. flour 12. dried beans	Look at Mary's shopping list. Then look at the list of items in Abdullah's store. Mary's Shopping List 1. oranges 4. powdered milk 2. eggs 5. biscuits 3. flour 6. jam Abdullah's Store 1. bread 7. mealie meal flour 2. salt 8. sugar 3. apples 9. curry powder 4. tins of fish 10. biscuits 5. coca cola 11. powdered milk 6. flour 12. dried beans Work with a partner. One person is Mary and the other person is Mr Abdullah. Make conversations like this. Mary: Good morning. Do you have any _____? Abdullah: Yes, I have some./No, I don't have any.

is to engage in the communicative interaction. By contrast, in the 'Going shopping' exercise, both Student A and Student B get to see each other's lists of products from the outset. No real gap in information is present. As mentioned in Ellis's definition, tasks can potentially feature two other types of gap, in addition to the 'information' gap type inscribed in the 'What can you buy' task. These are defined and exemplified in Table 6.8.

Another important feature of the 'What can you buy?' task is that it does not dictate to students what specific lexicogrammatical items to use to carry out the task. Students are able to draw freely on their linguistic (and extralinguistic) resources. On the other hand, exercises usually provide students with language exemplars that they are supposed to use (even if they may envisage some leeway in the extent to which these exemplars are modified). In the 'Going shopping' exercise, students are supplied with a model dialogue which they are explicitly told to stick to when they get to interact. Finally, a task works on the premise that whatever language is produced is a means to an end –

Table 6.8 Types of communicative gaps in tasks.

INFORMATION GAP	'a transfer of given information from one person to another – or from one form to another, or from one place to another – generally calling for the encoding or decoding of information from or into language' (Prabhu 1987: 46)	The 'What can you buy?' task above
OPINION GAP	'identifying and articulating a personal preference, feeling, or attitude in response to a given situation' (Prabhu 1987: 47)	AGONY AUNT(S) Is honesty always the best policy? Should we **always** tell the truth? Think about the following situations. Share your opinions on each one with your classmates. How many people share your point of view? How many have different ideas? 1. You saw your best friend's girlfriend out on a date with someone else. Should you tell your friend what you saw? Why? Why not? 2. Your friend has a new haircut. She is really happy with her new 'look' but you don't like it at all. In fact, you think it makes her look quite ugly. She asks for your opinion. Should you tell her what you really think? Why? Why not? (Adapted from Wisniewska et al. 2007: 163)
REASONING GAP	'deriving some new information from given information through processes of inference, deduction, practical reasoning, or a perception of relationships or patterns' (Prabhu 1987: 46)	WHO DO THEY LOVE? Lee, Tracy, Sid, and Kit are in love. Can you find who belongs together? Get together with a partner to read these clues and solve the puzzle. CLUES 1. Lee loves the person who speaks Swahili. 2. Tracy loves the person who tells amusing stories. 3. The teacher loves the writer. 4. The pilot loves the person who is interested in history. 5. Sid loves the person who plays the piano […] (Adapted from Wisniewska et al. 2007: 349)

and the end has to do with an extralinguistic purpose. In the 'What can you buy' task, the outcome is to end up with two different lists (items that Mary can buy at Abdullah's store and perhaps need not look for in a supermarket, and items that Abdullah does not stock and perhaps needs to order through his supplier). As regards the extralinguistic outcome of tasks, Ellis (2003: 8) points out that 'tasks involve a sleight of hand. They need to convince learners that what matters is the outcome. Otherwise, there is a danger that the learners will subvert the aim of the task by displaying rather than using language'. This would turn a task into an exercise, and the advantages for acquisition stemming from the Output Hypothesis would be lost.

It should be highlighted that while a teaching activity may have *some* of the features that have been singled out as distinctive for a task (cf. the examples of 'form/meaning/use' exercises presented in Chapter 1), only on condition that it include all the four features can it be defined as a task. It is indeed the sum of these features that results in the fact that learners 'orient' differently to a task vis-à-vis an exercise (Ellis 2009: 224). Another important caveat is that although tasks are often associated with speaking activities, and many of the examples that we will analyse below also fall into this category, in principle a task can involve any language skill and it often does rely on the integration of two and more skills.

In order to appreciate how tasks can be used to foster pushed output, hence output that is supposed to drive forward acquisition, four main issues will be tackled in the remainder of this section:

a. What kinds of options are available to researchers and teachers when designing and implementing tasks?

b. How do these options impact on the quality of output production?

c. To what extent can a task be focused, that is 'push' learners to produce output containing pre-determined lexicogrammatical features?

d. What kinds of activities can be carried out before and after task implementation to maximize language acquisition processes?

Several options have been singled out by researchers and methodologists (cf. e.g. Willis 1996; Skehan 1998; Ellis 2003; Nunan 2004; Willis and Willis 2007; Long 2015) with respect to how an output production task may be designed. Table 6.9 lists the main design variables held to potentially impact on learner output production.

In addition to task design variables, options in how a task may be implemented have been investigated. Table 6.10 lists the main task implementation options singled out by SLA and language teaching research. As Ellis (2012) points out, a task need not involve pair or group work but may also be performed in a lockstep fashion (the interaction occurs between the

Table 6.9 Task design options (from Ellis 2003: 118–137).

Task Design	Examples
Type of input provided: contextual support, number of elements, familiarity of topic	*Picture description task:* students carry out the task while viewing a picture vs having been shown the picture prior to the task and having it withdrawn during the task (contextual support); one vs more pictures to describe (number of elements); picture(s) may refer to an everyday event vs an event set in the past/a different culture (familiarity of topic).
Conditions of input provision: split vs shared information, number of task demands	*Map drawing task*: each learner may have the same whole picture of the street plan of a town vs they may each have partial pictures of the street plan (split vs shared information); the route in the map drawing task may have been preliminarily traced on the 'describer''s street plan vs it may be provided to them as a verbal description, hence requiring a further step (number of task demands).
Product outcome: closed vs open, convergent vs divergent, degree of structure	*Problem-solving task*: students solve a puzzle based on logical thinking. They are required to reach a predetermined outcome (closed outcome). *Discussion and decision-making tasks*: students discuss the pros and cons of globalization – the outcome is not predetermined in advance (open outcome); students need to agree on three things to bring on a week-long trip to a foreign country (convergent outcome); students discuss the pros and cons of social media but they are assigned different viewpoints and need to support their position (divergent outcome). *Presentation task*: students prepare a profile of their school for the upcoming open day: they need to complete a chart, design visuals, prepare a speech (rigidly structured outcome) vs they are free to design their presentation in any way they like (less structured outcome).
Process outcomes: discourse type	*Picture description task*: students are provided with pictures showing two characters involved in a car accident; they need to order the pictures and tell the story (narrative discourse type). *Decision-making task*: students are on a balloon that is losing altitude. One person needs to be heaved out of the balloon. Each student needs to argue their case (argumentative discourse type).

teacher and the whole class). It can be preceded by a pre-task (i.e. preparatory) stage and/or followed by a post-task stage (cf. below). Learners may play just one role (speaker or listener) or more than one (both speaker and listener). Role allocation may be random or based on individual learner factors such as language proficiency, degree of extroversion/introversion and so on. Prior to task performance, learners can be given time to plan ('strategic planning'), and this planning may be free (unguided) or students may be told what to focus on in their planning (e.g. content vs language). Planning/monitoring opportunities may also be afforded during task performance ('online planning'). The performance itself may be timed or untimed: students may be allowed to take any time they wish to carry out the task or may be given a time limit at the outset. Finally, the same task may be repeated (once or several times) or may be carried out only once.

Given the sheer variety of task options, it begs the question of which of them *work* best. In other words, which options lead to more learner production or rather better quality production – production that drives forward language development? Apart from fluency, which we have considered in the previous section, output production has been analysed from a psycholinguistic perspective (e.g. Skehan 1992, 1996, 1998, 2003) as consisting of another two main factors: accuracy and complexity. Accuracy is normally associated with 'correctness': in Skehan's (1996: 46) words, it is 'performance which is native-like enough through its rule-governed nature'. Complexity may be a more elusive concept. Complexity is said to be related to interlanguage change, hence to language development, to what researchers call the process of 'restructuring' interlanguage knowledge – 'the process by which the interlanguage system becomes more complex, elaborate, and structured' (Skehan 1996: 47). As a result of restructuring, new linguistic elements are integrated into a learner's interlanguage. Complex output may thus consist of language that is at the upper limit of a learner's interlanguage and result

Table 6.10 Task implementation options (from Ellis 2003: 118–137).

Task Implementation
• Lockstep vs pairwork or small group work
• With or without a pre-task stage
• Students as 'speakers' or 'listeners'
• Allocation of roles in a task according to learner factors
• Allocation vs non-allocation of planning time (guided/unguided)
• Timed vs untimed performance
• One instance or repeated task performance (with/without changes)
• With or without post-task stage

from the learner's testing hypotheses on recently acquired lexicogrammar. Alternatively, it may stem from the learners' use of a wider range of lexicogrammatical features, many of which, although perhaps still not fully automatized, are nevertheless 'at the cutting edge of development' (Skehan and Foster 2001: 190).

To better appreciate the difference between the concepts of accuracy and complexity with respect to learners' language production, it may be useful to refer to some of the 'measures' researchers have used to determine to what extent learners' interlanguage is accurate or complex (cf. Table 6.11).

Table 6.11 Measures of accuracy and complexity (from Ellis 2012: 207).

	Measure	Method of calculation
Accuracy	Percentage of error-free clauses	The learner's production is divided into clauses and each clause examined to see if it contains an error or if it is error-free. The number of error-free clauses is divided by the total number of clauses and expressed as a percentage.
	Target-like use of a specific grammatical feature	A specific grammatical feature is selected for analysis (e.g. past tense). Obligatory occasions for the use of this feature are identified and the number of times the learner supplies or fails to supply the target feature is identified. Accuracy is expressed as a percentage of correct suppliance.
Complexity	Amount of subordination used	The learner's production is divided into clauses and the number of (1) total clauses and (2) subordinate clauses is calculated. (2) is then divided by (1).
	Lexical richness (type-token ratio)	The total number of different words used (=types) is divided by the total number of words (= tokens) used.

As can be seen from Table 6.11, while accurate output has to do with conformity to norms, complex production is characterized by syntactic elaborateness and lexical variety, either of which may signal that the learner is trying to stretch their interlanguage and make their message more precise – key functions of language production according to the Output Hypothesis.

According to Skehan's (1998, 2003) Limited Attention Capacity Model (LACM), it is assumed that when learners engage in production, they tend to allocate their attention to either *what* they are going to say or *how* they are going to say it. The LACM is premised on the notion that attention is a process with limited capacity. When, as language learners, we focus on the content of a message, we usually do not have enough 'capacity' left to pay as much attention to the form of the message (and vice versa). As a result, our language production may tend to favour one of the three factors (fluency, accuracy and complexity) vis-à-vis the others – to use Skehan's words, there is a 'trade-off' between say fluency and accuracy, or accuracy and complexity. It may well be the case (Ellis 2012) that individual learner factors play a role too – for example, learners who are 'adventurous' in their language use and open to taking risks may be more apt to experiment with complex language vis-à-vis those learners who are less willing to leave safe territory and are more prone to stick to what they know is correct.

What are the effects of this differential focus on language acquisition and use? Skehan (1996: 49–50) points out that a focus on accuracy makes it 'less likely that interlanguage change will occur' and may also result in slow and perhaps halting speech. A focus on complexity boosts the chances that 'new forms will be incorporated into interlanguage systems' while a focus on fluency often results in faster speech and 'lower priority being attached to getting language right, or to the use of new forms'.

An important application of Skehan's LACM is related to the use of tasks as language learning tools. Researchers have started from the assumption that 'performance on a particular task can, at most, help *some* of the areas of language development, not all' (emphasis in the original, Skehan and Foster 2001: 233). Studies carried out in the past twenty years have shown that by manipulating task design and implementation options such as those mentioned earlier, it is indeed possible to engage psycholinguistic processes that underlie the emergence of any of the three aspects of production – fluency, accuracy and complexity (Ellis 2003, 2012). In this section, we will provide a brief overview of options impacting on accuracy and complexity, while the section 'Techniques and tasks for fostering speech fluency' will weigh in on the engagement of fluency through task design and implementation.

Table 6.12 summarizes the key task design and implementation options that have been shown to impact on accuracy and complexity in language production.

In order to develop learners' accurate language use, an English language teacher may, for example, decide to implement the 'Fortune cookie' task described in Figure 6.2. The task has a clear structure and as it requires written output in the form of 'fortune cookie predictions', it provides opportunities for planning during task implementation ('online planning').

Table 6.12 Task design and implementation options impacting on accuracy and complexity (from Ellis 2003: 118–137 and Ellis 2012: 218–223).

Option	Accuracy	Complexity
Contextual support	–	Tasks with no contextual support
Number of task elements	–	Tasks with many elements
Topic		–
Shared vs split information	–	Shared information tasks
Task demands	–	Tasks that pose a single demand
Closed vs open tasks	Open tasks	Open tasks with divergent goals
Inherent structure of the outcome	A clear inherent structure together with opportunities for planning	–
Discourse mode		Narrative task > descriptive task
		Argument > discussion
		Narrative > argument
Planning (strategic vs online)	Online planning, possible effect of strategic planning	Both strategic and online planning
Task repetition		Effective but dependent on learner proficiency and individual factors

---

FORTUNE COOKIE

In North America, Chinese restaurants traditionally give customers a fortune cookie at the end of the meal. This cookie is small and hollow. Inside you find a piece of paper that predicts something about your future. Work with another person.

STEP 1 Match the two parts of these fortunes.

1. You will help	a. a trip around the world
2. Your boss is going to	b. an A in this class
3. You will be lucky	c. to have a large and happy family
4. You are going to take	d. and win a lot of money
5. Your friends and family	e. are going to throw a big party in your house
6. You are going to get	f. give you a big rise
7. You will	g. make an important contribution in the world
8. You are going	h. is going to change dramatically
9. Your life	i. a friend in need
10. An interesting stranger is	j. going to enter your life

STEP 2 The writer of these fortunes has run out of ideas and needs some help. What kinds of fortunes do you like to receive? Write five examples. (Adapted from Wisniewska et al. 2007: 34-35)

Figure 6.2 The *Fortune cookie* task.

By contrast, the 'Mr Bean's birthday party' task in Figure 6.3 is arguably better suited to engage complex language output. The students are not provided with contextual support during task implementation (they first watch a video without taking notes and then tell the story), several elements are involved (the birthday party is attended by Mr Bean and other characters), information is shared by all task participants and planning time is provided.

MR BEAN'S BIRTHDAY PARTY

STEP 1 Work with a partner. Watch a video of Mr Bean's birthday party. Do not take notes.

STEP 2 After watching the video, you need to tell another pair what happened during Mr Bean's party. With your partner plan what you are going to say for a few minutes. Write brief notes.

STEP 3 Get together with another pair and tell each other about Mr Bean's birthday party. Do not look at your notes. Did the other pair remember the same events?

Figure 6.3 The *Mr Bean's birthday party* task.

Research based on Skehan's LACM into the impact of task options on language production is still ongoing (Long 2015). However, as also shown by Table 6.12, more clear effects seem to have been found for complexity. In other words, through the design or the implementation of a task it seems to be comparatively easier to engender a focus on complexity in learners' language production.

According to another influential psycholinguistic model, the Cognition Hypothesis (Robinson 2007), accuracy, complexity and fluency are not necessarily in competition with each other. Accuracy and complexity may be engaged *in tandem* vis-à-vis fluency as a result of manipulating a given set of task design options. By increasing the cognitive demands of a task, it is predicted that learners will be pushed to produce *both* more accurate *and* more complex output 'in order to meet the greater functional and conceptual communicative demands' (Robinson and Gilabert 2007: 162). For example (Long 2015), a task requiring an eyewitness account of a road accident may involve providing the account to a police officer at the scene of the accident or recounting the accident at a later stage, in the office of an insurance company. The second scenario places more cognitive demands on the learner and thus more naturally leads to more complex and potentially more accurate language use as a result of needing to provide more background detail (complexity) and a more precise description (accuracy).

Being aware of the effects of task design and implementation variables on language production is key to using tasks in the classroom as a way to foster pushed output. Another key issue that has important implications for material designers and language teachers is whether task variables can be manipulated in such a way as to engender the emergence of given lexicogrammatical features. In other words, can a teacher direct pushed output towards the use of targeted lexicogrammar while not foregoing the meaning orientation of tasks? To answer this question, we need to refer to the well-known distinction between 'focused' and 'unfocused' tasks. As they are originally pitched against traditional exercises, tasks are usually taken to be 'unfocused'. This means that, according to Nobuyoshi and Ellis's definition, 'no effort is made in the design and in the execution of a task to give prominence to any particular linguistic feature' (Nobuyoshi and Ellis 1993: 204). An example is the eyewitness account mentioned earlier. On the other hand, a task is 'focused' when one or a set of linguistic features are made prominent, 'although not in a way that causes the learner to pay more attention to form than to meaning' (Nobuyoshi and Ellis 1993: 204). What do we mean by making linguistic features prominent in a task? Obviously, we are not talking about instructing students to use given features or providing them with model sentences, as these practices would turn the task into an exercise, not dissimilar from the 'Going shopping' exercise that was analysed earlier. The issue has been tackled from a more theoretical perspective by Loschky and Bley-Vroman (1993) in what has become a seminal article in the literature on task-based language learning and teaching. The researchers posit three degrees of involvement of a lexicogrammatical feature in the implementation of a task:

> In task-naturalness, a grammatical construction may arise naturally during the performance of a particular task, but the task can often be performed perfectly well, even quite easily, without it. In the case of task utility, it is possible to complete a task without the structure, but with the structure the task becomes easier. The most extreme demand a task can place on a structure is essentialness: the task cannot be successfully performed unless the structure is used. (Loschky and Bley Vroman 1993: 132)

It is hence hypothesized that a task may be *more or less* focused. For example, a task involving making travel arrangements may lead to the use of the present simple (*The trains leaves at 9:30*), although other lexicogrammatical features are just as likely to be used (*I'm taking the 9:30 train*). This task would have the lowest degree of focus in that the targeted lexicogrammatical feature (the present simple) is 'natural' but by no means essential in carrying out the task. In a picture description task, deployment of a range of location expressions (prepositions and prepositional phrases) would be 'useful' to carrying out the task more efficiently (e.g. with fewer circumlocutions) but again the task might well be carried out without them. The highest degree of focus of a task is obtained when a given lexicogrammatical feature turns out to be 'essential' to task implementation. This is all very well in theory, but task essentialness is hard to turn into practice, as Loschky and Bley-Vroman seem to acknowledge. Output-oriented tasks for which a lexicogrammatical item is essential are extremely difficult to design in that 'the inherent redundancy of language and the availability of rich contextual clues in many tasks obviate the need for learners to use any particular grammatical structure' (Nobuyoshi and Ellis 1993: 205). Moreover, learners are adroit at relying on communication strategies 'to get round having to use a linguistic feature they do not know or cannot access easily' (Ellis 2012: 203).

As shown in Table 6.13, task essentialness is more naturally associated with comprehension-based tasks (examples of such types of tasks have been provided in previous chapters: IP activities, Chapter 3; consciousness-raising tasks, Chapter 4). One of the key benefits of task essentialness for language development is that it makes it more likely that learners will notice a lexicogrammatical feature and entertain hypotheses about its workings, and this is easier to achieve with tasks that are somehow controlled in their outcome (i.e. closed tasks, which require only one possible outcome). On the other hand, production-based tasks, which may be less controlled in their outcome (open tasks), tend to make the emergence of a lexicogrammatical feature at most a 'natural' consequence of task implementation. In terms of their effect on language acquisition, these tasks are more likely to foster the process of automatization of previous language knowledge rather than the process of hypothesis formation and hence development of new knowledge.

Studies that have put Loschky and Bley Vroman's proposals to the test have shown that emergence of *some* targeted lexicogrammatical features can to some extent be achieved in output production tasks through task design,

Table 6.13 Tasks and degrees of engagement of pre-determined lexicogrammatical features (Loschky and Bley-Vroman 1993: 142).

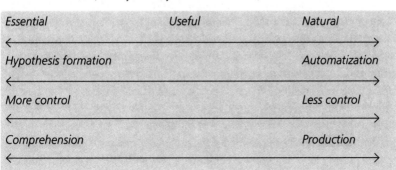

Essential	Useful	Natural
←――――――――――――――――――――――――――――――――――→		
Hypothesis formation		Automatization
←――――――――――――――――――――――――――――――――――→		
More control		Less control
←――――――――――――――――――――――――――――――――――→		
Comprehension		Production
←――――――――――――――――――――――――――――――――――→		

although the range of features investigated is still very limited and most of the studies have yielded disappointing results (for a review, cf. Samuda and Bygate 2008 and Ellis 2012). For example, question formation (Mackey 1999) appears to be easier to be elicited through a focused task than use of the passive voice (Boston 2010).

However, this is not the end of the story. If task essentialness is very difficult to obtain through design, attention to linguistic features can be more easily engendered methodologically, through special techniques deployed during the implementation of a task. Nobuyoshi and Ellis (1993) report on a small-scale study involving six learners who took part in two picture description tasks (for each task, the pictures were about an incident that had happened to a character). Three students made up the experimental group and the remaining three the control group. Each learner performed the task individually with the teacher. The tasks were repeated twice, with a one-week time lag between each administration. The first time, the experimental learners received 'clarification requests' (cf. Chapter 5) whenever they failed to produce the past tense or produced it incorrectly; in other words, the teacher signalled to the learners that she had a problem understanding the utterance, as in the example:

---

1. Learner: *Last weekend, a man painting, painting 'Beware of the dog'.*
2. Teacher: *Sorry?*
3. Learner: *A man painted, painted, painted on the wall 'Beware of the dog'.*
(Nobuyoshi and Ellis 1993: 205)

In (1) the learner fails to produce the correct past tense form.
In (2) the teacher signals misunderstanding, which leads the learner to reformulate their utterance (3).

It should be noted that all the teacher's interventions were as unobtrusive as possible and since she did not make explicit the source of the possible misunderstandings, they did not distract the learners from the overall message-orientation inherent in the tasks. Nevertheless, results showed that in most cases two of the three learners did reformulate their erroneous verb forms as a result of the teacher's clarification requests. During the second administration of the tasks with the experimental group, the teacher limited her clarification requests to only those occasions where she had genuinely failed to understand the learners. Even so, occurrences of grammatical use of the past tense in two learners' output matched or exceeded those of the first administration. As for the control group, they only received clarification requests for miscomprehension both times they did each task and did not show any significant gain in accuracy in past tense use between the two administrations. The study has important implications for language teaching as it shows that tasks can be made 'focused' 'if the focus is induced methodologically by means of requests for clarification directed at utterances containing errors in the feature that has been targeted' (Nobuyoshi and Ellis 1993: 209). Nobuyoshi and Ellis (1993: 209) also point out that 'focusing in this way need not disturb the communicativeness of a task' – provided it is done unobtrusively, the students will still orient to the activity as a task and not as a grammar-focused exercise.

Focusing through clarification requests enables students to produce language so that the first two functions of output for language acquisition as envisaged by the Output Hypothesis are exercised – noticing and hypothesis testing (cf. Section 6.3.1). A way of focusing a task so that learners are also led to use output to reflect on their interlanguage and extend their linguistic resources is shown in a well-known study by Samuda (2001), which revolves around the so-called 'Things in pockets' task. The task involves trying to piece together a profile of a 'mystery person' on the basis of the things they have in their pockets. The students are provided with the objects (e.g. pages from a diary, a pocket dictionary, a box of matches, etc.) and a chart aimed at guiding their hypothesis making. The chart is shown in Figure 6.4.

Learners work in groups and fill in the chart with their hypotheses. They subsequently report their findings to the class. The final outcome of the task is the creation of posters with short captions to describe a possible

How certain are you?

	Less than 50% certain (It's possible)	90% certain (It's probable)	100% certain (It's certain)
Name			
Sex			
Age			
Marital status			

Figure 6.4 Chart for the 'Things in pockets' task (Samuda 2001: 127).

profile of the 'mystery person'. This is a typical example of a task where given lexicogrammatical features (in this case, modal auxiliary verbs used to express degrees of possibility/probability, i.e. epistemic modality) may make the task implementation easier – more efficient and less circumlocuitous, but are by no means essential. Indeed, the students taking part in the study (who had little previous knowledge of this grammatical area, as shown by the results of a pre-test) conveyed how certain they were of their hypotheses in the first part of the task mainly through lexical means (*maybe*), often by 'mining' (borrowing) expressions from the task input (*it's possible, 90% certain*). This does not mean that the task failed in its purpose. On the contrary, it succeeded in creating what Samuda calls a 'semantic space', a 'need to mean', to express specific semantic meanings (epistemic modality) which the learners' interlanguage did not manage to fulfil, or fulfilled only partially. This way, students were led to notice a hole in their interlanguage. It is at this stage that the process of focusing the task is carried out – again, methodologically, during task implementation rather than by design. As the students report their findings, the teacher steps in to reformulate the guesses expressed by the students using modal auxiliaries:

---

1. T: *So lots of interesting ideas here. Paula, letters, uh schedule, opera, a busy man*
2. C: *Japanese classes*
3. T: *Yeah right, I forgot he's learning Japanese too (laughter)*
4. N: *And golf!*
5. T: *Oh yes very busy (laughter). Hmmm let's – why don't we look at how the language works here? Just for a minute uhh (looking at objects). Let's see now. Did you have anything here you thought was 'probable'? Like 90%*
6. Y: *Businessman*
7. T: *Businessman? 90%. Ok. So you're 90% certain he's a businessman, right? Here's another way to say this. You think it's 90% certain, so you think he must be a businessman. He must be a businessman (writes it on the board). So this (points to must be on board) is showing how CERTAIN how SURE you are. Not 100%, but almost 100%, 90%.*
8. A: *So 100% is 'be' or 'must'?*
   (Samuda 2001: 131)

The teacher (T) explicitly signals to the students that they are going to reflect on the way they have been expressing their speculations (5). To do so, she elicits an instance of the task input data and reformulates it using a modal auxiliary (7). This leads the students to start a process of metalinguistic reflection (8).

The teacher's methodological choices in leading students to focus on the use of the modal auxiliaries did seem to pay off as in the written posters created by the students, out of thirteen captions, seven contained the target features used accurately. The remaining captions expressed factual meanings and thus the use of modal expressions was not required.

Both the 'Picture description' and the 'Things in pockets' tasks are focused tasks as a result of the methodology which was used to implement them. However, the 'Picture description' task featured a 'reactive' approach by the teacher aimed at unobtrusively shifting the task focus on to a given lexicogrammatical feature (the past tense), through clarification requests uttered whenever the learners failed to use the past tense or used it incorrectly. By contrast, in the 'Things in pockets' task, the teacher's attempts at focusing the task on the use of modal auxiliaries followed a 'proactive' approach. After 'mining' input data, in the same way the students did in their initial task performance, she deliberately and explicitly introduced the targeted lexicogrammatical feature as a more precise and efficient way of encoding the meaning expressed lexically in the input data. This prompted learners to engage in metalinguistic reflection. While admittedly more obtrusive than the clarification requests illustrated in Nobuyoshi and Ellis's (1993) study, the teacher's proactive moves in Samuda's (2001) study were nevertheless treated 'as a "time-out" from task operations, but not from the bigger picture of the task as a whole' (Samuda 2001: 133), hence not detracting from the overall meaning orientation of the task.

A reactive approach to task focusing appears to be more suitable when a focused task is used 'diagnostically' (to find out what learners know about a given lexicogrammatical area) or for 'language-activating' purposes (e.g. to develop automaticity). Conversely, a proactive approach fits tasks which are used for 'knowledge-constructing' purposes (to build new language knowledge) (Samuda 2001). The role of the teacher is particularly crucial in focused task implementation and has been referred to as one of 'leading from behind' the task, 'to complement and support what the task has set in motion' (Samuda 2001: 120).

So far we have been concerned with task design and implementation. In the final part of this section, we will turn our attention from the task itself to what may happen before or after the implementation of a task. These two stages – while not essential to using tasks as a way to foster pushed output – have been hypothesized to play an important role in maximizing language acquisition processes. A selection of such options is listed in Table 6.14.

Table 6.14 Pre- and post-task options (adapted from Ellis and Shintani 2014: 142).

Pre-task phase	Modelling performance of the task	Students listen or watch the task being performed by 'experts'.
	Pre-teaching language	The teacher presents language that will be useful for performing the task.
	Schema developing	The teacher elicits and extends students' knowledge of the topic of the task.
	Strategic planning	The students are given time to prepare to perform the task before they actually perform it.
Main task phase		
Post-task phase	Repeat performance	Students are asked to repeat the task.
	Report	Students are asked to report the outcome of the task to the whole class.
	Language work	Students complete language exercises related to the linguistic problems that they experienced when performing the task.

How can task implementation be prepared so that learners may make the most of the learning opportunities provided by a task? Skehan (1996) highlights the fact that pre-task activities should target both the cognitive and the linguistic challenges posed by a task. In a task which asks students to discuss how strict their parents are and decide whose parents are the strictest (Willis and Willis 2007: 114–119), a pre-task phase might consist of a brainstorming activity in which students provide examples of actions they associate with strict parents and actions they associate with easy-going parents. This helps the students to 'develop a schema' for the task and, if needed, allows the teacher to 'pre-teach any language' (e.g. lexical items) that might be deemed useful and/or particularly challenging for the students. A recording (or a transcript of a recording) of proficient speakers that 'model the performance of the task' might also be provided. This would have the twofold aim of increasing the students' familiarity with the task type (thus lessening the cognitive burden) and feeding additional useful linguistic exponents. Finally, as was mentioned above, strategic planning, i.e. planning occurring before the task, might be usefully incorporated into the pre-task phase (cf. Subsection 6.3.3, 'Techniques and tasks for fostering speech fluency'). As shown in Table 6.15, Skehan (1998: 137–139) provides six main 'reasons for using pre-task activities' that highlight the kinds of beneficial effects a pre-task phase can have on lessening potential linguistic and cognitive challenges in task implementation.

Although the use of pre-task activities is advocated by both researchers and methodologists, Ellis (2003: 249) acknowledges that 'at best, all that the

Table 6.15 Reasons for using pre-task activities (from Skehan 1998: 137–139).

To introduce new language	New language may be introduced at this stage to kickstart interlanguage change.
To increase the chances that restructuring will occur in the underlying language system	Reorganization of the interlanguage system through the integration of partially acquired structures may take place.
To mobilize language	Language that has been recently learnt may be made accessible.
To recycle language	Language that has not been used for a while and is *specifically related to the task* may be activated.
To ease processing load	Task content is engaged so that the processing load during task implementation may be lessened.
To push learners to interpret tasks in more demanding ways	More demanding task interpretations may lead to more complex use of language during task implementation.

research to date has demonstrated is the likely effects of some of the procedures referred to above'. The option that has been more intensively investigated is strategic planning (Cf. Subsection 6.3.3, 'Techniques and tasks for fostering speech fluency'), for which robust research findings now exist about its effects on task implementation (for a recent study, cf. Nielson 2014).

What happens *after* a task has been implemented has also been the subject of research scrutiny and methodological proposals. The proposals which have been put forward are premised on the fact that learners need to be made aware of the kinds of post-task activities they will be required to carry out *before* they implement a task as 'learners' knowledge of what is to come later can influence how they approach attention-management during an actual task' (Skehan 1996: 55). As shown in Table 6.15, such activities might include the repetition of the task (e.g. in front of the whole class), a report to the class about the outcome of the task and language work. We will explore the benefits of task repetition in the next section. As regards task report, this is viewed as a key phase in Willis's 'framework for task-based learning' (see Table 6.16).

Table 6.16 Willis's (1996) framework for task-based learning.

Pre-task: Teacher introduces topic and task.
Task cycle:
Task: students carry out the task.
Planning: students plan how to report on task outcome.
Report: students report back to class.
Language focus:
Analysis
Practice

In Willis's framework, planning and report are integrated into the 'task cycle' as essential elements. In this proposal, planning comes after task implementation and is instrumental to the report phase. In the post-task planning stage students review what has taken place during the task and in so doing may be led to notice and reflect on gaps in their interlanguage knowledge. The actual report may include a writing component. With regard to the 'Strictest parents' task mentioned above, Willis and Willis (2007: 117) offer the following suggestions for the report activity:

> Learners might be asked to make notes to summarize their discussion. They could even be asked to write a report as a group, describing who had the strictest parents. These reports could then be read out, or put on an OHT for the class to see.

Another option envisaged for the post-task phase is labelled 'language work' in Table 6.15. To increase opportunities for noticing and metalinguistic reflection, students may be asked to work with samples from their output or other input. Lynch's (2001, 2007) proposal for this post-task option starts from the premise that opportunities for noticing are perhaps less forthcoming during actual task implementation than is thought quoting evidence from research suggesting that 'learners make relatively inefficient use of negative feedback on their ongoing L2 speech' (Lynch 2007: 311). The alternative advocated by Lynch is to provide 'offline feedback through post-task activities involving transcripts of learners' speech' (Lynch 2007: 312). These post-task activities are thought to enable learners to allocate more attentional resources to language than is possible during task implementation. In particular, transcribing is viewed as a powerful way of making 'learners' speech visible' (Lynch 2007: 312) and maximizing noticing opportunities.

Lynch's 2007 study experimented with two forms of post-task implementation transcribing: student-initiated (SI) and teacher-initiated (TI) transcribing. In SI transcribing, pairs of learners rehearsed and recorded a task, transcribed their performance, went over their transcript correcting and reformulating their speech where they thought fit and handed their reformulated transcript to the teacher, who provided a 'final' version of the transcript to be discussed by the original pair. In TI transcribing, after task performance was recorded, the teacher transcribed those parts which they thought needed correcting, handed over the partial transcript to the pairs of task performers, who corrected it and finally checked their changes with the teacher. Results from the study showed that while both SI and TI transcribing modes benefited the students, the possible longer-term effects for acquisition of the two transcribing modes appeared to differ. Students were asked to repeat the task the week following the transcribing sessions and four weeks later. Even after a month of engaging in the transcribing sessions, students who had experienced the SI mode appeared to display a higher degree of accurate use of the lexicogrammatical features that had been targeted in the transcriptions than students who had experienced the TI mode. Lynch (2007: 317) remarks that the main factor accounting for this difference was the 'greater depth of processing involved' in the SI mode.

As we have seen in this part of the chapter, tasks as language learning and teaching tools are a highly flexible resource that may be fruitfully used to foster pushed output in the classroom. Although task design variables can, to some extent, be manipulated to engender – e.g. – more accurate or more complex language use, it is how a task is actually implemented that seems to have more of an impact on the quality of learners' production – particularly, if pushed output is meant to lead to the emergence of pre-determined lexicogrammatical features. An example of how a focused task can be implemented in actual teaching practice will be provided in Section 6.4.1.

Techniques and tasks for fostering speech fluency

After examining the main features of L2 speech fluency and the possible challenges for learners (cf. Section 6.3.2), we will now consider how learners can be led to develop their ability to use an L2 more 'fluidly'. In particular, three main questions will be addressed in this section:

a. What type of output practice is most suitable for fluency development?
b. What task features can have a positive effect on L2 fluency?
c. How can fluency tasks be implemented through specific options, for example, planning and repetition?

Fluency has been one of the main concerns in Communicative Language Teaching (CLT) and traditionally viewed in its 'dichotomous' relationship with the other main feature of language competence, that is, accuracy. As Brumfit (1984: 51) explains,

> Language display for evaluation tended to lead to a concern for accuracy, monitoring, reference rules, possibly explicit knowledge, problem solving and evidence of skill-getting. In contrast, language use requires fluency, expression rules, a reliance on implicit knowledge and automatic performance.

By and large, this distinction between fluency and accuracy seemed to be justified for practical reasons as well as helping teachers take decisions about the content of lessons and the time to be allocated for different types of activities. However, despite being stressed in teachers' guides as an essential feature for second language competence, fluency has in fact turned out to be 'the neglected' component in classroom practice, as Bohlke (2014: 128) argues:

> Fluency activities are often the language activities that we find in the
> back of textbooks or listed only in teachers' manuals or resource books.
> This is unfortunate as these activities, [...], often go overlooked. They
> may be seen as less important or as optional activities that are worth
> doing but only if there is enough time.

In this regard, Rossiter et al. (2010) report that very few of the learning and teaching materials investigated in their survey include a full range of explicit, focused fluency activities. Similarly, Tavakoli and Hunter's (2017) study aimed at examining L2 teachers' understanding of speech fluency and their self-reported classroom practices for promoting it highlights that teachers often define fluency in a broad sense, and a large majority of the activities reported were more suitable for enhancing general speaking practice rather than specific fluency abilities. In the same vein, Gatbonton and Segalowitz (2005: 327) underline that

> although one component of fluency is automatic, smooth, and rapid
> language use, there are no provisions in current CLT methodologies
> to promote language use to a high level of mastery through repetitive
> practice. In fact, focused practice continues to be seen as inimical to the
> inherently open and unpredictable nature of communicative activities.

Proposals from SLA research support instead the idea that 'extended practice, under particular conditions and circumstances, will increase fluency by developing automaticity' (Segalowitz 2003: 401). The main issue teachers need to address is therefore what type of practice will be best for fluency development.

Opportunities for spoken production practice in the classroom have traditionally been provided through intensive drills and repetitive exercises aimed at the mastery of specific structures rather than at the practice of communicative use of the language. Gatbonton and Segalowitz (1988: 478) argue that the goal of this type of practice is 'the mastery of the structure of the utterances rather than the memorization of the utterances themselves'. By contrast, to obtain the automaticity that being fluent involves requires

> frequent opportunity to link together the components of utterances so
> that they can be produced without undue effort, so that what will be
> important will be the meanings underlying the speech rather than the
> speech itself. (Skehan 1998: 18)

What is needed then is a type of practice that requires learners 'to use target utterances repetitively while conveying genuine messages' (Gatbonton and Segalowitz 1988: 481). Practice should thus simulate the same conditions that apply in real-life communication, where 'processing and formulation of utterance must be done in real time' and where the primary focus is on message rather than linguistic accuracy (Johnson 1996: 45). Moreover, as part of the strategy for facilitating automatization, practice activities need to be designed so that utterances should contain no or limited challenging language. In this way, learners' attention will be shifted away from the forms that are being practised ('form defocus') so that it can be engaged in conveying the message in a fluent way (Johnson 1996: 175). An additional challenge for teachers is to set up fluency activities that will facilitate the transfer of automatized skills to contexts of real language use (Segalowitz 2003: 402).

Gatbonton and Segalowitz (1988: 484–489) suggest a number of features for effective fluency activities. Activities should be:

1. genuinely communicative – learners use specific target utterances from a genuine desire to communicate and receive information;
2. psychologically authentic – learners have the opportunity to experience some of the normal psychological pressure felt in real communication;
3. focused on only one or two language functions (e.g. directing, giving information, inviting) so that the majority of the utterances will be of the same type;
4. formulaic, that is involving the use of short memorizable utterances or multi-word constructions with a fix structure that can be usable in many situations;
5. inherently repetitive, that is, repetition is the means by which the activity goal is achieved.

In Table 6.17 we illustrate how these criteria apply in the analysis of a fluency activity called 'Family Tree' (Gatbonton and Segalowitz 1988: 482–489). The target language of the activity, which includes utterances to describe family roles and to talk about family relationships, can easily be adapted according to different learners' language levels.

Researchers investigating the influence of specific task variables on second language production have also singled out the variables which can best support fluency development. Drawing on Ellis (2003: 117–127)'s review of the research, we will consider here three types of task variables: (a) the type of input supplied by the task, (b) the type of demand required and (c) the type of outcome. For each variable, we will provide a description of types and examples of fluency tasks (see Table 6.18).

Table 6.17 Feature analysis of the fluency activity 'Family Tree' (from Gatbonton and Segalowitz 1988: 482–489).

Family Tree Students are divided into two groups (A and B) of at least six to eight. Each group will pretend to be members of an extended family and define what their relationships to each other are. Then each member of Group A interviews a member of Group B about the relationship in his/her group in order to draw a family tree. The members of Group B have the same task. Later, members of each group compare and discuss their information to agree on an accurate description of the other group.	
Genuinely communicative	The use of specific utterances is motivated by a need to find out about specific family relationships (*How are you related? I'm Y's brother*). To achieve the goal set for the activity, students have to use specific linguistic forms.
Psychologically authentic	Students are not given any time to study the utterances required to carry out the activity. While performing they have to decide what utterances to use and monitor what they say. This is meant to approximate the conditions of language use outside the classroom.
Focused	The activity highlights one or two language functions (asking and describing). It is therefore meant to elicit a limited number of utterances related to these language functions.
Formulaic	The activity elicits short utterances (*Who are you related to?*) or utterance frames (*How are you related to …? I'm Y's….*) that are usable in many other situations with little or no modification.
Inherently repetitive	The activity requires a great deal of repetition: students check the information with different students as large groups afford more opportunities to use the same utterances.

This type of analysis can help teachers carry out a theoretically motivated evaluation of oral production tasks paying attention to those variables that appear to have the greatest impact on fluency.

Besides investigating the effects of task variables on L2 oral production tasks, researchers have studied how specific 'procedural' options may affect the way a task is performed. In this final part, we will examine how planning and repetition can implement the design of fluency tasks. These two options can be somehow 'manipulated' by teachers to help learners gain the greatest benefit in terms of fluency in their spoken production.

As indicated by several studies, planning, and in particular strategic planning, has a deep effect on fluency resulting in faster speaking rate and fewer dysfluencies (Ellis 2005: 20). Strategic planning involves giving

Table 6.18 Effects of task design variables on L2 fluency (adapted from Ellis 2003: 117–127).

Design variables	Types of tasks	Examples of tasks
A. Type of input		
1. Contextual support	Tasks that provide contextual support such as a picture, a map or a diagram. Fluency is better promoted when the speakers can see the visual provided.	The learner narrates a story based on a series of pictures. The learner provides directions looking at a map with a route drawn on it.
2. Number of elements in a task	Tasks with few features that need to be manipulated by the speakers.	The learner narrates a story with two characters only happening in one place and at a single time without flashbacks. The learner provides directions looking at a simple map.
3. Topic	Tasks that involve familiar topics or routines.	The learner tells about a topic or a routine he/she is familiar with.
B. Task conditions		
Task demand	Tasks that pose a single demand.	The learner gives directions using a map on which the route to be taken is marked. The learner watches a video, then he or she tells the story.
C. Task outcomes		
1. Closed vs open outcome	Tasks with an outcome that is defined beforehand.	The learner has to work out a seating plan for the guests who will be attending a dinner party.
2. Inherent structure	Tasks with an outcome that has some kind of pre-structured form.	The learner has to explain to a partner how to get to a shop and buy something.

learners some time to prepare to perform the task considering what they are going to say and how they will need to say it. It was observed that during strategic planning learners 'give more attention to drawing up a conceptual plan of what they want to say rather than to formulating detailed linguistic plans' (Ellis 2008: 498). This explains why this type of planning has a stronger effect on fluency and complexity rather than on accuracy. Table 6.19 illustrates the variables that may be involved in strategic planning. Each variable may affect L2 fluency differently.

Investigation into the effects of guided and unguided planning showed that 'guided planners are more fluent than unguided planners'. Guided planning

Table 6.19 Variables in strategic planning in L2 production tasks (from Ellis 2005: 5).

Unguided planning	Learners can use their own devices or resources when planning a task.
Guided planning	Learners are given specific advice about what and how to plan (e.g. they may be told to focus on a specific language feature).
Participatory structure	The planning may be taken by the learners working individually, in groups or with the teacher.

Table 6.20 Planning guidelines for an instruction task (adapted from Sangarun 2005: 133).

A friend who lives in a different town is coming to see you next week. Follow these steps to plan the instructions you will give your friend.

1. Consider your friend's knowledge of your hometown.

2. Consider how you will explain to your friend:
a. how she or he will get from the train station to your school;
b. when and where she or he will meet you.

3. Also do the followings:
a. think of all the words you want to use in your message, and note only one word for one meaning;
b. think of transition words or phrases (*first, next, then…*) that will connect your instructions so that it is easy for your friend to follow them;
c. think of grammatical structures that play an important role in the task and write down the main parts of the grammatical structures.

can be provided in different ways. Table 6.20 presents an example of guided planning for an instruction task: learners are guided to plan the task both for content and language.

There is also some evidence that individual learner planning is most effective compared to teacher-led planning or group-based planning. Moreover, planning should not be viewed as something 'detached' or extremely time-consuming but should be incorporated into the whole sequence of task performance (Muranoi 2007: 71). Guidelines should be simple and take into account the learners' metacognitive skills and language level. They can be in the learners' mother tongue, if necessary.

Research has shown that repetition is another effective technique to enhance fluency skills. Repetition can be an inherent feature of the task, or can be part of the practice sequence. In particular, the repetition of the same task can help learners perform the task in a more fluent and complex way (Bygate 2001; Lynch and Mclean 2001). As a matter of fact, while

Table 6.21 Examples of retelling tasks aimed at fluency development in spoken production (Nation 1989: 383).

1. Marketplace

The learners are divided into buyers and sellers. The sellers are told what they are selling (furniture, books, holidays, etc.). Each seller prepares a sales talk to deliver to the buyers. The buyers circulate around the various sellers listening to the sales talks and finally making a decision about what they are going to buy. Each has to deliver their sales talk several times to the different buyers.

2. Messengers

The learners are divided into describers, messengers and makers. The describers have a model or an object to describe. It cannot be seen by the messengers or the makers. A messenger listens to a describer and then goes to a maker and tells the makers what to do. Because the task is complicated, the messenger will need to return to the describer several times for the same information. One describer can work with two or three messengers.

during the first performance learners tend to focus on message content and the basic language needed to convey it, during the repetition of the task they can rely on the previous work of conceptualization and encoding and switch their attention to the selection and monitoring of more appropriate linguistic aspects. Gains in oral fluency during task repetition also seem to be regardless of proficiency level or task type (Lambert et al. 2017).

One of the classroom activities that were found particularly effective to foster fluency by means of repetition is the 4/3/2 activity (Nation 1989), which will be illustrated later (cf. Section 6.4.1). In the activity, repetition is exploited by having learners tell the same story or giving the same talk about a topic three times to different listeners, decreasing the time from 4 to 2 minutes for each retelling. Research into the effectiveness of this type of activity showed that the technique increased the fluency with which the speakers delivered the talk; accuracy and also complexity seemed to be improved as a result of repeating the same items in the talk (Nation 1989: 382). Other activities that share the features of repetition and change of audience are illustrated in Table 6.21. These 'retelling' activities can be adapted for learners at varying proficiency levels.

In this section, we have considered what types of tasks are most suitable for L2 fluency development. We have also examined how fluency tasks can be implemented through procedural options such as planning and repetition. In the next part of the chapter, we will provide an example of the way fluency can be enhanced in actual teaching practice (cf. Section 6.4.2).

6.4 The principle in the classroom

This section aims to provide examples of the way a number of techniques and tasks aimed at fostering output production (cf. Section 6.3.3) can be implemented in actual teaching practice. The examples refer to two teachers who attempt to enhance spoken production in a focused task and a fluency task respectively. The tasks involve two different groups of students at a pre-intermediate level.

6.4.1 Ilaria dealing with a focused task

Video Extract 6

(a) You are going to watch an extract in which Ilaria, an Italian EFL secondary school teacher, is preparing her students to carry out an output production task. Analyse the task card with the instructions for the students.

Task card

You work for a match-making agency. Look at the photographs of different people.

1. Say what they have in common or do not have in common. Fill in the chart. Consider:

– their physical appearance
– their hobbies
– their likes and dislikes
– their jobs
– their habits
– their hopes for the future

Choose one person and match him/her with a perfect partner.

2. Write a report for your boss. Explain why it is a perfect match.

As a language teaching activity, a 'task' has distinctive features that tell it apart from an 'exercise'. To what extent does the 'Match-Making' activity satisfy the criteria for a task (Cf. Subsection 6.3.3, 'Output production tasks')? Provide reasons for your answers.

	Yes/No	Reasons
Is the activity mainly aimed at conveying a message?		
Is there a 'need' to close a 'gap' (through sharing information, discussion, reasoning and problem-solving)?		
Do learners have to use their own linguistic resources without having a model to follow?		
Is there a 'real' practical outcome?		

(b) Now watch the extract. In order to maximize language acquisition processes during the implementation of a task, a range of pre-task activities can be envisaged (Cf. Subsection 6.3.3, 'Output production tasks'). Which of the following activities did Ilaria carry out with her class prior to the task? Describe how the chosen activity(ies) was/were carried out.

Modelling performance of the task	
Pre-teaching language	
Schema developing	
Strategic planning	

6.4.2 Pushed output through focused tasks

(a) In a task students are free to use their own linguistic resources. However, the 'Match-making' task has been intended as a 'focused' task, in that it has been designed to elicit the use of specific lexicogrammatical features. Which language features do you think the task might make prominent? Watch another extract of Ilaria's lesson in which a group of students are carrying out the task. Which language features do they use to carry out the task? Are they the same language features you thought might be made prominent?

S1: *dislikes... dislikes, she dislikes...*
S2: *cats, she hates cats.*
S1: *no, she likes animals.*
S2: *yes but not cats*
S3: *not cats because dogs and cats are enemies*
S1: *but cats are so cute*
S3: *ok. habits?*
S2: *[...] she can like animals, but she can't like...*
S1: *cats.*
S2: *she cannot like cats. I don't know. so, habits. habits, yeah. habits. yes, she likes get up early every day.*
S1: *she runs in the park every day, maybe.*
S2: *yes.*
S1: *we said that she likes running, so why not. [...]*
S3: *In the park ... every day. with dogs.*
Ss 1 and 2: *runs with dogs.*
S3: *and her hopes for the future?*
S2: *she will be a great dog sitter.*
S1: *no, maybe she could want to change, to change her life, so become something completely different. something like...*
S3: *to to to open a big pet shop.*
S2: *she would open a dog shop.*
S1: *a dog shop.*
S3: *open a pet shop.*
S1: *so she doesn't change her life. all right.*

(b) Research into task-based learning has shown that by manipulating task features it is to some extent possible to lead learners to produce language that is either complex, fluent or accurate. The 'Match-making' task includes features that are predicted to foster complex language production. Complex output is held to be characterized by two main aspects: lexical richness and syntactic elaboration. Refer back to the extract above. Fill in the chart below with examples of lexical richness and syntactic elaboration.

| Lexical richness | Many different words are used rather than repeating the same words many times. | |
| Syntactic elaboration | Subordinate clauses are used. | |

(c) According to the Output Hypothesis, one of the main functions of output production is to lead learners to uncover possible 'holes' in their linguistic knowledge. Analyse the following examples from the students' interaction. What kinds of linguistic 'holes' do student 2 and student 5 seem to become aware of during the implementation of the task?

> S2: *[...] she can like animals but she can't like...*
> S1: *cats*
> S2: *she cannot like cats I don't know*

> S4: *[...]. getting up early in the morning 'cause she doesn't like*
> *to do this but he likes it. so how do we write this sound like –*
> *some difference such as getting up early in the morning which is*
> *something she doesn't like because of her being lazy but it would be*
> *too long so we're not writing that. which she doesn't like which is*
> *something she doesn't like. and we can say...*
> S5: *how to say 'pigra'?*
> Ss 4 and 6: *lazy, it's lazy*
> S5: *she's lazy stop*

(d) In a focused task the teacher may help students notice specific language features through special techniques. To do so, she can follow a 'reactive' or a 'proactive' approach (Cf. Subsection 6.3.3, 'Output production tasks'). Watch an extract of Ilaria's lesson in which a group of students are reading their task report to the class. Does the teacher use a reactive or a proactive approach to 'push' the students' output? Which specific lexicogrammatical features does she draw the students' attention to?

> S: *ok, Tracy and Pedro are a perfect match because she's a sportive*
> *woman, she play tennis and she trains a lot.*
> T: *ok, she, she?*
> S: *plays.*
> T: *she plays tennis, yes*
> S: *and she trains a lot and she loves watching all the types of sports*
> *Pedro is an actor but he loves watching matches of many different*
> *sports with he (?) friend*
> T: *can you repeat the last part?*
> S: *with his friend*
> T: *with his friends yes*
> S: *in the photo he has a big shoulder so we think he trains a lot in*
> *the gym.*
> T: *a big shoulder? just one?*
> S: *yes. eheh, the. the big shoulder.*
> T: *ah, he has big shoulders. ok.*

Second Language Acquisition in Action

6.4.3 Alessandro dealing with a fluency task

Video Extract 7

(a) You are going to watch a short extract in which Alessandro, an Italian EFL secondary school teacher, is dealing with a fluency task. What kind of fluency activities do you or would you use in the classroom? Do you or would you use different activities from those listed below?

• retelling activities	• guessing games	• reading aloud
• repetition drills	• role plays	• tongue twisters

(b) Watch the first part of Alessandro's lesson in which he introduces a fluency task called '4/3/2' (cf. Subsection 6.3.3 'Techniques and tasks for fostering speech fluency'). Complete the short description of the task provided below.

> Learners work in pairs with one acting as the ……….. and the other as
> ………….. The speaker talks for ……….. minutes retelling a previously
> read ………….while her/his partner listens and ……….words and
> expressions in a list. Then the …………. changes his/her partner giving
> the same information in three minutes, followed by a further change
> and a two-minute talk. The number of retellings and minutes for each
> retelling can be adapted according to the specific classroom context.
>
> (Maurice 1983, cited in Nation 2001)

(c) Now, watch another extract in which a pair of students carried out the '4/3/2' task. To what extent does the task satisfy the criteria for a spoken fluency task illustrated in a previous section of the chapter (cf. Subsection 6.3.3 'Techniques and tasks for fostering speech fluency')? Provide reasons for your answers.

Is the task genuinely 'communicative'?	Yes	Each speaker has to retell a story to different partners who do not know the story.
Is it 'psychologically' authentic?		
Is it focused on a particular language feature/function?		
Is the language used in the task formulaic?		
Is the task 'inherently' repetitive?		

(d) As pointed out, 'time pressure' has the effect of enhancing fluency during the task. Does the student seem to become gradually more fluent in his retelling of the story?

6.4.4 Fostering automaticity through increase of speed of output production

(a) The '4/3/2/' task involved a fourth retelling. Focus on the original text of the story that students had to prepare for their retelling and the transcriptions of the first and fourth retellings by one of the students carrying out the task. How is the student's first retelling of the story different from the original text? Does the content of the story change?

Original text of the story	First retelling	Fourth retelling
George Phillips of Meridian, Mississippi was **going up to bed** when his wife told him that she could see the light on in the garden. George opened the **back door** and went to **turn off the light**. He saw that there were people in the garden stealing things. He phoned the police. They said that all policemen were busy. George said, 'Okay', **hung up** and phoned the police again. 'Hello, I just called you **a few seconds ago** because there were people in my garden. Well, you don't have to **worry about** them now because I've just shot them.' Then he hung up. Five minutes later, three **police cars** and an ambulance arrived and caught the thieves. One of the policemen said to George: 'You said that you'd shot them!' George said: 'You said that all policemen were busy!'	*And he was going up to bed and mh but his wife eh told him ehm that ehm there were ehm light ehm on on the in the house and he went in the back door and turned off the light but he saw people that was that were mh stealing things and he called the police but the policeman said that mh all the the policemans are were busy and so he hung up and mh later he called again the police and said that mh to don't worry because they he has jus has just shot to the thieves and mmh hung up again and mmh few minutes ago uhm few minutes later four police cars and an and an ambulance ehm arrived to his house ehm and catch the thieves. And so that's it.*	*George was going up to bed but he saw a light in the back of the house so he opened the back door and he gone he turn turn off the light but he saw thieves that were steal- ing stealing thing and the called up the police but the police said that all the policemen were busy so he hung up and later he called an- other time but ehm and he said that don't mind because I've just shot the them and mmh he hu hung up another time; few minutes later he mh ehm some there were some police cars and an ambulance ehm in front of his house and the policemen were very mh surprised but he told that you told me that all the policemens were busy.*

(b) Go over the transcriptions of the student's retellings. How is the student's utterance fluency in the first retelling different from the fourth in the use of number of words, hesitations, repetitions, restarts and repairs? Fill in the table below with the data from your analysis. To what extent does the student manage to become more fluent?

Utterance fluency features	First retelling	Second retelling
Number of words		
Number of hesitations *(ehm, mm, uhm)*		
Number of repetitions of single words or group of words		
Number of restarts		
Number of repairs		

(c) To facilitate fluency the story also encouraged the use of formulaic language (highlighted in the original text). During the task the listener in each pair was asked to check if the speaker used these 'chunks' in his/her retelling of the story: *going up to bed, back door, turn off the light, hung up, a few seconds ago, worry about, police cars.* Go over the transcriptions of the first and fourth retellings above. To what extent did the student use the chunks in the original text during the following retellings?

(d) Research into the effectiveness of retelling tasks showed that besides fluency also accuracy and complexity seemed to be improved as a result of repeating the same items in the talk. In particular, output production was found to be characterized by flexibility/creativity in the use of chunks and more complex syntactic constructions. Analyse in more detail two extracts of the student's retellings of the story below and find evidence of the way the chunks and the structures underlined in the original text have been used.

Original text of the story	First retelling	Fourth retelling
George Phillips of Meridian, Mississippi was **going up to bed** when his wife told him that she could see the light on in the garden. George opened the **back door** and went to **turn off the light.** [...] 'Hello, I just *called* you	*And he was going up to bed and mh but his wife eh told him ehm that ehm there were ehm light ehm on on the in the house and he went in the back door and turned off the light [...] and mh later*	*George was going up to bed but he saw a light in the back of the house so he opened the back door and he gone he turn turn off the light [...] and*

Original text of the story	First retelling	Fourth retelling
<u>a few seconds ago</u> because there were people in my garden. **Well, you don't have to worry about them** now because I've just shot them.' Then **he hung up. Five minutes later, three police cars** and an ambulance **arrived** and caught the thieves.	*he called again the police and said that mh to don't worry because they he has jus has just shot to the thieves and mmh hung up again and mmh few minutes ago uhm few minutes later four police cars and an and an ambulance ehm arrived to his house ehm and catch the thieves.*	*later he called another time but ehm and he said that don't mind because I've just shot the them and mmh he hu hung up another time; few minutes later he mh ehm some there were some police cars and an ambulance ehm in front of his house*

6.5 Restructuring and planning

In this section, you will be asked to evaluate and adapt materials aimed at fostering students' pushed output and enhancing fluency in language production.

(a) Go back to Table 6.8. Analyse the 'Agony aunt(s)' task.

- Explain why it is held to be a 'task' rather than a language 'exercise'.
- What lexicogrammatical features do you think the task has been designed to make prominent?
- Review Table 6.12. Which design features of the task suggest that it is meant to 'push' learners to produce complex output? Which task implementation option(s) would you select in order to increase the chances that more complex output will be generated?

(b) Prepare four silhouettes of people doing different things and design a focused task.
- What are the learners expected to do in the task?
- What grammatical feature(s) is/are going to be made prominent through the task?
- Write a rubric for the task.

(c) Go back to Section 6.2 and review the 'Career moves' task in step d. Design an improved version of the task. How would you adapt the task so that

- it has a more well-defined practical outcome;

- it 'pushes' students to produce complex output;
- it potentially leads students to the use of given lexicogrammatical features?

Plan a suitable pre-task activity to introduce the task and lessen the linguistic and cognitive burden of task implementation. To increase the chances that students' output is 'pushed', what kind of post-task activity/ies would you design?

(d) Analyse the task 'A class photo' described below. The task has been designed to promote fluency and automaticity in output production. Consider these points in the analysis:

- Why can the task be considered 'communicatively genuine'?
- What makes the task 'inherently' repetitive?
- What language feature(s) will be made prominent in the task?
- To what extent are these features 'formulaic' and supposed to facilitate fluency?
- What kind of planning guidelines would you provide to help students prepare for the task (cf. an example in Table 6.8)?
- How would you increase the students' opportunity to use the same language features repeatedly throughout the task?
- Would you plan some post-task work focusing on the language that learners have used?

A class photo
Photographs will be taken of the class to be added to the teacher's souvenir collection. The students' task is to take turns telling one another where to stand and what pose to assume. The use of gestures is not allowed.
(Gatbonton and Segalowitz 1988)

(e) Choose one of the tasks described in Table 6.21. Analyse your task considering the variables that are supposed to facilitate fluency (cf. Table 6.18):

- the type of input supplied by the task
- the type of demand required
- the type of outcome.

Explain why the features of your task can be suitable to enhance learners' fluency.

Design the main teaching steps for the task including a pre-task stage and a post-task language focus.

6.6 Conclusions

The chapter has explored the role of output production in SLA, starting from the assumption that, according to Swain's Output Hypothesis, 'the act of producing language (speaking or writing) constitutes, under certain circumstances, part of the process of second language learning' (Swain 2005: 471). The analysis of the Output Hypothesis has enabled us to review the various functions that output is hypothesized to play in acquiring a second language. The use of 'tasks' as a way of fostering 'pushed output' has also been investigated in that task-based learning and teaching may represent 'the optimal context for the sustained and context-embedded type of output practices that theorists consider vital for L2 development' (Gilabert et al. 2016: 167). In particular, options in task design and implementation that empirical research has found to impact on the quality of learners' output (towards complex, accurate or fluent performance) and the much-debated issue of whether and how a task can be made 'focused' have been illustrated.

Since surfacing in the mid-1980s, the Output Hypothesis has been the target of considerable research effort. However, writing at the beginning of the twenty-first century, Shehadeh (2002: 601) pointed out that 'the question of whether and how learners' output, or output modification, helps with L2 learning' was 'still largely unanswered'. Fifteen years later, Gilabert et al. (2016: 160) noted that empirical work had still mostly focused on 'the processes associated with output practice' (cf. e.g. Izumi's work on noticing – e.g. Izumi 1999, 2002) while less emphasis had been placed on the investigation of 'internal processes [...] which are conducive to SLA'.

In the pedagogical realm, the large-scale adoption of tasks as teaching tools has been and still is an uphill battle, as documented by East's (2017) recent article. East remarks that 'teachers often struggle with differentiating a task from [...] more structured communicative activities' that might be found in mainstream communicative textbooks. Misunderstandings (cf. also Ellis 2009) persist with regard to the role of the teacher during task implementation (e.g. should the teacher take a step back and let the students get on with the task?). This may have a potentially disastrous impact on the effectiveness of task-based teaching as research has shown that the process of producing pushed output as a task is being carried out needs to be carefully supported. Besides task implementation, questions are still open with regard to the extent to which teachers resort to pre- and post-tasks phases and whether these actually work (Jackson and Suethanapornkul 2013).

In the second part of the chapter, we examined a number of aspects related to fluency in second language output production as the result of the learners' automatization of their linguistic knowledge, that is, the 'speed and ease' with which we perform a task (DeKeyser 2001: 125). We focused on speech fluency, not only in terms of 'performance', but distinguishing between its cognitive and utterance-related aspects. As production takes place in real time and requires continuous attention control, we also highlighted a number of attention-related factors that may place a special burden on learners' cognitive fluency. Finally, we analysed a number of 'fluency vulnerability points' that may occur at the different stages of the speech production cycle and affect the quality of learners' utterances in different ways. As Segalowitz (2010: 51) points out, a 'cognitive science' perspective on L2 fluency such as that illustrated in the chapter can provide 'a richer and more nuanced way of thinking about fluency compared to the lay view of fluency as simply a performance characteristic that lies on a single continuum stretching from low to high fluency'.

Moreover, a multidimensional perspective on fluency 'has yielded a number of ideas that might serve as criteria for instructional activities designed to promote fluency' (Segalowitz 2010: 177). These criteria highlight the importance of setting up tasks that are genuinely communicative, psychologically authentic, focused on only one or two language functions, involving the use of short memorizable utterances, and inherently repetitive. Research has also pointed to the positive effects for fluency development deriving from the use of specific task variables and 'procedural' options such as pre-task planning and task repetition. No doubt, second language teachers can take advantage of these insights to implement the design and use of fluency tasks in their teaching practice, as illustrated through the examples of tasks presented in the chapter.

6.7 Notes

1   According to Swain and Lapkin (1995: 372), Canadian immersion programmes were aimed at 'both academic achievement in the content areas studied and a high level of proficiency in the second language'.
2   Swain and Lapkin (1995: 372, cf. also Swain 1988) point out that 'only 15 per cent of the "public" talk of the students was greater than a clause in length'.
3   For example, the two sentences 'John failed because he didn't study' and 'John was failing despite supposedly having studied' convey roughly the same information, but reflect a difference in terms of the speaker's idea of what is important to underline in the message. The first specifies a causal connection between two events ('because'), while the second specifies a lack of causal connection ('despite') (Segalowitz 2010: 98).
4   These fluency vulnerability points are identified considering the stages in a model of the L2 speaker. The model is an adaptation of Levelt's (1999) model of the monolingual speaker and incorporating De Bot's model (1992) of the bilingual speaker.

6.8 Further reading

DeKeyser, R. (2001), 'Automaticity and automatization', in P. Robinson (ed.), *Cognition and Second Language Instruction*, 125–151, Cambridge: Cambridge University Press.

Ellis, R. (2003), *Task-Based Language Learning and Teaching*, Oxford: Oxford University Press.

Gatbonton, E. and N. Segalowitz (1988), 'Creative automatization: principles for promoting fluency within a communicative framework', *TESOL Quarterly*, (22) 3: 473–492.

Gatbonton, E. and N. Segalowitz (2005), 'Rethinking communicative language teaching: a focus on access to fluency', *The Canadian Modern Language Review/ La Revue canadienne des langues vivantes*, 61 (3): 325–353.

Kormos, J. (2006), *Speech Production and Second Language Acquisition*, Mahwah, NJ: Lawrence Erlbaum Associates.

Long, M. (2015), *Second Language Acquisition and Task-Based Language Teaching*, Malden, MA: Blackwell.

Lynch, T. (2001), 'Seeing what they meant. Transcribing as a route to noticing', *ELT Journal*, 55 (2): 124–132.

Lynch, T. (2007), 'Learning from the transcripts of an oral communication tasks', *ELT Journal*, 61 (4): 311–320.

Nobuyoshi, J. and R. Ellis. (1993), 'Focused communication tasks and second language acquisition', *ELT Journal*, 47 (3): 203–210.

Nunan, D. (2004), *Task-Based Language Teaching*, Cambridge: Cambridge University Press.

Samuda, V. (2001), 'Guiding relationships between form and meaning during task performance. The role of the teacher', in M. Bygate, P. Skehan and M. Swain (eds), *Researching Pedagogic Tasks. Second Language Learning, Teaching and Testing*, 119–140, London: Longman.

Segalowitz, N. (2003), 'Automaticity and second languages', in C. Doughty and M. H. Long (eds), *The Handbook of Second Language Acquisition*, 382–408, Oxford: Blackwell.

Segalowitz, N. (2007), 'Access fluidity, attention control, and the acquisition of fluency in a second language', *TESOL Quarterly*, 41 (1): 181–186.

Segalowitz, N. (2010), *Cognitive Bases of Second Language Fluency*, London: Routledge.

Skehan, P. (1998), *A Cognitive Approach to Language Learning*, Oxford: Oxford University Press.

Skehan, P. (2003), 'Task-based instruction', *Language Teaching*, 36 (1): 1–14.

Swain, M. (1985), 'Communicative competence: some roles of comprehensible input and comprehensible output in its development', in S. Gass and C. Madden (eds), *Input in Second Language Acquisition*, 235–253, Rowley: MA, Newbury House.

Swain, M. (1995), 'Three functions of output in second language learning', in G. Cook and B. Seidlhofer (eds), *Principles and Practice in Applied Linguistics*, 125–144, Oxford: Oxford University Press.

Swain, M. (2005), 'The Output Hypothesis. Theory and research', in E. Hinkel (ed.), *Handbook of Research in Second Language Learning and Teaching*, 471–483, Mahwah, NJ: Lawrence Elbaum.

Swain, M. (2006), 'Languaging, agency and collaboration in advanced second
    language proficiency', in H. Byrnes (ed.), *Advanced Language Learning: The
    Contribution of Halliday and Vygotsky*, 95–108, London–New York: Continuum.
Willis, D. and J. Willis (2007), *Doing Task-Based Language Teaching*, Oxford:
    Oxford University Press.

References

Aljaafreh, A. and J. Lantolf (1994), 'Negative feedback as regulation and second language learning in the zone of proximal development', *The Modern Language Journal*, 78 (4): 465–483.

Anderson, J. R. (1982), 'Acquisition of cognitive skill', *Psychological Review*, 89 (4): 369–406.

Anderson, J. R. (2007), *How Can the Human Mind Occur in the Physical Universe?* Oxford: Oxford University Press.

Andrews, S. J. (1999), 'Why do teachers need to know about language? Teacher metalinguistic awareness and input for learning', *Language and Education*, 13 (3): 161–177.

Andrews, S. J. (2007), *Teacher Language Awareness*, Cambridge: Cambridge University Press.

Angelova, M. (2005), 'Using Bulgarian mini-lessons in an SLA course to improve the KAL of American ESL teachers', in N. Bartels (ed.), *Applied Linguistics and Language Teacher Education*, 27–42, Berlin: Springer.

Badalamenti, V. and C. Henner-Stanchina (2007), *Grammar Dimensions 1*, 4th edn, Boston, MA: Thomson Heinle.

Bartels, N. (2003), 'How teachers and researchers read academic articles', *Teaching and Teacher Education*, 19 (7): 737–753.

Bartels, N., ed. (2005), *Applied Linguistics and Language Teacher Education*, Berlin: Springer.

Batstone, R. and R. Ellis (2009), 'Principled grammar teaching', *System*, 37 (2): 194–204.

Benati, A. (2005), 'The effects of processing instruction, traditional instruction and meaning-output instruction on the acquisition of the English past simple tense', *Language Teaching Research*, 9 (1): 67–93.

Benati, A. (2015), 'Structured input?' in J. I. Liontas (ed.), *TESOL Encyclopedia of English Language Teaching*, New York: Wiley.

Benati, A. (2016), 'Input manipulation, enhancement and processing: theoretical views and empirical research', *Studies in Second Language Learning and Teaching*, 6 (1): 65–88.

Benati, A. and J. F. Lee (2008), *Grammar Acquisition and Processing Instruction*, Clevedon: Multilingual Matters.

Benati, A. and J. F. Lee (2010), *Processing Instruction and Discourse*, London: Continuum.

Benati, A. and J. F. Lee (2015), 'Processing instruction: new insights after twenty years of theory and research and application', *International Review of Applied Linguistics*, 52 (2): 87–90.

Boers, F. and S. Lindstromberg (2008), *Teaching Chunks of Language: From Noticing to Remembering*, London: Helbling Languages.

Bohlke, D. (2014), 'Fluency-oriented second language teaching', in D. M. Brinton, M. Celce-Murcia, and M. A. Snow (eds), *Teaching English as a Second or Foreign Language*, 4th edn, 121–135, Boston, MA: Heinle Cengage Learning.

Borg, S. (1998), 'Teachers' pedagogical systems and grammar teaching: a qualitative survey', *TESOL Quarterly*, 32 (1): 9–38.

Borg, S. (2005), 'Teacher cognition in language teaching', in K. Johnson (ed.), *Expertise in Second Language Learning and Teaching*, 190–209, London: Palgrave Macmillan.

Borg, S. (2010), 'Language teacher research engagement', *Language Teaching*, 43 (4): 391–429.

Boston, J. S. (2010), 'Pre-task syntactic priming and focused task design', *ELT Journal*, 64 (2): 165–174.

Brumfit, C. J. (1984), *Communicative Methodology in Language Teaching: The Roles of Fluency and Accuracy*, Cambridge: Cambridge University Press.

Burgess, J. and S. Etherington (2002), 'Focus on grammatical form: explicit or implicit?', *System*, 30 (4): 433–458.

Burns, A. and J. C. Richards, eds (2009), *The Cambridge Guide to Second Language Teacher Education*, Cambridge: Cambridge University Press.

Busch, D. (2010), 'Pre-service teacher beliefs about language learning: the second language acquisition course as an agent for change', *Language Teaching Research*, 14 (3): 318–337.

Bygate, M. (2001), 'Effects of task repetition on the structure and control of oral language', in M. P. Bygate and M. Swain (eds), *Researching Pedagogic Tasks*, 23–48, Harlow: Longman.

Byrne, D. (1986), *Teaching Oral English*, Harlow: Longman.

Celce-Murcia, M. and D. Larsen-Freeman (1999), *The Grammar Book: An ESL/EFL Teacher's Course*, 2nd edn, Boston, MA: Thomson Heinle.

Celce-Murcia, M. and D. Larsen-Freeman (2015), *The Grammar Book: An ESL/EFL Teacher's Course*, 3rd edn, Boston, MA: Thomson Heinle.

Carrol, S. E. (2001), *Input as Evidence*, Amsterdam: John Benjamins.

Chaudron, C. (1988), *Second Language Classrooms. Research on Teaching and Learning*, Cambridge: Cambridge University Press.

Corder, S.P. (1967), 'The significance of learners' errors', *International Review of Applied Linguistics*, 5 (4): 161–170.

Council of Europe (2001), *The Common European Framework of Reference for Languages: Learning, Teaching, Assessment*, Cambridge: Cambridge University Press.

Cowan, R. (2008), *The Teacher's Grammar of English*, Cambridge: Cambridge University Press.

De Bot, K. (1992), 'A bilingual production model: Levelt's 'Speaking' model adapted', *Applied Linguistics*, 13 (1): 1–24.

De Graaff, R. and A. Housen (2009), 'Investigating the effects and effectiveness of L2 instruction', in M. H. Long and C. J. Doughty (eds), *The Handbook of Language Teaching*, 726–755, Oxford: Blackwell.

De Jong, N. H., M. P. Steinel, A. Florijn, R. Schoonen and J. H. Hulstijn (2013), 'Linguistic skills and speaking fluency in a second language', *Applied Psycholinguistics*, 34 (5): 893–916.

Declerck, R. (2006), *The Grammar of the English Verb Phrase. Volume 1: The Grammar of the English Tense System. A Comprehensive Analysis*, Berlin: De Gruyter.

DeKeyser, R. (1995), 'Learning second language grammar rules: an experiment with a miniature linguistic system', *Studies in Second Language Acquisition*, 17 (3): 379–410.

DeKeyser, R. (2001), 'Automaticity and automatization', in P. Robinson (ed.), *Cognition and Second Language Instruction*, 125–151, Cambridge: Cambridge University Press.

DeKeyser, R. (2003), 'Implicit and explicit learning', in C. Doughty and M. H. Long (eds), *The Handbook of Second Language Acquisition*, 313–348, Malden, MA: Blackwell.

DeKeyser, R., ed. (2007), *Practice in a Second Language: Perspectives from Applied Linguistics and Cognitive Psychology*, Cambridge: Cambridge University Press.

DeKeyser, R. (2015), 'Skill acquisition theory', in B. VanPatten and J. Williams (eds), *Theories in Second Language Acquisition. An Introduction*, 2nd edn, 94–112, London: Routledge.

Depraetere, I. and C. Langford (2012), *Advanced English Grammar. A Linguistic Approach*, London: Bloomsbury.

Donato, R. (1994), 'Collective scaffolding in second language learning', in J. P. Lantolf and G. Appel (eds), *Vygotskian Approaches to Second Language Research*, 33–56, Norwood, NJ: Ablex.

Donato, R. (2004), 'Aspects of collaboration in pedagogical discourse', *Annual Review of Applied Linguistics*, 24 (1): 284–302.

Doughty, C. and J. Williams, eds (1998), *Focus on Form in Classroom Second Language Acquisition*, Cambridge: Cambridge University Press.

East, M. (2017), 'Research into practice: the task-based approach to instructed second language acquisition', *Language Teaching*, 50 (3): 412–424.

Egi, T. (2007), 'Recasts, learners' interpretations, and L2 development', in A. Mackey (ed.), *Conversational Interaction in Second Language Acquisition: A Collection of Empirical Studies*, 249–268, Oxford: Oxford University Press.

Ellis, R. (1995), 'Interpretation tasks for grammar teaching', *TESOL Quarterly*, 29 (1): 87–105.

Ellis, N. C. (2005), 'At the interface: dynamic interactions of explicit and implicit language knowledge', *Studies in Second Language Acquisition*, 27 (2): 305–352.

Ellis, N. C. (2007), 'The weak interface, consciousness, and form-focussed instruction: mind the doors', in S. Fotos and H. Nassaji (eds), *Form-Focused Instruction and Teacher Education: Studies in Honour of Rod Ellis*, 11–33, Oxford: Oxford University Press.

Ellis, N. C. and D. Larsen-Freeman (2009), 'Language as a complex adaptive system (Special issue)', *Language Learning*, 59 (Suppl. 1): 1–26.

Ellis, R. (1994), 'Explicit/implicit knowledge and language pedagogy', *TESOL Quarterly*, 28 (1): 166–172.

Ellis, R. (1997), *SLA Research and Language Teaching*, Oxford: Oxford University Press.

Ellis, R. (2001), 'Investigating form-focused instruction', in R. Ellis (ed.), *Form-Focused Instruction and Second Language Learning*, 1–47, Malden, MA: Blackwell.

Ellis, R. (2002a), 'Methodological options in grammar teaching materials', in E. Hinkel and S. Fotos (eds), *New Perspectives on Grammar Teaching in Second Language Classrooms*, 155–179, Mahwah, NJ: Lawrence Erlbaum.

Ellis, R. (2002b), 'Grammar teaching – practice or consciousness-raising?', in J.C. Richards and W. A. Renandya (eds), *Methodology in Language Teaching*, 167-174, Cambridge: Cambridge University Press.

Ellis, R. (2003), *Task-based Language Learning and Teaching*, Oxford: Oxford University Press.

Ellis, R. (2004), 'The definition and measurement of L2 explicit knowledge', *Language Learning*, 54 (2): 227–275.

Ellis, R., ed. (2005), *Planning and Task Performance in a Second Language*, Amsterdam: John Benjamins.

Ellis, R. (2006a), 'Current issues in the teaching of grammar. An SLA perspective', *TESOL Quarterly*, 40 (1): 83–107.

Ellis, R. (2006b), 'Modelling learning difficulty and second language proficiency: the differential contributions of implicit and explicit knowledge', *Applied Linguistics*, 27 (3): 431–463.

Ellis, R. (2007), 'The differential effects of corrective feedback on two grammatical structures', in A. Mackey (ed.), *Conversational Interaction in Second Language Acquisition: A Collection of Empirical Studies*, 407–452, Oxford: Oxford University Press.

Ellis, R. (2008), *The Study of Second Language Acquisition*, Oxford: Oxford University Press.

Ellis, R. (2009a), 'Implicit and explicit learning, knowledge and instruction', in R. Ellis, S. Loewen, C. Elder, H. Reinders, R. Erlam and J. Philp (eds), *Implicit and Explicit Knowledge in Second Language Learning, Testing and Teaching*, 3–26, Bristol: Multilingual Matters.

Ellis, R. (2009b), 'SLA and teacher education', in A. Burns and J. C. Richards (eds), *The Cambridge Guide to Second Language Teacher Education*, 135–143, Cambridge: Cambridge University Press.

Ellis, R. (2009c), 'Task-based language teaching: sorting out the misunderstandings', *International Journal of Applied Linguistics*, 19 (3): 221–246.

Ellis, R. (2010a), 'Epilogue. A framework for investigating oral and written corrective feedback', *Studies in Second Language Acquisition*, 32 (2): 335–349.

Ellis, R. (2010b), 'Second language acquisition, teacher education and language pedagogy', *Language Teaching*, 43 (2): 182–201.

Ellis, R. (2012), *Language Teaching Research and Language Pedagogy*, Oxford: Wiley-Blackwell.

Ellis, R. (2016), 'Grammar teaching as consciousness raising', in E. Hinkel (ed.), *Teaching Grammar to Speakers of Other Languages*, 128–150, London: Routledge.

Ellis, R. and S. Gaies (1998), *Impact Grammar*, Hong Kong: Longman.

Ellis, R. and N. Shintani (2014), *Exploring Language Pedagogy through Second Language Acquisition Research*, London: Routledge.

Ellis, R., H. Basturkmen and S. Loewen (2002), 'Doing focus on form', *System*, 30 (4): 419–432.

Ellis, R., S. Loewen, C. Elder, H. Reinders, R. Erlam and J. Philp, eds (2009), *Implicit and Explicit Knowledge in Second Language Learning, Testing and Teaching*, Bristol: Multilingual Matters.

Erlam, R. (2008), 'What do you researchers know about language teaching? Bridging the gap between SLA research and language pedagogy', *Innovation in Language Learning and Teaching*, 2 (3): 253–267.

Erlam, R., K. Sakui and R. Ellis (2006), *Instructed Second Language Acquisition: Case Studies*, Wellington: Learning Media Ltd.

Favreau, M. and N. Segalowitz (1983), 'Automatic and controlled processes in the first and second language reading of fluent bilinguals', *Memory & Cognition*, 11 (6): 565–574.

Fotos, S. (1993), 'Consciousness-raising and noticing through focus on form – grammar task-performance versus formal instruction', *Applied Linguistics*, 14 (4): 385–407.

Fotos, S. (1994), 'Integrating grammar instruction and communicative language use through grammar consciousness-raising tasks', *TESOL Quarterly*, 28 (3): 323–351.

Fotos, S. and R. Ellis (1991), 'Communicating about grammar. A task-based approach', *TESOL Quarterly*, 25 (3): 605–628.

Fotos, S. and H. Nassaji (2011), *Teaching Grammar in Second Language Classrooms*, London: Routledge.

Freeman, D. (2007), 'Research fitting practice: Firth and Wagner, classroom language teaching, and language teacher education', *Modern Language Journal*, 91 (1): 893–906.

Gass, S. M. (2003), 'Input and interaction', in C. Doughty and M. H. Long (eds), *Handbook of Second Language Acquisition*, 224–255, Oxford: Blackwell.

Gass, S. (2010), 'The relationship between L2 input and L2 output', in E. Macaro (ed.), *The Continuum Companion to Second Language Acquisition*, 194–219, London: Continuum.

Gass, S. and A. Mackey (2015), 'Input, interaction, and output in second language acquisition', in B. VanPatten and J. Williams (eds), *Theories in Second Language Acquisition. An Introduction*, 2nd edn, 180–206, New York: Routledge.

Gass, S. and L. Selinker (2008), *Second Language Acquisition: An Introductory Course*, New York/Oxon: Routledge.

Gass, S. M. and E. M. Varonis (1989), 'Incorporated repairs in nonnative discourse', in M. R. Eisenstein (ed.), *The Dynamic Interlanguage: Empirical Studies in Second Language Variation*, 71–86, New York: Plenum Press.

Gatbonton, E. and N. Segalowitz (1988), 'Creative automatization: principles for promoting fluency within a communicative framework', *TESOL Quarterly*, 22 (3): 473–492.

Gatbonton, E. and N. Segalowitz (2005), 'Rethinking communicative language teaching: a focus on access to fluency', *The Canadian Modern Language Review/ La Revue Canadienne des Langues Vivantes*, 61 (3): 325–353.

Gilabert, R., R. M. Manchón and O. Vasylets (2016), 'Mode in theoretical and empirical TBLT research: advancing research agendas', *Annual Review of Applied Linguistics*, 36 (2): 117–135.

Goldberg, A. (2006), *Constructions at Work*, Cambridge: Cambridge University Press.

Green, P. S. and K. Hecht (1992), 'Implicit and explicit grammar: an empirical study', *Applied Linguistics*, 13 (2): 168–184.

Gutiérrez, X. (2016), 'Analyzed knowledge, metalanguage, and second language proficiency', *System*, 60 (1): 42–54.

Harley, B. and M. Swain (1978), 'An analysis of the verb system used by young learners of French', *Interlanguage Bulletin*, 3 (1): 35–79.

Hatch, E. (1978), 'Discourse analysis and second language acquisition', in E. Hatch (ed.), *Second Language Acquisition: A Book of Readings*, 401–435, Rowley, MA: Newbury House.

Hatch, E. (1983), 'Simplified input and second language acquisition', in R. W. Andersen (ed.), *Pidginization and Creolization as Language Acquisition*, 64–86, Cambridge, MA: Newbury House.

Howatt, A. P. R. (2004), *A History of English Language Teaching*, 2nd edn, Oxford: Oxford University Press.

Howatt, A. P. R. and R. Smith (2014), 'The history of teaching English as a Foreign language, from a British and European perspective', *Language and History*, 57 (1): 75–95.

Hulstijn, J. H. (2005), 'Theoretical and empirical issues in the study of implicit and explicit second-language learning', *Studies in Second Language Acquisition*, 27 (2): 129–140.

Izumi, S. (1999), 'Promoting noticing in SLA: an empirical study of the effects of output and input enhancement on ESL relativization', *Dissertation Abstracts International, A: The Humanities and Social Sciences* 61 (7), 2683–A.

Izumi, S. (2002), 'Output, input enhancement, and the Noticing Hypothesis: an experimental study on ESL relativization', *Studies in Second Language Acquisition*, 24 (4): 541–577.

Izumi, S. and M. Bigelow (2000), 'Does output promote noticing and second language acquisition?' *TESOL Quarterly*, 34 (2): 239–278.

Izumi, S., M. Bigelow, M. Fujiwara and S. Fearnow (1999), 'Testing the output hypothesis: effects of output on noticing and second language acquisition', *Studies in Second Language Acquisition*, 21 (3): 421–452.

Jackson, D. O. and S. Suethanapornkul (2013), 'The cognition hypothesis: a synthesis and meta-analysis of research on second language task complexity', *Language Learning*, 63 (2): 330–367.

Johnson, K. (1996), *Language Teaching and Skill Learning*, Oxford: Blackwell.

Kahng, J. (2014), 'Exploring utterance and cognitive fluency of L1 and L2 English speakers: temporal measures and stimulated recall', *Language Learning*, 64 (4): 809–854.

Kerekes, J. (2001), 'How can SLA theories and SLA researchers contribute to teachers' practices?', in B. Johnson and S. Irujo (eds), *Research and Practice in Language Teacher Education. Voices from the Field*, 17–41, Minneapolis, MN: Center for Advanced Research on Language Acquisition.

Kinginger, C. (2002), 'Defining the zone of proximal development in U.S. foreign language education', *Applied Linguistics*, 23 (2): 240–261.

Kormos, J. (2006), *Speech Production and Second Language Acquisition*, Mahwah, NJ: Lawrence Erlbaum Associates.

Kramsch, C. (2000), 'Second language acquisition, applied linguistics, and the teaching of foreign languages', *The Modern language Journal*, 84 (3): 311–326.

Krashen, S. (1981), *Second Language Acquisition and Second Language Learning*, Oxford: Pergamon.

Krashen, S. (1982), *Principles and Practice in Second Language Acquisition*, Oxford: Pergamon.

Krashen, S. (1985), *The Input Hypothesis: Issues and Implications*, London: Longman.

Krashen, S. (1994), 'The Input Hypothesis and its rivals', in N. Ellis (ed.), *Implicit and Explicit Learning of Languages*, 45–77, London: Academic Press.

Krashen, S. and T. D. Terrell (1983), *The Natural Approach*, New York: Pergamon.

Lambert, C., J. Kormos and D. Minn (2017), 'Task repetition and second language processing', *Studies in Second Language Acquisition*, 39 (1): 167–196.

Lantolf, J., ed. (2000), *Sociocultural Theory and Second Language Learning*, Oxford: Oxford University Press.

Lantolf, J. P. (2007), 'Conceptual knowledge and instructed second language learning: a sociocultural perspective', in S. Fotos and H. Nassaji (eds), *Form Focused Instruction and Teacher Education*, 35–54, Oxford: Oxford University Press.

Lantolf, J. and S. Thorne (2006), *Sociocultural Theory and the Genesis of Second Language Development*, Oxford: Oxford University Press.

Lantolf, J., S. L. Thorne and M. E. Poehner (2015), 'Sociocultural theory and second language development', in B. VanPatten and J. Williams (eds), *Theories in Second Language Acquisition. An Introduction*, 2nd edn, 207–226, New York: Routledge.

Larsen-Freeman, D. (1992), 'A non-hierarchical relationship between grammar and communication; Part I: theoretical and methodological considerations', in J. E. Alatis (ed.), *Georgetown University Round Table on Languages and Linguistics 1992*, 158–165, Washington, DC: Georgetown University Press.

Larsen-Freeman, D. (1997), 'Chaos/complexity science and second language acquisition', *Applied Linguistics*, 18 (2): 141–165.

Larsen-Freeman, D. (2001), 'Teaching grammar', in M. Celce Murcia (ed.), *Teaching English as a Second or Foreign Language*, 3rd edn, 251–266, Boston, MA: Thomson Heinle.

Larsen-Freeman, D. (2003), *Teaching Language. From Grammar to Grammaring*, Boston, MA: Thomson Heinle.

Larsen-Freeman, D., ed. (2007), *Grammar Dimensions*, 4th edn, Boston, MA: Thomson Heinle.

Larsen-Freeman, D. (2009), 'Teaching and testing grammar', in M. Long and C. Doughty (eds), *The Handbook of Language Teaching*, 518–542, Oxford: Wiley-Blackwell.

Larsen-Freeman, D. (2012), 'On the role of repetition in language teaching and learning', *Applied Linguistics Review*, 3(2): 195-210.

Larsen-Freeman, D. (2013), 'Transfer of learning transformed', *Language Learning*, 63 (1): 107–129.

Larsen-Freeman, D. (2014), 'Teaching grammar', in M. Celce Murcia, D. Brinton and M. A. Snow (eds), *Teaching English as a Second or Foreign Language*, 4th edn, 256–270, Boston, MA: Thomson Heinle.

Larsen-Freeman, D. (2015), 'Research into practice: grammar learning and teaching', *Language Teaching*, 48 (2): 263–280.

Lee, J. and A. Benati (2009), *Research and Perspectives on Processing Instruction*, Berlin: Mouton de Gruyter.

Lee, J. and B. VanPatten (2003), *Making Communicative Language Teaching Happen*, 2nd edn, New York: McGraw-Hill.

Leech, G. N. (1994), 'Students' grammar – teachers' grammar – learners' grammar', in M. Bygate, A. Tonkyn and E. Williams (eds), *Grammar and the Language Teacher*, 17–30, New York: Prentice Hall.

Leeser, M. (2004), 'Learner proficiency and focus on form during collaborative dialogue', *Language Teaching Research*, 8 (1): 55–81.

Leow, R. P. (2007), 'Input in the L2 classroom: an attentional perspective on receptive practice', in R. DeKeyser (ed.), *Practice in a Second Language: Perspectives from Applied Linguistics and Cognitive Psychology*, 21–50, New York: Cambridge University Press.

Levelt, W. (1999), 'Producing spoken language. A blueprint of the speaker', in C. Brown and P. Hagoort (eds), *The Neurocognition of Language*, 83–122, Oxford: Oxford University Press.

Lightbown, P. (2000), 'Anniversary article. Classroom SLA research and second language teaching', *Applied Linguistics*, 21 (4): 431–462.

Lo, Y.-H. G. (2005), 'Relevance of knowledge of second language acquisition: an in-depth case study of a non-native EFL teacher', in N. Bartels (ed.), *Applied Linguistics and Language Teacher Education*, 135–157, Berlin: Springer.

Loewen, S., Li F. Fei, A. Thompson, K. Nakatsukasa, S. Ahn and X. Chen (2009), 'Second language learners' beliefs about grammar instruction and error correction', *The Modern Language Journal*, 93 (1): 91–104.

Long, M. (1983), 'Native speaker/non-native speaker conversation and the negotiation of comprehensible input', *Applied Linguistics*, 4 (2): 126–141.

Long, M. (1990), 'The least a second language acquisition theory needs to explain', *TESOL Quarterly*, 24 (4): 649–666.

Long, M. (1991), 'Focus on form: a design feature in language teaching methodology', in K. de Bot, R. Ginsberg and C. Kramsch (eds), *Foreign Language Research in Cross-Cultural Perspective*, 39–52, Amsterdam: John Benjamins.

Long, M. (1996), 'The role of the linguistic environment in second language acquisition', in W. C. Ritchie and T. K. Bahtia (eds), *Handbook of Second Language Acquisition*, 413–468, New York: Academic Press.

Long, M. (2007), *Problems in SLA*, Mahwah, NJ: Lawrence Erlbaum.

Long, M. (2009), 'Methodological principles for language teaching', in M. H. Long and C. J. Doughty (eds), *Handbook of Language Teaching*, 373–394, Blackwell: Oxford.

Long, M. (2015), *Second Language Acquisition and Task-Based Language Teaching*, Malden, MA: Blackwell.

Long, M. and P. Robinson (1998), 'Focus on form: theory, research, and practice', in C. Doughty and J. Williams (eds), *Focus on Form in Classroom Second Language Acquisition*, 15–41, Cambridge: Cambridge University Press.

Loschky, L. and R. Bley-Vroman (1993), 'Grammar and task-based methodology', in G. Crookes and S. Gass (eds), *Tasks and Language Learning: Integrating Theory and Practice*, 123–167, Clevedon: Multilingual Matters.

Lynch, T. (2001), 'Seeing what they meant. Transcribing as a route to noticing', *ELT Journal*, 55 (2): 124–132.

Lynch, T. (2007), 'Learning from the transcripts of an oral communication task', *ELT Journal*, 61 (4): 311–320.

Lynch, T. and J. Maclean (2001), 'A case of exercising: effects of immediate task repetition on learners' performance', in M. Bygate, P. Skehan and M. Swain (eds), *Researching Pedagogic Tasks*, 141–162, Harlow: Longman.

Lyster, R. and L. Ranta (1997), 'Corrective feedback and learner uptake: negotiation of form in communicative classrooms', *Studies in Second Language Acquisition,* 19 (1): 37–66.

Lyster, R. and K. Saito (2010), 'Oral feedback in classroom SLA: a meta-analysis', *Studies in Second Language Acquisition,* 32 (2): 265–302.

Lyster, R., K. Saito and M. Sato (2013), 'Oral corrective feedback in second language classrooms', *Language Teaching* 46 (1): 1–40.

Mackey, A. (1999), 'Input, interaction and second language development: an empirical study of question formation in ESL', *Studies in Second Language Acquisition,* 21 (4): 557–587.

Mackey, A. (2007), 'Introduction', in A. Mackey (ed.), *Conversational Interaction in Second Language Acquisition: A Collection of Empirical Studies,* 1–26, Oxford: Oxford University Press.

Mackey, A. (2012), *Input, Interaction and Corrective Feedback in L2 Learning,* Oxford: Oxford University Press.

Mackey, A., S. Gass and K. McDonough (2000), 'How do learners perceive interactional feedback?,' *Studies in Second Language Acquisition,* 22 (4): 471–497.

Mackey, A., R. Oliver and J. Leeman (2003), 'Interactional input and the incorporation of feedback: an exploration of NS-NNS and NNS-NNS adult and child dyads', *Language Learning,* 53 (1): 35–66.

McCafferty, S. G. (1994), 'Adult second language learners' use of private speech: a review of studies', *The Modern Language Journal,* 78 (4): 421–436.

Meisel, J. M., H. Clahsen and M. Pienemann (1981), 'On determining developmental stages in natural second language acquisition', *Studies in Second Language Acquisition,* 3 (2): 109–135.

Muranoi, H. (2007), 'Output practice in the L2 classroom', in R. DeKeyser (ed.), *Practice in A Second Language: Perspectives from Applied Linguistics and Cognitive Psychology,* 51–84, Cambridge: Cambridge University Press.

Nassaji, H. (2012), 'The relationship between SLA research and language pedagogy: teachers' perspectives', *Language Teaching Research,* 16 (3): 337–365.

Nassaji, H. (2015), *The Interactional Feedback Dimension in Instructed Second Language Learning,* London: Bloomsbury.

Nation, P. (1989), 'Improving speaking fluency', *System,* 17 (3): 377–384.

Nava A. (2008), *Grammar by the Book. The Passive in Pedagogical Grammars for EFL/ESL Teachers,* Milano: LED Edizioni.

Nava, A. (2012), 'SLA in action: raising teachers' awareness of English lexicogrammar and its acquisition', in L. Pedrazzini and A. Nava (eds), *Learning and Teaching English: Insights from Research,* 91–115, Monza: Polimetrica.

Nava, A. (2017), 'Errors and learning/teaching English as a second/foreign language: an exercise in grammaticology', *Altre Modernità,* Special Issue, April: 79–97.

Nava, A. and L. Pedrazzini (2011), 'Good practice in teacher training: an experiential approach to raising Italian EFL trainee teachers' awareness of lexicogrammar and its acquisition', in G. Di Martino, L. Lombardo and S. Nuccorini (eds), *Papers from the 24th AIA Conference. Challenges for the 21st Century: Dilemmas, Ambiguities, Directions. Vol. 2. Language Studies,* 564–573, Roma: Edizioniq.

Nielson, K. B. (2014), 'Can planning time compensate for individual differences in working memory capacity?', *Language Teaching Research*, 18 (3): 272–293.

Nitta, R. and S. Gardner (2005), 'Consciousness-raising and practice in ELT coursebooks', *ELT Journal*, 59 (1): 3–13.

Nobuyoshi, J. and R. Ellis (1993), 'Focused communication tasks and second language acquisition', *ELT Journal*, 47 (3): 203–210.

Nunan, D. (1991), *Language Teaching Methodology. A Textbook for Teachers*, New York: Prentice Hall.

Nunan, D. (2004), *Task-based Language Teaching*, Cambridge: Cambridge University Press.

Nunan, D. and C. Lamb (1996), *The Self-directed Teacher*, Cambridge: Cambridge University Press.

Ohta, A. (2001), *Second Language Acquisition Processes in the Classroom: Learning Japanese*, Mahwah, NJ: Lawrence Erlbaum.

Ortega, L. (2007), 'Meaningful L2 practice in foreign language classrooms: a cognitive-interactionist SLA perspective', in R. Dekeyser (ed.), *Practice in a Second Language: Perspectives from Applied Linguistics and Cognitive Psychology*, 180–207, Cambridge: Cambridge University Press.

Ortega, L. (2012), 'Second language research for language teaching: choosing between application and relevance', in B. Hinger, D. Newby and E. M. Unterrainer (eds), *Sprachen Lernen: Kompetenzen entwickeln? Performanzen (über)prüfen*, Proceedings of the 2010 Annual Conference of the Austrian Society for Language Pedagogy, 24–38, Vienna: Präsens Verlag.

Parrott, M. (2010), *Grammar for English Language Teachers*, 2nd edn, Cambridge: Cambridge University Press.

Pedrazzini, L. (2012), 'SLA principles from practice: the Input Hypothesis', in L. Pedrazzini and A. Nava (eds), *Learning and Teaching English: Insights from Research*, 117–144, Monza: Polimetrica.

Pedrazzini, L. (2017), 'Dealing with students' errors: oral corrective feedback in the Italian EFL classroom', *Altre Modernità*, Special Issue, April: 98–117.

Pica, T. (1997), 'Second language teaching and research relationships: a North American view', *Language Teaching Research*, 1 (1): 48–72.

Prabhu, N.S. (1987), *Second Language Pedagogy*, Oxford: Oxford University Press.

Rebuschat, P. (2015), 'Introduction: implicit and explicit learning of languages', in P. Rebuschat (ed.), *Implicit and Explicit Learning of Languages*, xiii–xxii, Amsterdam: John Benjamins.

Robinson, P. (2007), 'Task complexity, theory of mind, and intentional reasoning: effects on L2 speech production, interaction, uptake and perceptions of task difficulty', *International Review of Applied Linguistics*, 45 (3): 193–214.

Robinson, P. and R. Gilabert (2007), 'Task complexity, the cognition hypothesis and second language learning and performance', *International Review of Applied Linguistics*, 45 (3): 161–176.

Rossiter, M. J., T. M. Derwing, L. G. Manimtim and R. I. Thomson (2010), 'Oral fluency: the neglected component in the communicative language classroom', *Canadian Modern Language Review*, 66 (4): 583–606.

Russell, V. (2014), 'A closer look at the Output Hypothesis: the effect of pushed output on noticing and inductive learning of the Spanish future tense', *Foreign Language Annals*, 47 (1): 25–47.

Rutherford, W. (1987), *Second Language Grammar. Learning and Teaching*, New York: Longman.

Rutherford, W. and M. Sharwood Smith (1985), 'Consciousness-raising and universal grammar', *Applied Linguistics*, 6 (3): 274–282.

Saito, K. and R. Lyster (2012), 'Effects of form-focused instruction and corrective feedback on L2 pronunciation development of Japanese learners of English', *Language Learning*, 62 (2): 595–633.

Samuda, V. (2001), 'Guiding relationships between form and meaning during task performance. The role of the teacher', in M. Bygate, P. Skehan and M. Swain (eds), *Researching Pedagogic Tasks. Second Language Learning, Teaching and Testing*, 119–140, London: Longman.

Samuda, V. and M. Bygate (2008), *Tasks in Second Language Learning*, London: Palgrave Macmillan.

Sangarun, J. (2005), 'The effects of focusing on meaning and form in strategic planning', in R. Ellis (ed.), *Planning and Task Performance in a Second Language*, 111–142, Amsterdam: John Benjamins.

Sarandi, H. (2016), 'Oral corrective feedback: a question of classification and application', *TESOL Quarterly*, 50 (1): 235–246.

Schmidt, R. (1990), 'The role of consciousness in second language learning', *Applied Linguistics*, 11 (2): 129–158.

Schmidt, R. (1994), 'Implicit learning and the cognitive unconscious: of artificial grammars and SLA', in N. Ellis (ed.), *Implicit and Explicit Learning of Languages*, 165–209, London: Academic Press.

Schmidt, R. (2001), 'Attention', in P. Robinson (ed.), *Cognition and Second Language Instruction*, 3–32, Cambridge: Cambridge University Press.

Schmidt, R. and S. N. Frota (1986), 'Developing basic conversational ability in a second language: a case study of an adult learner of Portuguese', in R. R. Day (ed.), *Talking to Learn: Conversation in Second Language Acquisition*, 237–326, Rowley, MA: Newbury House.

Schulz, R.A. (1996), 'Focus on form in the foreign language classroom: students' and teachers' views on error correction and the role of grammar', *Foreign Language Annals*, 29 (3): 343–364.

Segalowitz, N. (2003), 'Automaticity and second languages', in C. Doughty and M. H, Long (eds), *The Handbook of Second Language Acquisition*, 382–408, Oxford: Blackwell.

Segalowitz, N. (2007), 'Access fluidity, attention control, and the acquisition of fluency in a second language', *TESOL Quarterly*, 41 (1): 181–186.

Segalowitz, N. (2010), *Cognitive Bases of Second Language Fluency*, London: Routledge.

Selvi, A. F. and M. Martin-Beltrán (2016), 'Teacher-learners' engagement in the reconceptualization of second language acquisition knowledge through inquiry', *System*, 63 (1): 28–39.

Sharwood Smith, M. (1981), 'Consciousness-raising and the second language learner', *Applied Linguistics*, 7 (3): 239–256.

Sharwood Smith, M. (1993), 'Input enhancement in instructed SLA: theoretical bases', *Studies in Second Language Acquisition*, 15 (2): 165–179.

Sheen, Y. and R. Ellis (2011), 'Corrective feedback in language teaching', in E. Hinkel (ed.), *Handbook of Research in Second Language Teaching and Learning*, 593–610, London: Routledge.

Shehadeh, A. (2002), 'Comprehensible output, from occurrence to acquisition: an agenda for acquisitional research', *Language Learning*, 52 (3): 597–564.

Skehan, P. (1992), 'Second language acquisition strategies and task-based learning', *Thames Valley University Working Papers in English Language Teaching*, 1: 178–208.

Skehan, P. (1996), 'A framework for the implementation of task-based instruction', *Applied Linguistics*, 17 (1): 38–62.

Skehan, P. (1998), *A Cognitive Approach to Language Learning*, Oxford: Oxford University Press.

Skehan, P. (2003), 'Task-based instruction', *Language Teaching*, 36 (1): 1–14.

Skehan, P. and P. Foster (2001), 'Cognition and tasks', in P. Robinson (ed.), *Cognition and Second Language Learning*, 183–205, Cambridge: Cambridge University Press.

Soars, L. and J. Soars (1986), *Headway Intermediate, Student's Book*, Oxford: Oxford University Press.

Soars, L. and J. Soars (1996), *New Headway English Course Intermediate, Student's Book*, Oxford: Oxford University Press.

Song, M. J. and B. R. Suh (2008), 'The effects of output task types on noticing and learning of the English past counterfactual conditional', *System*, 36 (2): 295–312.

Spada, N. (2015), 'SLA research and L2 pedagogy: misapplications and questions of relevance', *Language Teaching*, 48 (1): 69–81.

Storch, N. (2007), 'Investigating the merits of pair work on a text editing task in ESL classes', *Language Teaching Research*, 11 (2): 143–159.

Swain, M. (1985), 'Communicative competence: some roles of comprehensible input and comprehensible output in its development', in S. Gass and C. Madden (eds), *Input in Second Language Acquisition*, 235–253, Rowley, MA: Newbury House.

Swain, M. (1988), 'Manipulating and complementing content teaching to maximize second language learning', *TESL Canada Journal*, 6 (1): 68–83.

Swain, M. (1993), 'The Output Hypothesis: just speaking and writing aren't enough', *The Canadian Modern Language Review*, 50 (2): 158–164.

Swain, M. (1995), 'Three functions of output in second language learning', in G. Cook and B. Seidlhofer (eds), *Principles and Practice in Applied Linguistics*, 125–144, Oxford: Oxford University Press.

Swain, M. (1998), 'Focus on form through conscious reflection', in C. Doughty and J. Williams (eds), *Focus on Form in Classroom Second Language Acquisition*, 64–82, Cambridge: Cambridge University Press.

Swain, M. (2000), 'The Output Hypothesis and beyond: mediating acquisition through collaborative dialogue', in J. P. Lantolf (ed.), *Sociocultural Theory and Second Language Learning*, 97–114, Oxford: Oxford University Press.

Swain, M. (2005), 'The Output Hypothesis. Theory and research', in E. Hinkel (ed.), *Handbook of Research in Second Language Learning and Teaching*, 471–483, Mahwah, NJ: Lawrence Erlbaum.

Swain, M. (2006), 'Languaging, agency and collaboration in advanced second language proficiency', in H. Byrnes (ed.), *Advanced Language Learning: The Contribution of Halliday and Vygotsky*, 95–108, London–New York: Continuum.

Swain, M. and S. Lapkin (1995), 'Problems in output and the cognitive processes they generate: a step towards second language learning', *Applied Linguistics*, 16 (3): 371–391.

Swan, M. (1994), 'Design criteria for pedagogic language rules', in M. Bygate, A. Tonkyn and E. Williams (eds), *Grammar and the Language Teacher*, 45–55, Harlow: Prentice Hall.

Tanner, R. and C. Green (1998), *Tasks for Teacher Education: A Reflective Approach*, Harlow: Longman.

Tavakoli, P. (2011), 'Pausing patterns: differences between L2 learners and native speakers', *ELT Journal*, 65 (1): 71–79.

Tavakoli, P. and M. J. Howard (2012) 'Teaching English to speakers of other languages: teachers' views on the relationship between research and practice', *European Journal of Teacher Education*, 35 (2): 229–242.

Tavakoli, P. and A. M. Hunter (2017), 'Is fluency being "neglected" in the classroom? Teacher understanding of fluency and related classroom practices', *Language Teaching Research*, Online First.

Tavakoli, P. and P. Skehan (2005), 'Strategic planning, task structure, and performance testing', in R. Ellis (ed.), *Planning and Task Performance in a Second Language*, 239–273, Amsterdam: John Benjamins.

Toth, P. D. (2006), 'Processing instruction and a role for output in second language acquisition', *Language Learning*, 56 (2): 319–385.

Ur, P. (1984), *Teaching Listening Comprehension*, Cambridge: Cambridge University Press.

Ur, P. (1988), *Grammar Practice Activities*, 1st edn, Cambridge: Cambridge University Press.

Ur, P. (2009), *Grammar Practice Activities*, 2nd edn, Cambridge: Cambridge University Press.

Ur, P. (2016), 'Grammar practice', in E. Hinkel (ed.), *Teaching English Grammar to Speakers of Other Languages*, 109–127, London: Routledge.

VanPatten, B. (1996), *Input Processing and Grammar Instruction: Theory and Research*, Norwood, NJ: Ablex.

VanPatten, B. (2003), *From Input to Output. A Teacher's Guide to Second Language Acquisition*, New York: McGraw-Hill.

Van Patten, B. (2004), 'Input processing in SLA', in B. VanPatten (ed.), *Processing Instruction: Theory, Research, and Commentary*, 5–32, Mahwah, NJ: Erlbaum.

VanPatten, B. (2007), 'Input processing in adult second language acquisition', in B. VanPatten and J. Williams (eds), *Theories in Second Language Acquisition*, 1st edn, 115–135, Mahwah, NJ: Lawrence Erlbaum Associates.

VanPatten, B. (2009), 'Processing matters in input enhancement', in T. Piske and M. Young-Scholten (eds), *Input Matters*, 47–61, Bristol: Multilingual Matters.

VanPatten, B. (2012), 'Input processing', in S. Gass and A. Mackey (eds), *The Routledge Handbook of Second Language Acquisition*, 268–281, New York: Routledge.

VanPatten, B. (2015), 'Input processing in Adult SLA', in B. VanPatten and J. Williams (eds), *Theories in Second Language Acquisition. An Introduction*, 2nd edn, 113–134, New York: Routledge.

VanPatten, B. and J. Williams (2015), 'Early theories in SLA', in B. VanPatten and J. Williams (eds), *Theories in Second Language Acquisition. An Introduction*, 2nd edn, 17–33, New York: Routledge.

Verspoor, M., W. Lowie and K. De Bot (2009), 'Input and second language development from a dynamic perspective', in T. Piske and M. Young-Scholten (eds), *Input Matters in SLA*, 62–80, Bristol: Multilingual Matters.

Vygotsky, L. (1987), *The Collected Works of L.S. Vygotsky Volume 1: Thinking and Speaking*, New York: Plenum Press.

Wajnryb, R. (1990), *Grammar Dictation*, Oxford: Oxford University Press.

Watanabe, Y. (2004), 'Collaborative dialogue between ESL learners of different proficiency levels: linguistic and affective outcomes', Unpublished M.A. Thesis, OISE, University of Toronto.

White, L. (1987), 'Against comprehensible input: the Input Hypothesis and the development of second-language competence', *Applied Linguistics*, 8 (2): 95–110.

Williams, J. (2005), 'Learning without awareness', *Studies in Second Language Acquisition*, 27 (2): 269–304.

Willis, J. (1996), 'A flexible framework for task-based learning', in J. Willis and D. Willis (eds), *Challenge and Change in Language Teaching*, 56–62, Oxford: Heinemann.

Willis, D. and J. Willis (2007), *Doing Task-Based Language Teaching*, Oxford: Oxford University.

Winitz, H. (1981), *The Comprehensible Approach to Foreign Language Instruction*, Rowley, MA: Newbury House.

Wisniewska, I., H. Riggenbach and V. Samuda (2007), *Grammar Dimensions 2*, 4th edn, Boston, MA: Thomson Heinle.

Wong, W. (2004), 'The nature of processing instruction', in B. VanPatten (ed.), *Processing Instruction: Theory, Research, and Commentary*, 33–63, Mahwah, NJ: Erlbaum.

Wong, W. (2005), *Input Enhancement: From Theory and Research to the Classroom*, New York: McGraw-Hill.

Wood, D., J. Bruner and G. Ross (1976), 'The role of tutoring in problem-solving', *Journal of Child Psychology and Psychiatry*, 17 (2): 89–100.

Wright, T. (2010), 'Second language teacher education: review of recent research on practice', *Language Teaching*, 43 (3): 259–296.

Author Index

Subject Index